Government by the Market?

Also by Peter Self

Cities in Flood
The State and the Farmer (*with H. Storing*)
Administrative Theories and Politics
Econocrats and the Policy Process
Planning the Urban Region
Political Theories of Modern Government

Government by the Market?

The Politics of Public Choice

Peter Self

© Peter Self 1993

First published 1993 by
THE MACMILLAN PRESS LTD
Houndmills, Basingstoke, Hampshire RG21 2XS
and London
Companies and representatives
throughout the world

ISBN 0–333–56972–5 hardcover
ISBN 0–333–56973–3 paperback

A catalogue record for this book is available
from the British Library.

Copy-edited and typeset by Povey–Edmondson
Okehampton and Rochdale, England

Printed in Hong Kong

To Hugh Stretton, fellow critic of public choice

Contents

Preface

In recent decades a powerful new paradigm of the proper scope and limits of government action has become dominant in Western democracies. This paradigm holds that governments should in general do less; that they should reduce or relinquish their previous responsibilities for maintaining full employment and a comprehensive system of state welfare; that they should privatise public services or their delivery wherever practicable; and that they should reform their own operations in accordance with market concepts of competition and efficiency. These beliefs in 'government by the market' rest upon propositions that the market system is inherently a better method for satisfying human wants and aspirations than recourse to government, and that the political process is subject to numerous imperfections and distortions. The aims of this book are to investigate the intellectual foundations of this new ideology, to examine the numerous public policies that have been (and are being) followed within its general rubric, and to evaluate these beliefs in terms of broader social values and understandings of 'the public interest'.

The intellectual basis for these new doctrines come from market theory and public choice thought. This book concentrates primarily upon the public choice element, because while market theory celebrates or defends the virtues of competitive markets (a subject taken up in Chapter 7), public choice concentrates upon the problems and limitations of the democratic political process. Thus it is able to provide a critically important collaboration to the advocacy of market theory by dealing specifically with issues of politics and political failure. Because public choice is in principle no more than an economic tool of analysis, its political uses have not been clearly recognised; and because of its economic language, public choice is a somewhat esoteric and unfamiliar subject for students of politics and the general public, at any rate outside the USA. However, public choice in simplified or popularised forms has contributed a lot to political debates and policies. In particular it has helped to erode the optimistic post-1945 belief in government planning and the welfare state, and to substitute the conclusion that the less governments do, the better.

Public choice theory represents the application of economic methodology to the study of politics. In principle it is an objective study not wedded to any particular political belief, but its inquiries are shaped by its strongly individualist and rationalist assumptions. These assumptions lead to a critical view of the political process owing to the many opportunities which it is said to provide for self-seeking behaviour, and an adverse view of the capacity of governments to satisfy individual wants compared with economic markets. Social choice (a related discipline) further brings in the intrinsic difficulties of making collective decisions upon a democratic basis.

The first three chapters offer a concise survey of public choice theories. My concerns have naturally been different from those of economic theorists. Public choice writers use an economic language which they do not usually relate to more conventional or traditional treatments of politics (an exception is James Buchanan, who does specifically relate his public choice theories to the history of political thought). In attempting to bridge this gap, I cannot do justice to the many sophisticated economic treatments of politics which occur in the literature, my concern being to present a readable analysis to a non-economist (although my interpretations and conclusions are also addressed to economists). The treatment has also to be selective in line with the wider purpose of the book of discussing the influence of ideas upon policies.

Thus I first take a critical look at the assumptions of public choice because they influence all that follows about the nature of politics. In Chapter 2 I try to pull together and evaluate some public choice theories about the behaviour of principal actors in the political process. Chapter 3 shows how certain strong conclusions by public choice writers have been utilised to build up the ideology of 'government by the market'. I want to stress here that a methodology based upon the idea of rational self-interest need not support these conclusions and can be turned instead into a strong critique of the market system. I recognise these alternative theories in the text, without having space to review them adequately, but I suggest that the highly individualist assumptions of public choice do point in a clear ideological direction. The public choice assumptions after all are those conventionally used to justify the market system in classical economics. Thus the main thrust of public choice writing, and still more of its political influence, have been to discredit democratic government and to extol the market system.

The next three longer chapters analyse the public policies pursued by political leaders in efforts to reduce the scope, range and costs of government and drastically to change methods of public administration and service delivery. These chapters are organised around the three themes of slimming the state, privatising welfare and restructuring government as key elements in a wide-ranging programme of political change. The examples are taken from English-speaking democracies where these political goals have been most evident, especially from Britain and the USA but also in some contexts from Australia, New Zealand and Canada. The Reagan and Thatcher years provide a laboratory for testing these policy innovations and the treatment is sometimes explicitly comparative. However, the general aim is not a comparative survey but an illustrative discussion of policies in a variety of arenas in order to demonstrate some of the goals and effects of this major shift in the relations between government and society.

This account of recent political history should have an intrinsic interest, whatever theoretical conclusions are or are not drawn. The influence of public choice thought (albeit in a popularised form) can be seen both in the general assumptions on which political leaders based their policies and also sometimes in the strategies which they pursued to disarm or overcome opposition. There is, however, a certain irony in the use or relevance of public choice thought in a policy context. The same critique of self-seeking political behaviour which supports the ideology of 'slimming the state' also suggests that the effort will be unsuccessful because of the necessary mobilisation of new interests (such as those embedded in the market system) and the costs of buying out existing interests. By the end of the 1990s it can be seen that the outcome of all these activities has been not so much to slim government itself as to alter quite drastically its economic and social responsibilities as well as its distribution of favours and sacrifices among the members of society.

The last three chapters revert to a more theoretical framework which revolves around the respective capacities of the market and political systems to satisfy individual wants and aspirations.

Chapter 7 investigates the performance of the market system against the claims of both public choice and market theory, and goes on to discuss the powerful impact of market ideology upon public policies, using a number of illustrations. Chapter 8 shows the failures of public choice and market theories to offer any tenable concept of the 'public interest' or to satisfy basic criteria of individual rights and social justice. The defects of the political system, including its tendencies to extremism and alienation and its liability to strong ethnic or group conflicts, are also sketched. Answers to these problems are sought in the concept of responsible and active citizenship and in Chapter 9 are further pursued through the search for a new policy paradigm that could enable democratic governments to realise social values which markets cannot satisfy.

Two points should be clarified about the purposes of this book. It nowhere suggests or supposes that public policies are likely to be closely based upon academic theories or prescriptions. Politics is a highly pragmatic activity which does not consistently follow any general principles of policy. Nonetheless it is the author's belief, which has grown stronger as the book has progressed, that ideas and ideology do count a great deal in politics, even though their application is much distorted by political considerations. They provide the essential basis of assumed social realities whereby political leaders explain and justify their policies to the public, backed by a media which keeps the range of 'realistic' options within narrow limits. It is usual here to refer to Keynes' aphorism that every practical man is the slave of some defunct economist. In respect of current policies the economists in question are alive, kicking and influential, but otherwise there is truth in Keynes's statement.

Secondly, in criticising the 'self-interest' assumption of public choice, I do not mean to revert to an idealistic tradition about the state which assumes extensive public-spirited behaviour. While self-interest and altruism both exist, the former is generally the more dominant motive; but the directions and degrees of self-interest depend very much upon the structure of opportunities within a given political and economic system, and upon the ethical norms (or their absence) which regulate behaviour in that system. In *The Culture of Contentment* (1992) J. K. Galbraith reaches the gloomy conclusion that highly irrational and short-sighted public policies will continue to be pursued because they suit the perceived self-interest of the affluent majority of the population (by which he means a majority of those voting and holding effective power, not a majority of the whole population). This view that the 'affluent' are myopic even about their own longer-term interest does not wholly square with the assumption of *rational* egoism, and seems to me to be too gloomy a view of the propensities and future of the human species. What seems truer is that a shift to more aggressive and short-sighted forms of self-interest is being brought about by the retreat of democratic governments from responsible economic and social policies.

This situation raises a political issue which is now crucial (although often not recognised as such) for the life and future of democratic societies. How far must or should significant social goals be sacrificed in order to comply with the criteria of economic efficiency imposed by the workings of the international market system? Government policies have increasingly been guided by this assumed requirement, even at the cost of rising unpopularity. Political conflict and extremism have grown because of it. I am not of course reducing political events to a single cause, but suggesting that the drift from a more democratic and pluralist model of government to a less open and more authoritarian one can be partly at least explained in these terms. One lesson from this book is that governments, whether acting individually or collectively, need to recover more room for manoeuvre in the service of social goals.

I am grateful for comments on parts of the book from individual scholars. My thanks are especially due to Hugh Stretton, who read the whole draft and on particular chapters to Rudolf Klein, Harvey Feigenbaum, Phyllis Colvin, Jonathan Boston, Patrick Dunleavy, John Nethercote, Carol Weiss, Maurice Kelly, Bob Goodin, Jan Lamboy, Campbell Sharman and Peter Williams. I am also grateful for some constructive suggestions on public choice issues from my publisher's reviewers, Keith Dowding and Ian Holliday. None of these individuals have any responsibility for the use made of their advice. I have also benefited from seminar discussions on parts of the book at the Australian National University and several other Universities.

The Research School of Social Sciences in the Australian National University provided me with a supportive and friendly base for research and writing over two years as a Visiting Fellow in the urban research and politics programmes. My special thanks go to Penny Hanley in urban research for help with the bibliography and to Christine Treadwell in politics who word-processed successive drafts with accuracy, speed and patience. My publisher, Steven Kennedy, actively helped with advice and encouragement over the design of the book. My wife Sandra did her best to keep me to a timetable and tolerated my absorption in the book with much kindness.

Canberra *Peter Self*

1
Economic Interpretations of Politics

In the last thirty-five years a powerful new body of political thinkers has emerged, collectively known as the 'public choice' school. These thinkers model the study of politics upon the methods and assumptions of neo-classical market economics. Their writings have not only introduced a new intellectual view of the nature of politics but have had a considerable influence upon the conduct of politics and public policy, as this book will demonstrate.

The origins of the public choice school lie in the study of public finance and public goods by such writers as Wicksell and Lindhal. For some time the interest of economists was focused upon the question of what governments should do to remedy various forms of market failure, and upon the provision and financing of those 'pure public goods' which only governments can supply. Subsequently this concern was widened and reversed as economists started to compare the methods and problems of collective decision-making with those of competitive markets providing private goods. The rapid growth of governments after World War Two was an obvious stimulus to this field of study and contributed towards a radically different and more critical approach to the workings of government than traditional political science provided.

Public choice developed primarily in the USA and is still heavily concentrated there, although its influence has spread, especially to other English-speaking countries. It has produced a prolific volume of work which reflects the somewhat different approaches of the Virginia School led by James Buchanan and Gordon Tullock, who founded the Public Choice Society in 1963, and the Chicago School, represented by such writers as Mancur Olson and George Stigler. Earlier, in 1957, Anthony Downs had written his path-breaking *Economic Theory of Democracy*. The founding fathers, such as Buchanan, Tullock, Olson, William Riker and Anthony Downs, wrote some original works which advanced bold theories in fairly non-technical language. Later American writers have concentrated more upon testing hypotheses about specific issues of American politics. More broadly, and especially outside America, the economic approach has influenced the growth of 'rational actor' models of politics, which share a similar economic methodology but reach different conclusions.

This chapter provides a brief introduction to the basic assumptions of public choice thought and considers some of the critical issues which they raise. Its aim is to lay the ground for the review in Chapter 2 of the positive theories of public choice, and in Chapter 3 of its normative theories, which taken together have produced a body of beliefs or ideology with a potent influence upon political life.

Comparing economic and political systems

A well-known text-book gives the following definition of public choice:

> Public choice can be defined as the economic study of non-market decision-making, or simply the application of economics to political science. The subject matter of public choice is the same as that of political science: the theory of the state, voting rules, voting behaviour, party politics, the bureaucracy and so on. The methodology of public choice is that of economics, however. The basic behavioural postulate of public choice, as for economics, is that man is an egoistic, rational utility maximiser.
>
> (Mueller, *Public Choice*, Cambridge University Press, 1989, pp. 1–2)

Mueller notes that traditionally 'political man' (or woman) is supposed to be concerned with the public interest and 'economic man' with his private interest, but public choice rejects this dichotomy. Buchanan and Tullock (1962, pp. 20–3) ask why we should assume that an individual 'changes gear' when he moves from the private to the public sphere. He is still the same person, and it is reasonable to assume that his basic motives and interests will remain the same. What will change are the constraints and rules under which he operates, which will be critical for the rational calculation and pursuit of his private interest.

This leads to the other element in Mueller's definition – the special conditions of collective action or 'non-market decision-making'. What is the relationship between the economic and political systems? Many writers, such as Schumpeter (1943), have stressed the close cultural and institutional linkages between market capitalism and parliamentary democracy. Marxist theorists have made precisely the same point from the opposite viewpoint of arguing the dependence of liberal democracy upon capitalist interests (MacPherson, 1962). Before Marx the great classical economists such as Smith, Ricardo and Malthus stressed the significance for political behaviour of the conflicts of interest between different economic classes.

However the economic model used by mainstream public choice is the neo-classical one of perfectly competitive markets. Markets are assumed to work through voluntary exchanges between free individuals, each pursuing his or her private self-interest. Markets move towards an equilibrium point where no individual would profit from buying or selling a different product, or from changing his or her occupation. However this equilibrium point is continually moving with changes in individual tastes, costs of production, or the arrival of new products. If, in the homely example, individuals start demanding more coffee and less tea, the production of these commodities will shift until the marginal revenue that can be earned from either product equals the marginal cost of its production. By such continual marginal adjustments markets are said to respond spontaneously to consumer demands, thereby achieving 'allocative efficiency'.

Actual market systems do not satisfy the strong requirements of this ideal model, for example over perfect competition, full information or in other respects. However public choice theorists can still utilise this model to map certain features of political life. Following this approach, voters can be likened to consumers; political parties become entrepreneurs who offer competing packages of services and taxes in exchange for votes; political propaganda equates with commercial advertising; government agencies are public firms dependent upon receiving or drumming up adequate political support to cover their costs; and interest groups are co-operative associations of consumers or producers of public goods. Moreover the whole political system can be viewed as a gigantic market for the demand and supply of 'public goods', meaning all outputs supplied through a political instead of a market process (and including regulations and transfer payments as well as goods and services).

The 'political market' is cruder and harder to study than the market system. Market transactions can be measured and analysed in the common unit of money. Political transactions involve voting, which can be counted like money but which covers only a part of politics. Political action involves the exercise of authority, power and influence. Laws and government decisions can be known but influence is often elusive or secretly exercised. Nonetheless power or influence is in some ways the analogue of money, because it is the means through which political actors pursue their goals.

Moreover the individual citizen has much less scope for expressing her preferences through voting than the consumer has in the market-place. In theory all resources flow and adjust to the changing demands of market consumers; public choice theory suggests many ways in which the *political* process does *not* respond to the demands of citizens. In addition government action involves coercion which supposedly does not apply in market exchanges. Because collective decisions involve coercion and cannot satisfy all individual preferences equally, most public choice writers regard government as being intrinsically a less desirable means for satisfying individual wants than the market place, except for essential public goods. This conclusion is disputed by those who look to government to correct the inequalities and instabilities of the market place. This basic issue will recur later.

Basic assumptions: self-interest and rationality

A basic assumption of public choice thought is that individuals act as 'rational egoists' who pursue their private interests in both economic and political life. This is an arguable and slippery starting-point requiring elucidation. It will be convenient to deal with the two ideas of 'egoism' and 'rationality' separately.

The concept of self-interest

Ever since Adam Smith argued that it was the self-interest of butchers and bakers which (in a competitive market) promoted the general prosperity, it has been widely accepted that the market system works through the private pursuit of economic gain. This statement can be questioned. Other motives play a necessary part in economic life (see Chapter 7) and it can also be argued that the dominant role of self-interest is not so much the *cause* as the *consequence* of competitive markets. If full competition truly existed, as the theorists propose, an individual trader would need to act purely self-interestedly in order to survive. Ironically 'rational economic man' then becomes not the freely choosing individual which public choice theorists celebrate but a mechanistic figure controlled by external forces (Hollis and Nell, 1975).

Even so the pursuit of private gain is generally pursued and (subject to some moral as well as legal constraints) legitimised within the market system. The ultimate motive need not be a selfish one; I may want to make a lot of money in order to give to charity or an ailing friend. However public choice writers stress that the market relationship itself is instrumental and impersonal in its nature. Market consumers look for the best buy and while a few individuals may (for example) boycott South African oranges, even a socialist will usually buy a hi-fi set on purely personal preference without regard to the labour policies or other practices of the company making it.

Do these same instrumental and self-regarding motivations apply also in politics? In the past even neo-classical economists have doubted the comparison. Edgeworth, one of the founders of this school, believed that self-interest was the first principle of economics but thought also that trade (like war) involved 'the lower elements of human nature' which need not apply elsewhere (Sen, 1982, pp. 84–8). No less a market advocate than Mrs Thatcher seemed to hold much the same view when she told the Church of Scotland (rather smugly) that, while the worthy clergy and she herself did not need the spur of large economic incentives, businessmen needed them if they were to generate wealth (Raban, 1989).

Public choice theorists reject this line of thought as mistaken and hypocritical. Why should private, personal interest cease to be relevant when a voter votes, an interest group campaigns, or a politician seeks office? Although they made reservations, for example conceding the existence of altruism, the early public choice writers took self-interest to be the most realistic assumption about political behaviour (Downs, 1957, pp. 27–8; Buchanan and Tullock, 1962, p. 30). A more recent study stays with the hypothesis that 'private interest will dominate decision making in a large number of cases' (Crain and Tollison, 1990, p. 3).

These contentions do not accord with popular ideas of how politics *should* be conducted. For example, Robert Lane's survey of American attitudes found that self-interest was viewed as fruitful and beneficial within a market context, but as harmful and in need of constraint in a political one (Lane, 1986). On the other hand, public opinion tends also to be highly sceptical of the actual motivations and behaviour of politicians, bureaucrats, and so on. It is this 'credibility gap' to which public choice theory draws attention. The public's expectations of politics are held to be unrealistic. Public choice writers may have performed a service in seeking to expose some of the cant and self-interest which surrounds politicians' frequent appeal to the 'public interest', but their opposite assumptions may not be valid either.

Conflicting motives in politics

Altruism appears to be a much more widespread factor in political than in market behaviour. Certainly this is true of voting behaviour (see Chapter 2). In economic terms this means that an individual's own 'utility' is increased by contributing to the 'utility' of others, whether particular groups or the whole community. Public choice theorists explain this factor as a sort of 'psychic income', but this rather cumbrous explanation still weakens the concept of self-interest as a workable assumption. Self-interest can have little explanatory force unless it can be contrasted with altruistic behaviour.

Faced with much contrary evidence about political behaviour, Howard Margolis reverts to a dual explanation. Politics (he argues) exhibits both selfish and altruistic tendencies. However he retains economic methodology by suggesting that an individual will seek a balance between these tendencies and will experience diminishing utility if he or she becomes either too selfish or too altruistic (Margolis, 1982). There is some similarity here to Hirschman's suggestion of a public–private cycle, whereby individuals go into public life with altruistic motives or ideals, experience disillusionment, revert to the world of private interests and gain, find *that* in turn unsatisfying, and repeat the cycle (Hirschman, 1982). However, while Hirschman's account is at least suggestive about the existence of broad social cycles of political engagement and disillusion, Margolis' account offers a weak basis for predicting how individuals will behave in particular political situations.

Another important factor in political life, which does not have any parallel in the market-place, is the influence of ideology. Even if (very implausibly) ideology is defined or written off as simply a rationalisation of private self-interest, it clearly has the capacity to stimulate and energise political action, as subsequent chapters will demonstrate. Moral rules or standards also play an important part in political life. As Etzioni (1988, pp. 41–3) points out, moral norms differ basically from personal preferences, being generalised in rules, symmetrical in application and expressing commitments which often run counter to personal inclination. Thus they are not the same as a personal taste for altruism. Moral rules are relevant in all walks of life, including market behaviour. Their greater relevance to politics may reflect the fact that politics offers more opportunities for deviant behaviour (for example, behaviour which contradicts the intended function of some office) than does a properly policed market-place. In their critique of public choice theory, March and Olsen (1984, p. 21) stress the significance of 'normatively appropriate behaviour', meaning the rules and standards which guide political life. These rules and standards may be lax or firm. The laxer they are, the greater the scope for seeking private advantage by opportunistic behaviour.

Public choice theorists can offer two defences against these criticisms. One is to stress the instrumental character of much political behaviour. For example, whatever a politician's motives or ultimate goals, he needs to get elected to pursue them. Similarly, whether a bureau chief seeks only a bigger salary for himself or believes in the social value of his bureau's function, he will still want to maximise his bureau's budget and output (Niskanen, 1971). These arguments are not watertight, but they do draw attention to the importance of personal incentives and constraints in particular political or bureaucratic situations. The second defence is to claim that the self-interest assumption, while not always true, is prevalent enough to serve as a useful hypothesis for political analysis. Thus Brennan and Buchanan (1985) argue that the concept of 'homo economicus', while perhaps 'descriptively less relevant in the political setting than in economic markets' is still a 'useful fiction' for 'reasoned speculation' (1985, pp. 51; 65–6). The value of the public choice approach 'lies in its ability to generate testable hypotheses and predictions about political behaviour' which 'have been found to hold in a variety of cases' (Crain and Tollison, 1990, p. 4). Thus public choice defends its assumptions by their ability to yield significant and testable predictions about political behaviour. This test will be examined in the next chapter.

The rationality assumption

Public choice theory assumes that individuals are rational actors and choosers. It also assumes, as in the earlier quotation from Mueller, that a rational individual will be a utility maximiser. This concept is elusive. It is used as a basis for economic 'laws' of supply and demand; for example, if the price of some product increases because of higher costs, less of it will be demanded since consumers now find it relatively more expensive. This is not always true, however; for example, a higher price for some luxury article can occasionally stimulate more sales because of its snob value as conspicuous consumption. Snob value can be incorporated into the individual's 'utility function', but this concept becomes circular if it covers every choice which a consumer makes.

Equally the concept of maximisation is dubious. It is open to Herbert Simon's contention that most individuals and organisations are content to 'satisfice', that is to take the first course of action which seems good enough rather than to go on to find the best possible option (Simon, 1957). Simon reached this conclusion from discovering that organisations usually respond to a new situation or challenge by adapting an existing programme, not developing a new one. However 'satisficing' may also be rational when the costs of innovation are included. Public choice theorists use the costs of acquiring information as a rational explanation for some aspects of voting behaviour (see Chapter 2).

These considerations need not undermine the concept of economic rationality. The rationality of the market system depends upon the opportunities which it provides for rational choice, not upon the assumption that these will always be fully taken. There will always be individuals who are too lazy or other-worldly to make rational market choices. This is economically irrational, although not necessarily so in terms of some wider scale of human values. There is enough uniformity in mass market behaviour to make predictions possible. The concept of 'revealed preference' enables predictions to be based on the aggregate choices actually being made without bothering about individual psychology.

The same concept can be applied to political elections which also 'reveal' the preferences of the electors by the way they vote; but the reasons for political voting seem to be too diverse (as the conflicting interpretations of election results show) to permit extrapolation to future elections. Politics do not involve the massive volume of individual transactions from which laws of market behaviour can be plausibly deduced. There are no comparable criteria available for judging the rationality of political behaviour in terms of the requirements of the political system.

It does not follow that rational individual behaviour produces rational results. For example, individual farmers may behave rationally in responding to a fall in farm prices by increasing output to maintain their incomes; but the effect is to reduce farm prices further. In markets as well as politics rational egoism has some perverse effects.

However, public choice theory links rationality closely with self-interest. This frequent association seems due to the idea that self-interest offers a simple and plausible basis for defining the scope of rationality. Even so self-interest has many political expressions, such as the pursuit of power, glory or social status and esteem. Some public choice writers argue that these apparent goals cover up opportunities for material gains (Laver, 1981). This simplification keeps public choice theory consistent with its economic origins but is a very strained and cynical interpretation of political behaviour.

This concept of rationality can be criticised as narrow, one-dimensional and short-sighted. It does not delve into the deeper roots of individual behaviour. Jon Elster has stressed the multiple sides of individual personality and the internal conflicts and arguments which revolve around the exercise of choice (Elster, 1985, pp. 1–34). Amartya Sen contends that individual preference cannot be adequately represented on a one-dimensional scale, but involves higher level or meta-choices between different orderings of personal goals, such as moral versus selfish standards of behaviour and short versus long-term interests. Individual rationality is a complex construction. A concept of rationality based upon a narrow or materialist view of self-interest leads to perverse and contradictory results which produce 'rational fools' (Sen, 1982, pp. 84–108).

Social choice theory

Economists' usual definition of rationality entails a consistent set of preferences. The assumption among most economists is that an individual's 'utility' cannot be measured but can be expressed as an order of preferences. A rational preference ordering needs to be transitive: for example, if I prefer A to B and B to C, I will also prefer A to C. (There are other conditions of rationality which need not be discussed here.)

Once again individuals do not necessarily order their preferences in a consistent manner. No less an intellectual body than the French Academy voted to meet in Versailles rather than in Paris, in Fontainebleau rather than in Versailles, and finally in Paris rather than Fontainebleau – thus producing Condorcet's famous paradox of an irrational deadlock caused by intransitive preferences. The 'irrationality' of this distinguished body could have occurred from 'strategic voting' by one or more members who reasoned that a delayed decision would assist their preferred option; or it might reflect some members changing their minds as they heard more evidence (in which case another voting round would solve the problem), or possibly merely the uncertainty or ambivalence of some members.

The concept of preference is important for voting rules. Illogical voting by an individual affects the rationality of the collective result. The nature of voting rules strongly affects the results of elections and other collective decisions. These issues are the subject matter of an important related discipline known as *social choice*. Social choice theory is primarily relevant for normative questions about democratic decision-making which figure in Chapter 3. Social choice theory must assume rationality but need not assume self-interest; provided individual preferences are consistently ordered, we can examine logical ways of combining them without bothering about motivation.

To conclude this section, economics produces sophisticated models of the logic of choice but usually within a narrow concept of rational action. The models cover the 'costs' and 'benefits' of alternative ways of satisfying individual wants or alternative methods of combining individual preferences. These models do not inquire at all deeply into the sources of human motivation (although some economists like Sen do so) but treat rationality as an instrumental value for pursuing egocentric ends. Public choice theory generally stays with this limited notion of rationality, without investigating its fuzzier meanings. Logical consistency of action is assumed, but its specific goal is left to be filled in by the political context in which the individual is pursuing his personal advantage, or borrowed from traditional economic beliefs, such as that all work or effort is a cost (pain) done for the benefit of consumption (pleasure). This dualism comes out in the assumption that acts such as voting or political participation necessarily involve some personal cost. Given these theoretical limitations, public choice theory (as will emerge) is surprisingly robust. This robustness stems in part from its analysis of the contradictions which the assumption of rational egoism produces.

The problem of co-operation

The pursuit of rational self-interest often frustrates social co-operation. Many of the consequent problems can be modelled as games or game-like situations (for a useful summary see McLean, 1987, pp. 125–53). The theory of games has a special attraction to public choice theorists because in a game the objective is clear (to win or to achieve the maximum score or 'pay-off'), the rules are clear and the only problem is to find the most logical strategy for an individual to pursue. The best-known logical problem analysed in public choice is that of the 'prisoner's dilemma'. Although by now extremely familiar, it merits a brief discussion as providing the paradigm case of the way a rationally selfish strategy pursued by each of two individuals leads to a bad result for both of them, and it has strong implications for political behaviour.

The prisoner's dilemma

Two prisoners are sitting in separate cells and each is being urged to confess and help convict the other. The pay-offs are as in the matrix below. Each prisoner reasons that if he defects and the other prisoner stays mum, he will get the best result of a light sentence (6 points). If, however, he stays mum and the other defects he will get the worst result (0). Either way the dominant selfish strategy for each prisoner is to defect, which lands them both with a substantial jail sentence (2 points each), whereas both could achieve a much better result by tacitly co-operating and staying mum (4 points each).

		B	
		Co-operates	Defects
A	Co-operates	4/4	0/6
	Defects	6/0	2/2

The question arises of how, if every individual is a rational egoist, social norms of co-operation develop. One public choice theory is that this process occurs through super-games whereby individuals gradually learn the benefit of co-operation. To test this thesis, Robert Axelrod organised two computer tournaments each of 200 iterated plays of 'prisoner's dilemma', with a prize for the most successful strategy. This was won both times by a psychologist, Anatol Rapoport, with a fairly simple strategy of 'tit for tat' whereby a player co-operates the first time round and thereafter follows his opponent's moves. This strategy is robust, because it eschews opportunism and fosters predictability (thereby opening a window for co-operation), but it does not provide a sure strategy for establishing co-operation between selfish individuals (Axelrod, 1984).

Axelrod suggests that biological evolution shows a balance being struck between self-assertion and willingness to co-operate. The 'tit for tat' strategy is based upon just such a balance: the individual will retaliate if pushed around but resumes co-operation as soon as his opponent/partner is willing. This theory has some relevance for political and international conflicts; for example, it may suggest that balanced retaliation is often a preferable strategy to the pursuit of complete victory or 'unconditional surrender'. For a time in World War One British and German soldiers evolved a mutual strategy of refraining from shooting at each other at meal times (ibid., pp. 73–87). A parallel governmental strategy of requiring the enemy countries to disgorge their territorial gains rather than to surrender completely might have shortened the war and prevented its later renewal in more virulent form. Clearly, however, international conflicts are often driven by blind passions of anger and revenge, not rational calculations of self-interest.

The theory of games now figures in strategic studies of international conflict. The nuclear arms race represented a kind of iterated prisoner's dilemma since each big power could have saved substantial resources and increased its own (and the world's) safety by mutual restraint from adding to its nuclear arsenal. However, so long as each power thought it possible to achieve a dominant or impregnable position, or believed that the other power was bent upon doing so, no real co-operation was possible. Co-operation depended upon the introduction of a 'mutual assurance game' whereby trust in the other's intentions could be gradually increased through successive bilateral arms reductions. These developments were influenced by gradual acceptance of the unrealism of either side achieving an impregnable defence, but in fact the growing internal weakness of one power (the Soviet Union) undermined the equality of the relationship and created a new situation.

The Cuban missile crisis of 1960 can be compared to a game of 'chicken'. In this game two motorists race side by side down a two-way road, the first to draw back losing the game and reputation. The US government faced the problem that, if it did not stop the export of nuclear missiles from Russia to Cuba, the country's safety could be endangered and its reputation for firm action would suffer (similarly the need to protect America's reputation as the guarantor of another country's existence was the main official reason for military intervention in Vietnam); but equally American armed intervention could trigger off a nuclear conflict. The attempts made within the American government to put a figure on the probability of nuclear war were useless in this unique situation, but it took the risk and the Russians drew back from confrontation.

The theory of coalitions

The limitation of games theories is of course that real life cannot be reduced to the simplified conditions but complex strategies which distinguish games. Also, with the exception of two-person, zero-sum games of opposed interests (where one person's gain is the other's loss), no unique optimum strategy can be found for winning most games (Riker and Ordeshook, 1973, Chs 5 and 8). However some political situations, such as the formation of coalitions, can be modelled in a somewhat analogous way to game problems to show problems of co-operation.

One example is the demonstration by Buchanan and Tullock (1962, pp. 131–45) of the problem of cyclical majority voting. They imagine a group of farmers collectively deciding upon the repair of their roads. It will pay a bare majority of farmers to form a coalition which will repair only their own roads at the expense of the whole group. However if side-payments are possible, alternative and successive winning coalitions will be formed through bribing individuals to change sides. The result becomes completely indeterminate. In practice it may be suggested that farmers are unlikely to be so narrowly egocentric and short-sighted as to behave in this way. A substantial majority might, for example, agree upon a policy of repairing all roads according to a technical schedule of priorities, even if some would do better from this arrangement than others.

In some legislative situations co-operation depends upon a process of 'log-rolling'. The classic case is the 'pork barrel' in the US Congress, whereby legislators exchange support for their pet local projects. These arrangements can be generalised to produce a legislative quasi-market in which legislators form fluctuating coalitions to support or oppose particular measures, based upon calculations of 'political opportunity costs' to their own interests. This behaviour derives from a legislative system with weak party discipline and strong local interests. One result of log-rolling is to slow up decisions, as shown in the periodic 'budget crises' due to Congressional failure to pass the necessary appropriations bills. Party discipline can be seen as a device of enforced political co-operation which expedites decision-making by moving the bargaining process to within the party and strengthening the role of party leadership.

The best known theory of political co-operation is William Riker's thesis that a coalition will consist of a bare majority because anything more will dilute the rewards of office among an unnecessarily large number of individuals (Riker,1962). The thesis is most plausible if it is assumed that politicians are interested only in the personal rewards of office. It can be extended (although more dubiously) to cover distinctive policy or ideological goals, since these also will be diluted within a larger than necessary coalition, but conversely these goals can also be an obstacle to numerically 'rational' partnerships between possible coalition members. Riker applied his thesis to American Presidential elections; for example, he argued that President Johnson's victory in 1964 was unnecessarily large owing to the accident of inheriting Kennedy supporters after Kennedy's assassination and adding his own substantial Southern supporters. Johnson could afford to lose many of his Southern supporters because of his civil rights stand but later he also lost many Kennedy supporters because of the Vietnam war. The argument that Johnson suffered because his coalition was too large is not very convincing. More relevant tests of Riker's thesis are the formation of coalition governments in Europe (see Chapter 2).

The free rider theorem

The leading example of the political application of the problem of group co-operation is the free rider theorem (Olson, 1965). Olson postulates that a rational individual will not incur the cost and trouble of supporting an organisation formed to pursue some jointly beneficial goal, in circumstances in which his own contribution will make a negligible difference to the result and he can enjoy any eventual benefits without contributing. In other words he will 'free ride' on the backs of others. This theorem is a strong inference from the assumption of rational egoism, and it has been widely applied to political life. Besides Olson's application of it to interest groups, the theorem has been used to analyse barriers to voting and perversions in the demand and supply of public goods (see Chapter 2). It can also be extended to extra-legal or illegal activities such as tax evasion and non-compliance with laws.

Olson attacked the pluralist belief that voluntary organisations develop out of motives of mutual concern and co-operation. Instead he explained their growth in terms of hard-headed calculations of self-interest. His chosen examples are economic interest groups, such as farm organisations, trade associations or trade unions, who seek political benefits such as subsidies, protection or minimum wages which will apply to all relevant individuals, whether they join the organisation or not. He finds that many such organisations also offer commercial or advisory services, such as insurance, discounted goods, marketing assistance and information that are geared to members' economic interests. Members are attracted by these 'selective incentives' which then provide the necessary basis for the political activities of the organisation. At a later stage the problem of co-operation may be overcome by the organisation acquiring coercive sanctions, such as the trade union closed shop, or special legal privileges, such as the right of professional bodies to control entry and conditions of work. Olson's theory is considered further in Chapter 2.

These various problems of co-operation between rational, self-seeking individuals are important for public choice theory in two ways. In the first place they illustrate the limitations upon rational choice in politics, especially when contrasted with the economists' conception of free market exchanges. On the other hand it is vital that basic rules be somehow established if forums of voluntary exchange are also to exist. Some rules, for example over property and contract, are basic 'public goods'. In the second place they suggest the importance of institutional rules for determining how self-interest is pursued and how problems of co-operation are solved or shelved. The distinctive contribution of mainstream public choice lies in the marriage between theories of rational action and the operation of institutional rules.

Alternative public choice

Some writers accept the 'rational actor' model of public choice but deduce from it quite different conclusions. These alternative versions of public choice thought are important both for the criticisms which they offer of the dominant American literature and for their fusion of economic methodology with older traditions of political science such as pluralism or Marxism.

The common assumption of all rational actor models is methodological individualism which means that:

> all social phenomena – their structure and their change – are in
> principle explicable in ways that only involve individuals – their
> properties, their goals, their beliefs and their actions.
> (Elster, *Making Sense of Marx*, Cambridge University Press, 1985, p. 5)

This assumption rejects social and historical determinism and stresses the micro-foundations of social behaviour which are rooted in the beliefs, purposes and choices of individuals. It is an assumption now accepted by some Marxists, as the above quotation from Elster suggests, as well as by economic individualists.

However, within this framework, there are marked differences between what may be called strong and weak versions of methodological individualism. The strong version assumes that the individual is generally mistress of her fate and forms her goals and preferences independently. This is the usual approach of market economists and mainstream public choice writers who, while not denying social influences, treat individual preferences as 'exogenous' and rarely inquire into their origins. The weak version of individualism, while rejecting determinism, stresses the ways in which individual preferences are formed and circumscribed by economic and social conditions. There follows a brief review of some criticisms of mainstream public choice from this perspective.

(a) *The formation of preferences.* Patrick Dunleavy uses public choice methodology to develop a concept of 'group identity'. He argues that an individual can rationally identify his private interest with that of a group which reflects his structural situation in society; for example, a factory worker can identify with his local trade union and perhaps with a Labour Party which reflects his interest as a worker. These are 'endogenous preferences', based upon the logic of structural cleavage and conflict and groups formed on this basis have a 'compact identity set' and relatively homogeneous interests. Alternatively or additionally, an individual may identify with a cause group or minor political party which corresponds with her personal beliefs, values or lifestyle ('exogenous preferences'). Such groups have a more unstable identity and more diverse interests (Dunleavy, 1991, pp. 45–78).

This distinction between endogenous and exogenous preferences is useful but overdrawn. In the former case it is not necessarily clear what organisation (or none) will most rationally serve an individual's economic interest. Personal preference and judgement play a not inconsiderable part. In the latter case, socialisation may strongly influence the cause (if any) which an individual supports. Dunleavy's analysis is also open to the 'free rider' objection: why should a rational egoist join a trade union in the first place?

Nonetheless the general argument about the social formation of preferences is hard to deny. Public choice theorists cannot offer any worthwhile predictions about political behaviour unless they assume that all (or anyhow most) individuals in the same situation will share similar preferences or interests sufficiently to override their individual differences. This is the necessary basis for predictions about the behaviour of groups of bureaucrats, politicians and so on, however the group is defined. Anthony Downs (1957, p. 30) made the simple assumption that all members of a political party share the same dominant interest in election, even though he admitted that it was unrealistic in terms of individual behaviour. On the other hand a public choice analysis that assumes all preferences to be both 'exogenous' and selfish would reduce group behaviour to a set of conflicting personal goals. The structural and social factors which give cohesion to the group could not figure in the analysis.

Dunleavy's postulate of 'group identity' seems to revert to a pluralist approach, since it suggests the need for motives of empathy and loyalty among members of the group and not just self-interest. Moreover, to the extent that generalisations are easier to make about group than about individual behaviour, pluralism also re-emerges. While individual motivation is often complex and uncertain, the behaviour of an organised group can be at least better hypothesised in terms of rational action since its objectives are usually limited, specific and observable, even if exposed to internal conflict and change. As pluralists contend, the diverse interests of individuals are channeled into a variety of group interests. Public choice theory introduces significant insights into issues of group co-operation, but in the end it too has to hypothesise groups as unitary actors, despite the contradiction this involves with the strong version of methodological individualism.

(b) *Social power*. Mainstream public choice, reflecting neo-classical market theory, shows little recognition of the existence of social power. Buchanan and Tullock (1962, pp. 12, 23–7) deny that power or class relations play much part in politics, and attribute political conflicts to the different interests of independent individuals. As in market theory, the power base of these conflicting interests is left out. By contrast alternative versions of public choice stress the existence of highly unequal individual resources in both market and political spheres, which overlap and reinforce each other. As a consequence the wants of poor individuals may be difficult to express through the political options actually presented to them. Poor individuals also typically possess less relevant information. Both points can be illustrated by the fact that voting in elections is generally lower among the poor than among the rich.

Social power can be used to change the incentive structure of other individuals (Dowding, 1991, pp. 142–8). A historical example was the capacity of an employer to threaten sanctions against any workers who voted the wrong way – a source of political power that has been widely but not wholly countered by the device of secret ballots (and secret ballots are now attacked by some conservative adherents of public choice as contrary to open transactions). Considerable wealth is now necessary when standing for political office in some countries, especially the USA, and this wealth can be used to persuade voters to change their minds. In many countries direct bribes are still used as political inducements. These are examples of the capacity of well-endowed individuals to change the 'incentive structure' of others.

Governmental power can be used to change both the opportunities and the preferences of individuals. Public choice writers stress the ability of politicians to win votes by a selective distribution of economic favours. However the ability of governments to discipline individuals through policy changes which narrow their options and change their expectations is an unfamiliar idea in the mainstream literature. Mainstream public choice stresses the responsiveness of government to political demands, not the independent interest of a party in power in shaping individual preferences to suit its own ends (Dunleavy, 1991).

(c) *Marxist public choice*. Marxist public choice sounds paradoxical since its political conclusions run directly contrary to most mainstream theorists. The interest of some Marxists in public choice lies in showing that issues of class conflict and exploitation can be explained in terms of the rational action of individuals (insofar as choices are open to them) and need not be ascribed to some mysterious, deterministic historical law. However this form of Marxist revisionism views public choice as only one way of understanding political behaviour, not (as the mainstream theorists do) as an exclusive and adequate methodology (Elster, 1986, p. 220) and it uses economic methodology to reject the idea that the market system is based upon voluntary exchange.

The Marxist version of rational choice argues that class conflict and exploitation can be explained by exchanges between differently endowed individuals in a competitive market setting. Workers under capitalism are in a weak position to understand or pursue their own interests and welfare. Instead their preferences, 'have been formed under conditions of inadequate opportunity, have been warped, more generally, by capitalist society' (Roemer, 1986, p. 194). This treatment of preferences is quite contrary to the meaning of rational choice as understood by mainstream public choice.

Elster (1985) uses rational choice analysis to consider how far workers can overcome their collective action problem of organising effectively to defend their interests. Such motives as deriving a positive personal utility from the welfare of fellow workers, feeling guilt or shame at failure to help others in the same adverse situation and the social pressures of a shared lifestyle can all help to establish 'a conditional preference for co-operation'. These motives are quite likely to be found among dependent groups of workers but are much less likely among capitalists, among whom collective action will usually emerge only from the experience of iterated games of rationally selfish competition. This analysis of workers' co-operation is 'rational', in the sense that basically the worker will not proceed too far beyond his perception of his own self-interest but will take some risks to improve his position and that of his close associates. Consequently revolution is unlikely, both despite and because of the existence of systematic power relations. In similar vein Elster applies games theory to strategies of conflict and co-operation between the three classes of land-lords, bourgeoisie and workers and between capitalists, workers and state.

Conclusion

This brief excursion into alternative versions of rational choice shows the versatility of this concept and the many directions in which it can be turned.

> Pluralists, élitists, statists can all use the rational choice method . . . but the method itself will not generate the thesis which will prove the most empirically robust.

(Dowding, *Rational Choice and Political Power*, Edward Elgar, 1991, p. 175)

However the claim of mainstream public choice is that it *has* a methodology which is fully adequate and empirically robust, whereas alternative versions make a more selective or limited use of this methodology. Moreover mainstream public choice is firmly and strongly anchored in the neo-classical economic tradition. It may be that the assumptions embedded in that tradition are untenable or have to be heavily modified. It may be too that strong and pertinent criticisms of the market model can be made from within the public choice framework itself. None-theless the strong individualism of mainstream public choice, and its affinity with market theories, give it a potent political appeal and application which will emerge later.

2
Theories of Political Behaviour

This chapter will review some of the theories about political behaviour which have been derived from public choice's distinctive methodology. We will consider the role of actors in the political process: voters, parties, interest groups, bureaucrats, politicians. This review leads naturally on to a central subject of public choice: the demand and supply of public goods. The chapter's conclusions deal with the validity of these theories – how true are they and do they justify their assumptions? As we are dealing with a large body of work the coverage is necessarily selective and condensed, with a stress on those theories with strong political implications.

Voters

The initial problem about voters which public choice theorists must face is why they bother to vote at all. Voting involves the individual in only a small amount of effort, yet the possibility that a single vote will affect the election result is microscopically tiny; so why should a rational egoist vote at all (Downs, 1957)? The situation seems different in a marginal constituency, and the fact that voting is often higher there might lend some support to Downs' hypothesis, but even in marginal constituencies it is almost unknown for the result to turn upon one single vote. Perhaps the egoistic voter in question is not rational enough to calculate the odds correctly.

We need not waste much time on this subject, however, since most public choice theorists admit that voters are influenced by other motives, such as party loyalty, a sense of duty, or the need for self-expression. The 'rational egoist' hypothesis may help to explain why many people never vote and why polling is low in adverse circumstances – for example, Labour used to pray for a fine polling day in Britain because some of their supporters would not turn out to vote after work on a wet evening. However the theory cannot explain the decline in voting often attributed to political apathy, since the narrow equation of cost and influence has not changed.

The larger problem for the voter is how to use her very limited power effectively. Public choice theorists view voting as essentially a referendum over the preferred supply and cost of public goods; but at a general election the voter is faced with a choice between two or more comprehensive packages of proposals which she must take as a whole and cannot disaggregate. This is sometimes known as the problem of 'full supply'. In the market-place the housewife can balance her preferences for tea and coffee, and will at least get what she pays for. In the polling booth, neither of these conditions applies. She has to accept a proposed increase in defence expenditure, which she may not want, along with an increase for health, which she may favour; and she has to accept the consequent increase in taxation on both counts. Again she has no assurance that the party of her choice will, if elected, deliver what they promise. They may find excuses for delay or fail to deliver through economic circumstances.

Despite these problems the usual public choice assumption is that voting will express the individual's estimate or expectation of her private financial interest (Tullock, 1976). This assumption seemed to fit various electoral studies which reached the unsurprising conclusion that economic depression in a particular region or industry produced electoral swings against the government. However this general conclusion did not imply a close correlation between personal economic situation and voting behaviour. The general hypothesis of 'pocketbook voting' has now been extensively investigated and largely disproved. Leif Lewin has summarised the results of numerous studies of voting behaviour in North America and many European countries. In almost every case there *is* a relationship between the way the individual views the state of the economy or the competence of the government and how she votes; but little relationship between her vote and her personal financial status (Lewin, 1991). Of course the voter will hope that what is best for the national prosperity will also in due course benefit him or herself; but this is a different kind of judgement from 'pocketbook voting'.

There is some correlation between economic class and voters' attitudes; for example (quite naturally) industrial workers tend to be more worried about unemployment than about inflation, while middle-class voters show the reverse bias. However Lewin's general conclusions seem to hold even when allowance is made for class and party affiliations (Lewin, 1991, pp. 47–8). In the USA individual positions on such issues as unemployment and the Vietnam War correlated better with ideological beliefs than with personal self-interest which they often contradicted (Reich, 1988, pp. 25 and 39–41). One American survey of voting concluded emphatically that 'in general, symbolic attitudes (liberal–conservative, party identification and racial prejudice) had strong effects, while self-interest had almost none' (Sears *et al.*, 1980).

Faced with this evidence, some public choice theorists have fallen back on the concept of 'expressive voting'. The argument is that, since the rational voter knows that she can make virtually no difference to the outcome, she is free to take the moral reward of casting a 'public interest' vote at no real cost to herself (Brennan and Walsh, 1990, pp. 97–144). This argument ties in with Schumpeter's earlier observation that there is something rather theatrical and unreal (to the ordinary voter) about political contests, and with Buchanan's view that individuals are much more careless and indifferent about matters of public than about private concern. Brennan and Walsh's argument has a curious implication. If most individuals did in fact vote on a public interest basis then the results would not have the perverse effects which many public choice writers claim. However 'expressive voting' is not necessarily benevolent or public spirited since it can be rooted in strongly emotional attitudes (such as racial prejudice) or in personal likes or dislikes for particular politicians.

Tullock's concept of 'pocketbook voting' looks more plausible in the context of referenda on single issues (such as occur in Swiss cantons and American states) or in the election of a single-purpose local authority such as an American school board. However even in such contexts many voters seem to be altruistic. A Swedish vote on a proposal to tax mortgage interest did not find (as might be expected) most home-owners opposed and most renters in favour; 'the voter's self-interest was less important than his ideological position' (Lewin, 1991, p. 54). In an American study quoted by Mueller, (1989, pp. 367–8) 40 per cent of voters were ready to have their property rates increased in the interest of equalising taxes across districts.

Generally it seems that voting behaviour is much too complex to be captured by any single theory. Traditionally most voting reflected party loyalties and this is still a significant factor (see below). Voting on economic issues has grown in importance and reflects mixed judgements upon the existing state of the economy and the perceived ability of parties to manage it better (here judgements on competence are as important as those on policies) (Kiewiet, 1983). It might be concluded that voting is 'sociotropic', for example based not on private self-interest but on some view of what is best for the country (Lewin, 1991 p. 45). However this view is too simple and optimistic when account is taken of both the superficial knowledge and weak interest of many voters as well as of the intrusion of strong passions and prejudices which are ignored by the rationalism of public choice.

Parties

One of the earliest and best public choice books was Anthony Downs' lucid *An Economic Theory of Democracy* (1957). Downs set up a model of party behaviour based upon assumptions which he conceded to be somewhat unrealistic – namely that the voter is a rational egoist and that in a democracy the sole aim of a political party is to achieve or retain office. Policies must therefore be designed so as to maximise votes.

Using this model Downs developed some fascinating insights into party behaviour and competition. His strongest insight was that a rational voter (and still more, one supposes, an irrational one) will not incur the high personal cost involved in being adequately informed about policy issues. (He was right on that score: most voters get only superficial information about politics and even the well-informed can usually cover only a few issues.) Consequently it is quite rational for a voter to choose a party representing his or her general position on the political spectrum, and for the party to develop its ideology as a short guide to that position. If we now assume that the political spectrum can be viewed in terms of a single left–right dimension, the behaviour of parties will be a function of the distribution of voters along that spectrum, together with the particular rules of the electoral system.

Suppose further that these rules are biased towards a two-party system and that the preferences of voters are concentrated in the middle of the spectrum ('single-peaked preference distribution'). Then it will pay both parties to take up policy positions close to each other in the middle of the spectrum, each seeking to command all votes to the left or right (an analogy is two ice-cream sellers standing together in the middle of a long beach). If now the middle block of voters move in either direction, the parties will move with them. However the voters well to the left or right of the centre will dislike this arrangement and if they become too alienated or more numerous they will compel the parties to move apart.

This last point was strongly developed in *Exit, Voice and Loyalty* (1970) by Albert Hirschman, who pointed out that, compared with the ability of market consumers to change their custom from one firm to another, citizens had only a weak capacity to 'exit' from one party to another and consequently needed to rely on using their 'voice' within the party. Since the more extreme party members will usually care more about its policies than those near the middle (who have much less to hope or fear from a change of government), they will exert a stronger voice within the party ranks and will raise that voice if dissatisfaction sets in with moderate policies. The stronger ideology of party 'activists' is a well-known fact and is paralleled by similar behaviour within interest and cause groups (Moe, 1980).

A further point is that in a dominant two-party system like the British or American, a third party has little hope of achieving office unless it can replace one of the major parties. Theoretically this might happen if (through the stronger 'voice' of their extremists) the main parties moved far enough apart for a third party to capture a large zone of middle ground.

A mixture of Downs' and Hirschman's theories gives a plausible interpretation of British politics. After a strong left-ward move by the electorate in wartime, Labour won the 1945 election handsomely, the Conservatives then moved to the left, embracing much of the programme of the 'welfare state', Labour moved back somewhat to the right as normality returned, and the two parties, despite their rhetoric, then followed very similar policies over most issues for almost three decades. Even the eventually divisive issue of inflation was one on which both parties would have liked to reach the similar solution of a statutory incomes policy. It was the failure of both the Wilson and the Heath Governments to achieve this result which ushered in the fiercer politics of the 1970s.

British politics in the 1980s supported Hirschman's thesis. As no consensus on the answer to Britain's economic problems was found, the two main parties moved further to the right or left under the influence of their extremists. The Conservative Party held together but the Labour Party split. A group of Labour moderates called the 'gang of four' formed a new party, the SDP (Social Democratic Party), which subsequently joined with the small Liberal Party to form a centralist bloc, the Alliance. The Alliance won over 25 per cent of the vote in the 1983 election, but, since its supporters were geographically dispersed, the British electoral system translated this success into less than 4 per cent of seats. Hence the new party failed to win enough middle ground to replace Labour, but its intervention pushed Labour into moving back towards the right to protect its flank. By 1992 both main parties were beginning to gravitate back towards a new centrist zone well to the right of the previous 'consensus'.

However the evidence suggests that Downs' theory, while offering some valuable insights into party behaviour, has too narrow a view of political goals. For example, a historical study of European Socialist parties concluded that they would have been much more successful if they had adjusted their policies to win middle-class votes, but their goals and ideologies precluded this strategy (Przeworski and Sprague, 1986).

More specific public choice tests have been concerned with coalition theory. Riker's 'minimum numbers theory' – the argument that a coalition will be based upon a bare majority in order to maximise gains to its members – has emerged as (at most) only one factor in the complex politics of coalition formation. The formation of coalition governments in European countries is much influenced by the 'policy distance' between parties, for example, parties usually try to form coalitions with partners whose ideologies are not too different, regardless of any law of numerical expediency. Also important are institutional rules, personal loyalties and long-term party strategies (Laver and Schofield, 1990; De Swaan and Mokken, 1980).

A more straightforward example of the vote-maximising assumption is the theory of the 'political business cycle', which argues that a government will court popularity by stimulating the economy or cutting taxes before an election (Nordhaus, 1975; MacRae, 1977). Striking examples of this behaviour are not hard to find, but extensive research has shown that the theory applies only to a limited number of cases and is not generally true (Lewin, 1991, pp. 62–71).

Once again the theory is weak because it overlooks distinctive party goals. For example, left-wing governments tend to increase public expenditure initially and later to be pushed by external pressures into retrenchment, and right-wing governments to behave in the converse manner. In British politics these tendencies help to explain why Conservative governments have more often inflated the economy before an election and Labour ones have behaved 'more responsibly'. Moreover a more critical attitude towards inflation, especially by right-wing voters, has reduced the scope for achieving quick popularity by this means.

Downs' theory reflects an optimistic view of the power of voters by supposing that party policies, through the competition for office, will broadly reflect the distribution of preferences among the electorate. Hence the key role of the median voter in two-party contests. Later public choice theories, especially of the 'alternative' variety, stress instead the powerful instruments that a government can bring to bear to change or 'shape' individual preferences among the electorate (Dunleavy, 1991). Parties in office do not respond passively to changing electoral preferences, but promote particular interests and ideologies with all the means at their disposal.

It is possible to rescue both the 'political business cycle' and the 'median voter' theory in a weak form. Thus it does appear that governments tend initially to pursue their own distinctive goals and interests, but pay more attention to the median voter and public opinion generally before an election. The median voter plays a mild bell-wether role in this unsurprising conclusion.

Interest groups: formation

Before public choice theories appeared on the scene, interest groups had already been extensively studied by pluralists. Indeed for the more extreme pluralists, starting with Bentley (1949), almost all politics could be reduced to the interplay and competition of group interests. Parties consisted of aggregations of specific interests. The public interest consisted in the institutional and conventional 'rules of the game' which regulated group conflicts. Bureaucracy and government could also be divided into agencies and administrative groups with their own distinctive policies and interests (for a pluralist analysis of government, see Self, 1985, pp. 79–107).

As with voting, the 'free rider' theorem poses an initial problem for public choice theorists as to why so many active interest groups should exist at all. Olson's theory of 'selective incentives', introduced in Chapter 1, does not explain the initial formation of these groups. The only way in which such a group will emerge, on a strict reading of the free rider assumption, is when some individual or organisation has sufficient private interest in the outcome to carry the whole cost of promoting some common benefit. A favourite example is the case of the multi-millionaire Howard Hughes, who bought a local TV station so that he could view Westerns all night, thereby conferring this benefit on all other viewers (possibly local citizens with teenage children would not see this as a benefit). More seriously a big firm could find it profitable to organise and pay for a lobby group even though other firms would 'free ride' on its efforts. Relaxing the theorem a little, this example suggests that an interest group will be easiest to form where there are a few major beneficiaries, and more generally that small groups should be easier to form than large ones – especially if account is taken of the social sanction of public opinion.

Further research by Moe (1980) on American economic interest groups, such as farm and business organisations and trade unions, underlines the actual complexity of motivations among members of these organisations. While material incentives such as Olson suggests are often quantitatively the main reason given for membership, other motives are also significant. Ideological and political goals figure strongly in the calculations of leaders and of the more active members, especially in some of the larger organisations. Additionally 'solidarity' motives play a part, usually the secondary one of the social satisfaction derived from working together in a common cause. Moe also suggests that solidarity motives are a stronger and more direct reason for the participation of workers in European trade unions.

The many co-operative services provided by early trade unions in Britain or by farm organisations in the USA seem to have sprung from their members' belief in mutual support, rather than from any necessity for 'selective incentives'. These traditional motivations are weaker among the more affluent and individualistic car workers in the Luton factory studied by Goldthorpe *et al* (1968), although the 1980s miners' strike in Britain showed that appeals to solidarity still strongly influence the behaviour of workers in the old heavy industries. There is also some problem in explaining how interest groups can provide commercially attractive services in the face of outside competition unless they can draw on some mutual loyalty. The not infrequent failures of such enterprises point the moral. There are bodies, such as large motoring organisations, which individuals join wholly to obtain certain services, without necessarily supporting the political propaganda waged on their behalf. Generally, though, selective incentives are an inadequate reason for the growth of interest groups.

Olson's and Moe's analyses are concerned only with *economic* interest groups. As Olson concedes, ideological motivations are likely to play a much larger part in the behaviour of specifically political bodies, such as parties and (still more) cause groups pursuing welfare or environmental goals. While the material interests of its members can figure in the behaviour of any organisation, it strains common sense to assume that the members of Greenpeace, for example, are primarily swayed by such concerns. Solidarity motivations will also be important whenever individuals gain mutual pleasure and support from pursuing a common task, and the 'displacement of goals' – whereby the pursuit of an original goal is replaced by the secondary aim of holding the organisation together – is a familiar development.

Interest groups: influence

A simple model of interest group activity can be based on the distribution of costs and benefits among the relevant actors (Wilson, 1980).

		COSTS	
		Concentrated	Diffused
BENEFITS	Concentrated	1	2
	Diffused	3	4

Square 1 represents a tug-of-war between two or more interest groups, for example over getting government contracts or licences, being accepted as the representative body of a profession, or locating a public facility. Here both costs and benefits are concentrated on specific groups, although a wider public may be affected by the outcome. Square 4, where both benefits and costs are widely diffused, covers such issues as the extent to which a universal system of social security can be afforded. Here a generalised interest (that of taxpayers) is pitted against an equally generalised one (that of consumers). This is usually regarded as the realm of party rather than interest group politics, but in practice the design of a general scheme will to some extent concentrate costs or benefits on specific groups.

The main focus of public choice theory is squares 2 and 3, especially the former, where the interest group has the opportunity to gain a concentrated benefit for its members while diffusing the cost among a wide public; for example a vulnerable industry will get tariff protection (paid for by consumers); a farm organisation will get subsidies (paid for by taxpayers); a professional organisation will get monopoly powers of self-regulation (paid for by less competition and higher service costs); and so on. Because the cost in each case is so widely diffused it is likely to be of little concern to any one individual.

Square 3 represents the converse situation where the cost of some measure is concentrated upon a particular group for the benefit of a broader constituency. The regulation of industries and the control of monopolies provide many examples. Here the industrial pressure group is on the defensive and may lose the first round; however it will now work to influence or 'capture' the relevant public agency, often with considerable success. Another familiar example is that where a group of residents form an *ad hoc* pressure group (or utilise an existing one) to oppose some unwanted development, such as an airport or power station or public housing estate. Here, however, they are usually faced by a developer (public or private) seeking to supply some necessary service or utility. The residents' group sometimes wins, but usually only through shifting the facility to a location where the opposition is less or the residents are poorer and weakly organised.

From this analysis it can be argued that many minority interests have a political opportunity to exploit majorities, which varies with their organisational strength and political influence. The former factor depends on such things as ease of organisation (geographically concentrated miners are better placed than widely dispersed farm workers); financial resources (an advantage for big corporations); know-how, contacts and energy (environmental groups are more successful in middle-class than working-class areas); and possible use of sanctions (whether, for example, a strike will inflict serious injury upon the economy).

However pressure groups cannot succeed unless they can also win the support of politicians. Public choice theorists stress the significance of an exchange relationship between politicians and interest groups for mutual advantage. The advantages to the politicians, on the rational egoist model, include such things as electoral support, campaign contributions and personal financial payments such as retainers, company directorships or, in some cases, direct bribes. In this way, according to some theorists, the general public becomes the silent, disregarded paymaster of special interests.

How widespread is this form of political transaction? It is certainly pervasive in the USA. There the ability of special interests to exploit the state with the connivance of politicians has been extensively documented (see, for example, McConnell, 1966). The machine politics of the big cities worked through politicians buying votes with favours and getting a cut from lucrative contracts. Big city machines have declined, but Congress continues to offer a more dignified version of the same relationship.

In order to get and stay elected, Congressmen need to satisfy local interests with such things as public works, subsidies and defence contracts. One study concludes that a rational Congressman gets on best by combining 'position statements' on the big issues of the day, which show his respect for public opinion, with special favours to local interests (Mayhew, 1974). As the chairmanship of Congressional committees goes with seniority, the successful Congressman is increasingly able to deliver Federal benefits to his area and to secure higher financial support for himself (Crain and Tollison, 1976). Because the Federal bureaucracy is fragmented into numerous bureaus serving specialised clienteles, the bureau chief also needs to secure or actually to create a supportive interest group, as well as seeking budgetary and legislative help from Congress. Hence the famous 'iron triangles' of Federal bureau, Congressional committee and favoured interest group, held together by the mutual exchange of favours.

In parliamentary systems with highly disciplined parties and strong executive government, as in Britain, there is less scope for multiple exchanges of specialised favours. In Britain, 'respectable' interest groups follow the more formal pattern of direct relationships with government departments. Although the personalised element is generally absent, this relationship often amounts to an exchange of political favours. The main political linkages with an influence upon policy are the incorporation of trade unions within the constitution of the Labour Party and the looser Conservative Party links with financial and business interests who provide substantial campaign contributions. Parliament is less involved directly in political deals, although many MPs accept retainers from interest groups and sometimes help to persuade Ministers to favour particular interests (Richardson and Jordan, 1979).

Most 'mainstream' public choice judges interest groups by the implicit standard of a beneficent market model. Thus all claims by minority interests come to be regarded as exploitative 'rent-seeking' behaviour that is endemic throughout the political system (Buchanan, 1989). Consequently little distinction is made between interest group claims in terms of their equity or desirability; for example, some claims attempt to remedy inequalities and instabilities within the market system or to help deprived minorities.

The most critical public choice account of interest groups is Olson's *Rise and Decline of Nations* (1982). Olson argues that most interest groups impose economic costs which slow down a society's capacity to adopt new technologies and to reallocate resources in response to changing conditions; in other words, interest groups build up protective barriers against market change and economic growth. He contends that the relatively slow economic growth of Britain or the USA, compared with that of Germany or Japan, can be traced to the durability and entrenched character of interest groups in the former countries, whereas Germany and Japan had to rebuild their institutions from scratch after the war. Olson's theory represents the apogee of a market critique of politics and comes curiously from a writer who had previously argued the extreme difficulty of forming interest groups at all.

Bureaucrats

Bureaucracy seems to have a particular fascination for public choice theorists. They are unable to accept the traditional view that bureaucrats are guided, at least to some extent, by a sense of public service backed up by established conventions and the need for peer approval. Instead they postulate that bureaucrats are primarily motivated by their private interests over pay, status and personal convenience or ambition.

Tullock (1965) diagnoses the pathology of bureaucracy as residing in the ability of officials to substitute their own interest for their supposed function. Thus a bureaucrat may distort information if that assists his career. Tullock claims that in the State Department (of which he was a member), foreign representatives often busy themselves with entertaining visiting Senators who can help their career in Washington, rather than in advancing American interests. While such anecdotal evidence may be true, it hardly comes to grips with deeper questions about the integrity of bureaucracy. However it is true enough, as Tullock says, that the hierarchical structure and large size of public bureaucracy does offer many opportunities for individual officials to distort information or to modify political goals, if it suits them to do so.

Public choice theory ascribes much of the growth of government to the private interests or ambitions of bureaucrats. C. Northcote Parkinson's famous 'laws' of bureaucratic expansion (the 'multiplication of subordinates' and 'work expanding to fit the time available') gave a rather mechanistic account of this process. Downs (1967) argued that a government bureau will seek to expand its 'policy space' so as to stabilise its environment and provide more rewards for its members. Moreover, once a new agency has been established, it will prove almost impossible to abolish it. Downs' bureau theory cannot be universalised, but it does seem to accord with the near immortality of US Federal agencies; even the Reagan Administration failed to pick off its number one target of the Economic Development Bureau, owing to Congressional protection. However, in countries where bureaucratic careers are not tied to particular agencies, and the agencies have less or no legislative protection, they are periodically merged and occasionally abolished.

The best known public choice theory about bureaucrats is Niskanen's (1971), probably because it is logically and mathematically elegant. Niskanen argues that all the possible goals of a bureau chief, except ease in managing his bureau, are positively and monotonically related to the size of his budget. A larger budget will increase the bureaucrat's salary, status and power, and will also coincide with his own probably high evaluation of the bureau's work. The bureau is assumed to hold a monopoly of an unpriced public good whose output cannot be economically measured, and to have a bilateral monopoly relationship with its political sponsors. Given the bureau's control of information and the difficulties of judging its efficiency, Niskanen predicts that the bureau chief will be able to extract a substantial surplus from his political 'masters' to his own advantage.

The consequence, says Niskanen, is that bureaus produce a much larger output than is actually wanted. However, as a general theory, Niskanen's is empirically wrong in almost all its facts.

1. The salary of a bureau chief is *not* closely related to the size of his bureau (and the same goes for department heads). Some of the smallest government departments, such as the US Treasury, State Department and Justice Department, command the highest salaries and prestige.
2. Bureaus are not necessarily monopolistic. In the USA many have overlapping functions and, in the words of one witness, 'duplicate each other and compete for clientele as if they were the corner grocer' (Self, 1977, p. 101).
3. Political controllers are not so starved of information as Niskanen claims. They get help from numerous legislative inquiries and new initiatives such as the Management Information System for Ministers (MINIS) in Britain.
4. In any case bureau chiefs and other line managers are subject to the control of 'super-bureaucrats' located in central agencies, such as the Treasury or Ministry of Finance.
5. It is impossible to say that bureaus produce an excessive output if there is no objective way of valuing the output. It might actually be more plausible to argue that bureaus pad their staff and expenses rather than produce too much.

Niskanen's theory seeks to explain the real enough phenomenon of bureaucratic growth under favourable economic circumstances. In these conditions centralised controls, while not negligible, may certainly be weak, and bureaucratic interest will often be supportive of the political pressures for expanded public services. Niskanen's theory is too narrow an interpretation of this situation and becomes much less relevant when retrenchment sets in. The smart bureaucratic act is then likely to be 'bureau-shaping', for example controlling other bureaucrats from a high status office – a theory considered further in Chapter 6.

In many democracies, the strongest administrative interests are not departments or bureaus but cohesive and prestigious groups, such as the administrative class in Britain and the various *grands corps* in France. The popular British comedy series, *Yes, Minister*, was written under the inspiration of public choice theory (Borins, 1988). In this series both the departmental head, Sir Humphrey Appleby, and the Minister act to maximise their own careers, initially in opposition but eventually in collusion. Additionally, Sir Humphrey is a strong defender of the privileges of both his administrative and his social class; for example, subsidies for Covent Garden Opera, of which he is a trustee, are all right, but subsidies for a provincial football club? The French *grands corps* are a still stronger example of collective privilege within bureaucracy. A member of one of these bodies belongs in effect to an exclusive club, which opens to him a range of privileged positions within both government and industry through the system of *'pantouflage'* which also enables the official to return to his administrative base (Suleiman, 1974).

The collective defence or aggrandisement of particular administrative agencies or groups is a well-worn theme of traditional political science. However earlier writers also observed the institutional and normative restraints upon this kind of action, which are more dismissively treated or ignored by public choice theorists. Pluralistic accounts of the complex interplay of bureaucratic and political interests, such as Wildavsky's *The Politics of the Budgetary Process* (1964) and Sayre and Kaufman's *Governing New York City* (1960), did not point to any blanket condemnation of bureaucracy as such.

The main thrust of public choice theory is to take a much more critical view of bureaucracy than earlier pluralist writers. They stress the many opportunities which individual bureaucrats have to pervert political goals to their own advantage. This individualist treatment is strongly biased towards American conditions, since the more usual problem is the collective self-interest of bureaucratic groups or agencies. That bureaucratic groups have privileges which they defend is plain enough, and it is also clear that they often wish to defend their chosen policies and to delay or prevent unpalatable political directions. However these facts do not constitute an adequate analysis or evaluation of the relations between bureaucrats and politicians in a democracy.

Guy Peters (1987) offers five models of these political–bureaucratic relationships. At one extreme, politicians are in effective command and bureaucrats comply with their wishes; at the other, bureaucrats are in control and govern by virtue of their expertise. The former model produces the variable outputs of political choice, the latter produces stability and continuity of government. No democratic political system closely accords with either model, but in principle the American system comes closest to the first model and the French system closest to the second. This being so, it seems surprising that the American public choice theorists should concentrate upon the ability of bureaucrats to avoid political control. The explanation may lie in the dual control over bureaucracy exercised by the political executives in the Administration and by Congress. The former are handicapped by their brief tenure and lack of government experience (Heclo, 1977) and the protection of bureaus by Congressional committees; and Congressional control is exercised through legislative rules and financial appropriations and by building political alliances with administrative agencies.

Peters' other three models portray two forms of co-operation and one of conflict between the participants. Without going into details here, these models are closer to reality. However in recent years some Western governments, influenced or encouraged by public choice theory, have sought to strengthen their control over bureaucracy. The outcomes of these policies are discussed later (Chapter 6), but one unsurprising result has been a heightening of adversarial relations.

Demand and supply of public goods

Public goods are central to public choice analysis, one of whose basic purposes is to uncover and reveal the nature of preferences for public goods (Frey, 1983). But what are public goods? Are they likely to be undersupplied or oversupplied? And how will they be distributed? The possible answers to these questions turn upon the combined impact of the various actors in the political process.

Economic definitions of public goods

The economic concept of 'pure public goods' will not take us far because there are so few goods which are genuinely in this category. A pure public good is a jointly supplied one from which individual consumers cannot be excluded (Musgrave, 1959, pp. 9–12). Favourite examples are defence, police and the administration of justice, but police forces can be and increasingly are privately provided. Other examples are lighthouses, parks and streets, but parks could be and sometimes are charged for through controlled entry, and the use of streets may eventually be financed through electronic meters in cars. A further frequent part of the definition – namely that consumption by one individual shall not affect that of others – is also vitiated by congestion of roads, beaches and other public facilities.

However neo-classical economics can supply other circumstances in which the provision of a public good *may* be justified:

1. If, through economies of scale or other technical reasons, public provision is more cost-effective per unit supplied. Some consumers will still suffer a loss in terms of their private preferences, but this result can be accepted provided individual gains are sufficient to compensate individual losses (the Pareto principle). Many public utilities could be or anyhow were justified on this basis.
2. If there are substantial 'externalities' resulting from private decisions which affect many other people. A familiar example is the control of pollution.
3. If the public considers, on moral or social grounds, that some forms of consumption are good or bad. Education is a 'merit good' because it is believed to contribute to economic growth and civic responsibility. Drugs, tobacco, alcohol and perhaps gambling are 'merit bads'.
4. If a redistribution of wealth would increase the utilities of poor individuals by more than the losses to rich individuals, after allowing for any consequent 'disincentive' effects.

The application of these economic guidelines is highly controversial. Each principle can be interpreted restrictively or positively. Under (1), one issue is whether the winners should actually compensate the losers or whether it is enough that they *could* do so. Under (2), argument centres on the costs and benefits of control. Under (3), the imposition of merit goods and bads may be resisted as detrimental to free individual choice or be favoured for its social and economic effects. Under (4), comparisons between individual utilities may be ruled out on principle (Pareto again) or a very positive view taken of the increases in welfare which redistribution can bring.

These issues spill over from economic analysis into strongly contested political debate. This fact suggests that economic criteria for the supply of public goods are bound to be either very narrow (pure public goods) or very open-ended and debatable. However mainstream public choice writers do quite often (tacitly or otherwise) use restrictive market criteria in their theories of public goods.

The political nature of public goods

The more realistic and relevant definition of public goods is as all those goods which are or may be demanded and supplied through the political process. This is a very open-ended list; almost every possible good has at some time been supplied by some government. It is helpful to relate the analysis of public goods to the three basic functions of modern government: to regulate, to redistribute income and to provide goods or services.

The first two functions are unique to government. Powers to regulate may sometimes be delegated by government to a private body (such as a professional organisation regulating its members), but the source of their power stems from government. Only government can ultimately provide the coercive sanctions which all forms of regulation require unless voluntarily agreed. Equally only government can compulsorily take from one private pocket and hand to another, although private organisations and firms can voluntarily make welfare payments or cross-subsidise their products. However any substantial redistribution of resources hinges on the coercive capacity of governments to tax and subsidise. The public provision of goods and services is in a different category, because most such goods can be supplied by the market sector, although often in a different form. In addition these three functions of government are often combined into a package of measures (involving for example regulation, subsidies or incentives, advisory and technical services) designed to achieve some particular goal.

This elementary classification of the powers of government clarifies some puzzles about the size of government. This question of size can be tested by public expenditure, public sector employment, volume of laws or range of services, and all tests give different results. For example, despite much talk of deregulation, the regulatory powers of governments continue to grow. However the 'regulatory state' is relatively inexpensive, compared with defence or the big social programmes, and makes fairly modest although professionally significant demands upon manpower. Hence the marked growth in statutory regulation does not show up clearly in the statistics of government expenditure, despite its significance for the workings of society.

Most government expenditure is allocated either to goods and services or to transfer payments. In the latter case wealth is redistributed but there is no direct government claim upon resources. However the resource effects of transfer payments vary: some transfers are straightforward redistributions of income, such as social security payments; some are tied to particular forms of consumption, such as grants for the arts or for sport; some represent a stimulus to particular economic activities, such as export subsidies, or compensation to producers for unstable market income, such as farm price guarantees.

The effect of privatising the delivery of public services is to reduce public employment, perhaps drastically, but not necessarily public expenditure. A greater use of transfer payments instead of direct provision of services has the same effect. More of the work of government then consists of moving money rather than providing goods. An important variant is that governments can mandatorily require employers or other agents to provide specific services or welfare payments, and there is a long history of such arrangements in some European countries. This tactic has the effect of disguising the full cost or range of the 'welfare state'.

The market in public goods

Public choice theorists offer different versions of the way this complex market in public goods operates. The comparison with economic markets suggests that there should be some equilibrium level of demand and supply, reached theoretically at the point where the median taxpayer's marginal satisfaction from public goods equals his marginal willingness to pay for them; but this test is plainly unrealistic (Frey, 1983). A political test of collective democratic preference is, as the public choice theorists stress, extraordinarily hard to operationalise. Hence their judgements about public goods rest upon perceived distortions in the political process when compared either with the theoretical market model or some ideal model of preference aggregation.

The undersupply thesis

Initially public choice thinkers were disposed to think public goods would be systematically undersupplied. One reason was the 'free rider' problem of organising individuals to demand some public good which they would all like to have. Another was that citizens have an obvious incentive to consume as much as they can of a free or subsidised public good, but an equally strong incentive to minimise their tax contributions and disguise their real demand (Samuelson, 1954). The net effect will be Galbraith's (1978) picture of private affluence and public squalor, 'the luxury picnic by the polluted stream'.

The oversupply thesis

These initial theories have become strongly reversed. Groups demanding public goods are not the fragile creations which the free rider theorem suggests. Instead the dominant school of public choice stresses the capacity of rent-seeking interest groups and self-seeking bureaucrats to expand public services and expenditure. Politicians are also prone to oversupply public goods, because of the shortness of the electoral cycle, the need to increase or maintain their popularity, and the ability (as with bureaucrats) to achieve impressive public works at a minute personal cost. In cases such as the Concorde aircraft's development, bureaucratic experts and pipe-dreaming politicians could launch a vastly extravagant but highly prestigious project at minute personal cost (Self, 1985, p. 66). Another example is the initiation of major reforms promising substantial public benefits most of whose costs will accrue later – a case of 'symbolic politics and deferred costs' (McLean, 1987, pp. 36–9). McLean quotes the case of the US Environmental Protection Act of 1970 which set rigorous standards for discharges into rivers, motor car emissions and other sources of pollution and a rigid timetable for their implementation. Politicians could take immediate credit for a sweeping environmental reform, but the costs to industry came in later and could not be sustained. However an alternative explanation is that industrial interests lobbied successfully to have the Act much modified (Wilson, 1980).

Buchanan and Wagner (1977) argue that budgetary deficits due to overspending are a natural consequence of electoral competition since voters are more responsive to quick rewards than to eventual costs. Government overspending also reflects public ignorance about the real costs of public policies and concessions to interest groups. Buchanan, Tullock, Olson, Niskanen, Crain, Tollison and other public choice writers concur in the belief that public goods will be substantially oversupplied, owing to the self-interest of politicians, interest groups and bureaucrats, often acting in coalitions and backed by the ignorance and short-sightedness of voters.

The mismatch thesis

Another theory is that public goods will be systematically misallocated. Breton (1974) argues that government is a monopoly supplier of much wanted and valued public services. It will extract a surplus from these goods by undersupplying them, which it will use to confer special benefits on its supporters or other favoured interests. Thus the public goods market is not so much inflated as distorted. Breton sees politicians as extracting a surplus from the electorate for their private benefits and bureaucrats as doing the same from politicians.

The distributional effects

The traditional view of democratic politics was that wealth will be transformed from a rich minority to a poor majority via the distribution of taxation and public goods. Downs (1957) reached this conclusion on the basis of the likely distribution of voters' preferences. However another theory, sometimes known as 'Director's Law' after a head of the US Bureau of the Budget, argues that it is the middle class who will benefit at the expense of both rich and poor (Stigler, 1970). This is a version of the 'median voter' theory. 'Director's Law' might partly explain why, in the 1980s, programmes which benefited the large middle mass of the population, such as social security or health insurance, proved much more resistant to tax cuts than more specialised programmes for the poor, unemployed or minorities (see Chapter 4). This theory conflicts with Breton's thesis that basic services will be milked to finance special favours.

The time cycle

Contradictions between these various theories can be better understood, if not resolved, by placing them in a time perspective. In the 1950s and 1960s period of both economic and governmental growth, the 'undersupply' thesis seemed plausible. By contrast in the 1970s situation of stagnant economic growth and problems of governmental 'overload' and fiscal crisis, the thesis of oversupply came into its own. Public choice theories about the self-exciting propensity of the 'political market' towards continuous expansion offered a plausible explanation of current events and pointed a finger at the alleged culprits.

More recently the situation has again changed. Political leaders, armed to some extent with the public choice analysis of 'oversupply', have made efforts to pull back the spending coalitions and to cut the supply of public goods. Consequently the Buchanan-Wagner 'fiscal illusion' seems to have been reversed. Voters have apparently become more persuaded of the benefits associated with tax cuts than with public goods, although opinion polls actually show equivocal or balanced attitudes. Recent history might therefore suggest that the over-supply thesis was the product of a particular period and not a general law.

The paradox of public goods

Looking at the conditions of many public services – queues for health treatment, overcrowded classrooms, unkempt parks, pot-holes in roads – it is hard to accept the thesis that they are 'oversupplied'. The counter-claim is that the provision of a free or cheap service inevitably inflates the demand for it and thereby produces a situation of inadequate supply for consumers but excessive cost for taxpayers. This gap becomes large when, as with the British National Health Service, the demand for free treatment is elastic and the costs of medical technology are rising. Buchanan contends that in such circumstances chronic under-funding is inevitable, however efficient or equitable the service itself may be (Buchanan, 1965).

This paradox reflects the different conditions under which public and market services are provided. Commercial services produce an equilibrium between supply and demand by pricing; public services as a rule do not and hence produce an inevitable political tension over their financing. If the political gap between demand and willingness to pay grows too wide, one solution is to introduce some element of price rationing, as has happened to some extent with once free health services, or to cut the scope of the service.

The alternative is somehow to increase resources for the service. If it can be shown that the public service is more efficient and equitable than commercial provision, the service would seem to be undersupplied. Some public choice writers would want to separate the 'efficiency' and 'equity' tests and apply only the former to the public–private comparison. However the efficiency of a service also depends upon whether it is perceived as equitable – for example the perceived equity of the British health service contributed to a social ethic of consumer constraint and medical responsibility. Public choice analysis doubts the reality or durability of these motivations.

Distributional coalitions

Finally in this section the distributional theories of public choice need more attention. If the preferences of voters were indeed decisive, Downs' theory that the distributional interests of the majority will prevail would be correct. However, as other public choice writers have pointed out, this assumption cannot hold, because of the variety of particular interests able to influence the pattern of distribution.

Moreover the distributional impact of public goods is extraordinarily complex. The simple distinction sometimes made by economists between 'allocative goods', which serve a necessary productive function and are widely used, and 'distributional goods' that are concerned with social equity, cannot be sustained. All public goods have some distributional effect and redistribution of wealth can take place in all directions, not just from richer to poorer. Political decisions on the supply of particular goods and on tax changes or concessions are made seriatim with little or no attention to their cumulative distributional effects. Faced with the problem of 'full supply' the individual voter cannot keep up with the effects of numerous political changes, although he or she may have some idea of the general direction in which a government is moving. Hence there is plenty of scope for political manipulation and confusion. Public choice writers correctly stress the voters' lack of information for judging policy effects.

Public choice writers, basing their theories upon American institutions, exaggerate the distributional impact of special interests elsewhere. Congressional 'log-rolling' and the 'iron triangles' of spending coalitions between Congressional committees, bureau chiefs and interest groups are unique American phenomena. In European countries parties pursue policies which (whether mildly or strongly) favour the distributional interests of broad sectors of society and relate the claims of interest groups to this criterion. Although the providers of a public service have some obvious affinity of interest with groups pressing for its expansion, other bureaucrats are specifically located or trained to resist sectional claims. Theories such as Breton's of the dominance of pay-offs to special interests over the maintenance of basic services are exaggerated as general propositions.

Moreover politicians need not be confined to exchanges with existing, well-established interests. They also have opportunities to mobilise and articulate 'latent interests', particularly if large sections of society are politically neglected. A famous example was President F. D. Roosevelt's 'New Deal' coalition of poor farmers, unemployed or low-paid workers and ethnic minorities, which tilted the distribution of public goods more towards the wants of the poor majority (Truman, 1951). The New Deal can be seen as an illustration of Downs' thesis about redistribution, but Roosevelt's coalition did not endure or permanently upset the unequal influence of interests in American politics. Indeed Roosevelt himself proceeded by establishing new agencies to help deprived groups, not by attacking the position of established interests and agencies, and President Kennedy later followed the same strategy in his 'war on poverty'.

This window of opportunity for new political entrepreneurs is not confined to the mobilisation of a poor majority. In the 1980s new entrepreneurs claimed to be mobilising latent interests such as those of taxpayers and consumers against the active interests which (they claimed) had caused the growth of government. That history belongs to Chapter 4, but the point here is that these new coalition builders sought to co-opt middle-income voters into a political alignment with the rich, not the poor. This development may reflect a long-term shift in the structure of society that produces a 'culture of contentment', dividing the interests of a comfortably off majority from a poor, neglected minority (Galbraith, 1992); or it may reflect more limited shifts in society which political leaders have been able to exploit and accentuate under favourable circumstances.

Thus a theory of public goods has to build upon analysis of all the elements in the political process. The public choice approach seems to offer more insights into political bargaining about public goods within a limited forum such as Congress than into wider issues of their supply and distribution. Majority opinion clearly has some effect upon the supply of public goods, but it is an open question as to how far majority opinion can be mobilised or manipulated by political entrepreneurs.

How true are public choice theories?

Public choice theory has introduced a new and distinctive methodology into the empirically oriented tradition of political science (although there have been previous methodological fashions – for example, systems theory). Its logical–deductive basis claims scientific credibility and enables it to proceed from assumptions about individual goals to hypotheses about how these goals will work out under given institutional rules and conditions. This approach has served the purpose of vigorously questioning existing political beliefs and offering some stimulating new theories and insights, especially for games-like and rule-bound situations where the goals of the actors can be plausibly known or inferred. Thus public choice throws interesting light on the *tactics* pursued by politicians, interest groups or bureaucrats to achieve their objectives. Its weakness is that assumptions taken from the different world of market economics are too narrow and open-ended to explain political behaviour adequately. For example are politicians:

1. teams of neutral brokers trying to maximise votes;
2. entrepreneurs exchanging particularist favours;
3. advocates and beneficiaries of sectional interests;
4. members of a collective conspiracy for exploiting an ignorant electorate; or
5. individual mavericks who will follow whatever course offers the biggest material rewards?

Of course all these hypotheses may be partly true, but each theorist seems too keen to dredge up his own crock of gold from the well of economic assumptions to compare and integrate them.

On a public choice analysis, an individual politician will support his party or government only so long as it suits his private interest. Individual resignations from office or switches of party allegiance are rather rare and often personally unprofitable acts, but they sometimes have a substantial political impact. Biographical evidence suggests that such decisions are usually made formally on some issue of principle, sometimes combined with the expectation of future political advantage. However there seems no way of predicting where or why such deviant behaviour will occur. Thus the 'rational egoist' basis of public choice thought does not actually enable us to understand some of the most critical acts in politics.

As stated earlier, public choice thinkers stress that the test of their assumptions and methods lies in the fruitfulness of their predictions. On this basis the better-known theories do not perform well. There is by now plenty of evidence that voting does not follow personal financial interest; that parties pursue other goals than maximising votes; that interest groups grow for other reasons than economic incentives; that bureau chiefs do not simply try to maximise their budgets. The theories are wrong because they exclude or underrate other important motives in political behaviour, such as ideological and policy goals, emotional identifications and prejudices, and moral standards and constraints.

On the other hand the theories (or some of them) do explain aspects of political behaviour previously neglected. While the assumption of 'rational egoism' does not hold closely, the public choice approach does uncover the personal incentives (or lack of them) which influence behaviour in particular situations – for example, the reaction of bureaucracies to political change. Olson's theory of 'selective incentives' does reveal one element in the growth of interest groups; Downs' 'Economic Theory' captures interesting aspects of voter and party behaviour. The 'free rider' theorem is far from being a complete barrier to co-operative action, but it does explain a common obstacle. Viewed as exploratory models (as some theorists like to regard them), these theories may enlarge understanding of politics but can *explain* behaviour only in very limited contexts.

Public choice writers often distance themselves from traditional political science and neglect its evidence and insights. For example, pluralist writers have offered many detailed and critical studies of the operations of interest groups. Public choice analysts cover much of the same ground translated into economic language such as 'rent-seeking'. There is one important difference, however. Pluralism viewed society itself as composed of diverse interests. Particular interest groups were criticised for excessive claims, but not over the intrinsic legitimacy of their advocacy. Public choice often views all interest groups critically for securing unjustified 'rents' at the expense of taxpayers or consumers and as inimical to the efficiency of the market economy. This significant difference derives as much from normative as from positive theories of politics (see next chapter); but it intrudes into the explanatory analysis. These limitations have not stopped public choices theories from being politically influential. The reasons for this outcome will be explored in the next chapter.

3
The Creation of a New Ideology

This chapter first reviews normative public choice theories about the desirable role of democratic political institutions. It then shows how key elements of public choice thought have been fused with economic theories of the market to form a distinctive and highly influential ideology. Finally it analyses the transformation of public choice and market theories into the realm of actual politics and policy-making.

The limits of democratic choice

A central problem for social choice theory is to determine how the individual preferences of the members of a society are to be translated into collective political decisions. Welfare economists had earlier developed the concept of a 'social welfare function'; to express in an equation some concept of the total welfare of society. A SWF could express the preferences of a dictator or ruling party, but on the assumption that the welfare of each individual should count equally, a democratic SWF would theoretically take the form of $SWF = a^u + b^u + c^u \dots n^u$, where n equals the total members of the society and u equals the personal utility of each individual. However, the concept of assessing and adding together the welfare functions of all individuals presents insuperable problems of measurement and comparison. It is more meaningful in the context of democracy to seek ways of aggregating the preferences expressed by each individual over a restricted range of options. The SWF can now be redefined as a procedure for devising a social ordering of a set of options from the preference orderings of each individual.

Kenneth Arrow's famous 'impossibility theorem', which has had a considerable influence upon public choice thought, demonstrates the severe logical limitations upon this form of democratic decision-making. Suppose, for example, that there are only three voters choosing between three options (abc), and that their rankings are abc, bca and cab, it can be shown that a majority of two to one exists against each possible option. It thus becomes logically impossible to choose between the options in a democratic manner. Without going into the technical details of the 'impossibility theorem', Arrow has shown that, if a choice involves more than two alternatives and if the preferences of individuals are sufficiently diverse, no unique and transitive SWF can be constructed unless some part of society dictates to the rest (Arrow, 1963; Downs, 1957, pp. 18, 60–1).

Arrow's theorem has attracted an enormous volume of commentary without being successfully rebutted (for a brief analysis see McLean, 1987, pp. 154–76). But what precisely does the theorem show? It reveals the impossibility of any theory of an absolute popular democracy, but it does not imply that a democratic vote between three or more alternatives will necessarily or always fail Arrow's test since individual preferences may be more homogeneous than in the above example. It does not mean either that the heated debates which occur over the design of fair voting systems are meaningless or unimportant, but it does mean that they have to be placed within a broader democratic context than the act of voting itself. A referendum between only two alternatives does not run into the Arrow problem, but its 'meaningfulness' depends upon the perceived relevance and importance of the choice being made. For example the French (1992) referendum on the Maastricht Treaty did not allow voting in favour of some qualified version of the Treaty but those in that position still had to make an important choice. Even allowing for Arrow's theorem, proportional representation will normally allow a closer representation of voters' policy positions than single-member voting, although it may not give as much scope for judging individual candidates or produce as much governmental stability – if that is electorally desirable. Complex electoral systems which allow for multiple preference orderings can still be more formally democratic than cruder systems despite their exposure to Arrow's problem, but their acceptability hinges upon the weight given to other elements in the democratic process.

Although social choice theory does have relevance for the choice of voting rules, the real world of politics is rather far removed from Arrow's theoretical problem. In practice voters are often given an effective choice between only two alternatives, for example to choose between Party A and Party B. Agenda setting is determined by political leaders, guided or supplemented by movements of opinion within political parties, by the influence of the media and the bureaucracy, and possibly by changes in public opinion. The alternative programmes on offer may cover only a very narrow range of possible options. 'Non-decisions' are as significant as 'decisions' in setting out the issues which voters are asked to decide. Political propaganda also plays a substantial part in the articulation of relevant issues.

Liberalism v. populism

Riker (1982) argues that social choice theory has demonstrated that no democratic system can produce results which accord even roughly with the wishes or preferences of the population. If the choice is confined to two parties majority voting will provide a reasonable answer, but it is too restrictive to confine popular choice to only two options and once more options are introduced, Arrow's theorem applies. Moreover there is no way of preventing 'strategic voting', in situations where the individual will gain by disguising his real preference. Finally the populace can exert little or no influence over agenda setting which determines the alternative policies that are submitted for popular choice. Riker does not conclude that the concept of democracy is meaningless but that it must be understood in a restricted way as a safeguard for the protection of basic rights and prevention of abuses of power through periodic opportunities to change office-holders. Democracy can work as an instrument of control, not of decision-making, and only makes sense if coupled with constitutional safeguards for restricting the role of government (Riker, 1982).

However there is an important strain in public choice thought which rejects Riker's conclusions. If individual preference is the ultimate criterion for public policy (the usual public choice assumption) and if (an important if) *political* preference is to be accorded the same status and respect as market preference, every effort should be made to discover what the public actually want and to implement their preferences. These efforts need not be confined to the act of voting, important as that is; social surveys, public opinion polls, cost–benefit analysis and other devices for ascertaining what people want can be used. Bruno Frey, a public choice economist, stresses the need to frame economic advice so as 'to induce decision-makers to act according to the preferences of individuals', which should be the basic political criterion (Frey, 1983, p. 193).

From this standpoint it may not matter that an ideal system of democratic choice is impossible, when so much could be done at least to enlarge its present scope. Obvious measures would include more frequent elections, an extensive use of referenda, and perhaps powers for electors to remove representatives who vitiate their mandate. These nostrums of popular democracy are not new. In the early nineteenth century, the Chartists were advocating annual parliaments and referenda (as well as full adult suffrage) on the very public choice argument, put strongly by Bentham, that this would eliminate the influence of 'sinister interests' (read today, greedy pressure groups). An important goal of some public choice writers today is to make bureaucracies directly accountable to the publics they are supposed to be serving. For example, Vincent Ostrom (1973) has put forward a comprehensive programme for controlling bureaucracy through multiple elected bodies (see Chapter 6).

Other public choice writers object that expanding the range of popular decisions increases the opportunities for majorities to exploit or dictate to minorities (Buchanan, 1986, pp. 229–39). A partial answer to this problem can be sought through systems of political devolution, which make it possible for public policies to vary in line with the different preferences of local electorates, while dissatisfied citizens get the opportunity to move to another jurisdiction. Thus a public choice case for maximising the instruments of democratic choice can be made out, despite the Arrow problem and other difficulties, but it still encounters the many obstacles to rational collective choice stressed by other writers.

Buchanan's constitutionalism

A very different normative critique of the political process comes from James Buchanan and others in the Virginia School. Buchanan rejects the whole conception of a social welfare function as a mathematical monstrosity, which tries to establish a false aggregation of individual utilities. He grounds his thought upon the individual's capacity for attending to his own interests and engaging in mutually beneficial trade with others, whether in the market or the political realm. Political economy should mean, not devices for adding up preferences, but the study of the appropriate rules for regulating these exchanges and thereby facilitating the individual's pursuit of his or her own ends.

Unfortunately the pursuit of material self-interest in politics (which Buchanan assumes to be the universal case) vitiates the purposes of political exchange. The individual in his private capacity can foresee and influence the consequences of his actions, but he cannot do this in his collective capacity – although collective decisions *do* affect his welfare in unforeseeable ways (Buchanan, 1986, pp. 229–39). Majority decisions may sometimes be a necessary way of reaching public decisions but they still thwart the wants of the minority (Buchanan and Tullock, 1962). The individual is coerced into decisions that he does not wish (Buchanan does not consider that an individual may be frustrated or coerced in his private transactions because these are voluntary). Worse still, office-holders have plentiful opportunities to exploit or bribe the public. For example, Buchanan regards it as a universal law that politicians will run up budget deficits to help their re-election.

Buchanan still recognises and indeed emphasises the vital role of government in establishing a 'moral order' of lawful transactions without which the market could not function at all, and in providing some necessary public services. His solution to this dilemma is a constitutional agreement which will restrain the opportunities for private political gain and restrict the size and scope of government. This constitution should include more stringent safeguards than mere majority voting in order to check the incursions upon individual interests of transient or tyrannical majorities (Buchanan and Tulloch, 1962). These safeguards could include familiar features of the American constitution, such as the separation of powers and the need for qualified and concurrent majorities on constitutional or other important issues. However even the American constitution needs to be greatly strengthened to ward off governmental excesses, and Buchanan has been an advocate (along with Milton Friedman and others) of strong constitutional limits being placed upon levels of taxation and public expenditure.

Following his mentor, the Swedish economist Wicksell, Buchanan believes that agreement to the constitution ought to be unanimous because no individual should be coerced into such a basic commitment. He admits that this result is unlikely in practice (Buchanan, 1986, pp. 55–69). Still he pins his hopes to the idea that any individual who thinks reflectively about her long-

term, permanent interest will favour strong constitutional safeguards for her personal liberty and property against political
exploitation. To do this, Buchanan has of course to persuade his
audience of the prevalence and inevitability of political exploitation and the feasibility of making a clear distinction between
constitutional and political issues. His appeal goes, so to speak,
from drunk political Philip to sober constitutional Philip. It is
none too easy to accept this dramatic change of personal attitude
which contrasts strongly with Buchanan's assumptions elsewhere
that the same 'homo economicus' rules in politics and the market-
place.

There is an obvious parallel here with Rawls' (1971) 'veil of
ignorance', behind which an individual is assumed to will
minimum rules of social justice without knowing what particular position in society he will himself occupy. Buchanan rejects
Rawls' concern with the probable outcome of the chosen rules,
insisting that the only legitimate contract is a purely procedural
one; but in practice rules are quite reasonably judged in part by
their outcomes and constitutional laws cannot in reality be
insulated from political changes and pressures. If one were to
accept Buchanan's contract theory, there seems to be no reason
why all or even most reflective individuals should agree with
Buchanan's set of constitutional rules. Some of them, for example,
might favour a rule which restricts the permitted level of
economic inequality and prevents any individual from acquiring
more than a specified proportion of the society's wealth. Since
government must police the market system, such a rule could
logically fall within the ambit of constitutional law; and indeed
(although Buchanan does not accept it) Rawls' principle that
social inequalities must be justified by their utility to the least
advantaged members of society seems to point in this direction.

Thus Buchanan's constitutional theory in its pure form is hardly
likely to prove operational or indeed consistent with the public
choice assumption of rational self-interest. Nonetheless it offers an
influential argument for a very limited conception of the role of
government which goes further than the arguments of Riker and
others who draw negative conclusions from social choice theory.

The construction of ideology

Before discussing the ideological uses of public choice thought, it
is necessary to clarify the meaning given here to the word

ideology. This is difficult because 'ideology' now carries a heavy load of different meanings and implications but no better word seems available. It is generally agreed that an ideology comprises a cohesive set of beliefs and values, of positive and normative assumptions about the nature of the world. An ideology has a practical and social function; it helps an individual to interpret social or political events and to find her way in a confusing world (Boudon, 1989).

An ideology has a somewhat closed or insulated character and often invokes strong emotional attachment. However, unlike many definitions of the word, the one used here does not imply that an ideology need be impervious to questions about its truth or falsehood. The social theories or beliefs which underlie an ideology are assumed capable of being examined and tested in varying degrees, although there may be strong resistance to the process. Equally the values implicit in an ideology may be exposed and submitted to informed moral judgement. While ideology involves deviation from scientific objectivity, one which is inevitable where strong social beliefs and interests are involved, the deviation is not necessarily so large (although it often may be) as to preclude appeals to relevant evidence and experience.

Following the Marxist tradition, ideologies are frequently treated as mere intellectual rationalisations or justifications of the material interests of their adherents. Public choice theory, with its stress upon the dominance of selfish material goals, logically shares the same interpretation. Both are 'economistic' doctrines. Certainly there is a strong element of rationalisation present in ideological beliefs. However this is an inadequate explanation since (as has already been shown) many individuals appear to support political ideologies which run contrary to their material interests. Moreover an ideology is capable of incorporating altruistic or moral beliefs and values.

A broad definition of ideology means that the term is not necessarily opposed to the concept of rational action. It is rational for an individual to base her actions upon some set of beliefs and values about the nature of society; indeed it would seem irrational not to do so. Of course many individuals do not possess an explicit or coherent intellectual system of this kind, or they reply upon some fragmentary system, but rationality suggests the advantage of making one's beliefs as coherent as possible without slipping into dogmatism or resistance to further evidence. Some might prefer the term 'social philosophy' for this kind of belief, but the border line with ideology is not clear. It is interesting that the original meaning of the word was almost the opposite of present usage – namely the scientific study of social ideas (Boudon, 1989, pp. 24–5).

These points can be clarified by considering political ideologies. Socialism and conservatism are intellectual constructs of considerable complexity and a wide range of meanings. They have a fairly insulated character, but not one so complete as to prevent meaningful discussion about their social assumptions and values; if that were not so, political debate would be meaningless. Because these are complex belief systems, experience and evidence are unlikely as a rule to move an adherent from one camp to the other, but they may and do influence individuals to change their position within one of the camps. The ideologies of political parties are much more flexible, pragmatic and elusive, but they are certainly open to debate. The 'Keynesian welfare state' can also be seen as an ideology (in the broad sense used here) which had a wide influence on individual beliefs about the capacities and responsibilities of government in the post-1945 period. Its theories and values were and are open to amendment.

Ideologies perform essential political functions of informing the public, mobilising supporters and energising leaders and other activists. As Downs (1957, pp. 100–2) points out, a party's ideology is an economical way of informing the public about its policy stance. An effective ideology will mobilise political supporters to share the general beliefs and goals of a party, interest group or politician. Chapter 2 showed not only that ideology was a significant motive in politics, but that strongly held beliefs stimulate individuals to greater activity and influence within pressure groups and parties.

Since politics works a great deal through argument and persuasion, it is reasonable to suppose that a politician is likely to be more effective if he genuinely believes in what he is doing. A coherent body of values and beliefs helps. Of course his ideology may be a narrow and dogmatic one yet still gain many adherents, and he may dose his ambition with copious draughts of ideological medicine. This is a familiar pathology of politics. The once fashionable belief that we are seeing the 'end of ideology' cannot be sustained and there is no political answer to a bad ideology except the effective presentation of a better one.

Any critique of a particular ideology has to analyse its foundations, and submit it to the test of available evidence about its assumptions and outcomes.

Public choice ideology

Mainstream public choice theories have been fused with market theories and converted into a powerful new ideology which has become politically dominant over the last two decades. This new ideology has overthrown or undercut the previous dominant ideology often described as the Keynesian welfare-state.

In both these cases the dominant ideology is a joint product of economic and political thought. The Keynesian–welfare state combination stressed the limitations and failures of market economics and the beneficial capacities of the state for promoting both social welfare and economic prosperity. The new ideology reverses this approach and argues the general beneficence of markets and the many failures of politics. Public choice thought plays a vital part in this new synthesis because it claims to expose the grave intrinsic defects of the political process, especially when compared with the merits of market choice. Without this demolition job on the role of government, market ideology could not have flourished in the 1980s. As Buchanan puts it, 'In a very real sense, public choice theory offers a theory of governmental-political failure that is on all fours with the theory of market failure that emerged from the theoretical welfare economics of the 1950s' (Buchanan, 1986, p. 256).

Unfortunately there is as yet no good name for this new composite ideology. 'Government by the market', suggesting the dominance of a market-based view of the role of politics and government, perhaps adequately conveys its meaning. This section discusses the development of the new ideology.

The transformation of political thought

In the 1950s, especially in America, the dominant view of the political process was of a beneficent pluralism. It is true that many case studies by political scientists demonstrated the perverse impacts of strong sectional interests. However these impacts were seen as deviations from a generally harmonious political process. Pluralism held that a citizen rationally entrusted his various interests to different political organisations. The claims of different interests would be sifted and reconciled according to 'rules of the game' that were constitutionally or conventionally recognised, and the resultant public policies would be implemented by an expert and politically impartial bureaucracy (or, more realistically, by a bureaucracy which also balanced a diversity of interests). The result would be a process of 'disjointed incrementalism', which might look untidy but had the merit of maximising agreement or consensus over the chosen policies (Self, 1985, pp. 79–107).

The concept of political 'systems theory' (Easton, 1953) involved a similar stance since it translated the policy process into a series of logical stages. The political demands of individuals were converted into interests; the claims of interest groups were aggregated into party programmes; the programmes were translated into legislation and policies; and the political inputs thus clarified were translated into administrative or judicial outputs of interpretation, implementation and arbitration. Although, on both the pluralist and systems interpretations, inequalities and abuses of power would occur, the political system itself was accorded a high degree of legitimacy and responsiveness to social demands.

Public choice theorists view the political process as a great deal less responsive to individual wants and a great deal more exposed to the self-regarding manipulations of its principal actors or participants. To summarise the conclusions which are often drawn about the role of the individual citizen:

1. As a voter he has a negligible capacity to affect political outcomes.
2. Because of this situation he has little incentive to acquire the information needed to make informed judgements.
3. In any case problems of preference aggregation distort the results of elections.
4. The 'free rider' problem deters him from more active forms of political participation.
5. He has much less incentive to think or act rationally or constructively about public affairs compared with his own private interest.
6. Insofar as he does participate, he will be primarily concerned with his own material self-interest.

Mueller (1979, p. 105) concludes that 'the assumption that the electorate is ignorant and greedy underlies much of the public choice literature'. McLean (1987, p. 52) points out that the severe limitations upon rational voting are bad news for the voter but, up to a point, good news for politicians because they increase their discretionary powers and scope for manipulation. Thus public choice theory has fathered two further propositions:

1. Interest groups, bureaucrats and politicians, singly or in combination, can and do manipulate the political process for personal gain at the general expense. Interest groups gain from the mismatch between the 'concentrated benefits' which they seek and the diffused costs which they impose, and from the gains to politicians or bureaucrats of a mutual exchange of favours. Bureaucracies are difficult or impossible to control effectively because of their size, near-monopoly of information and resistance to any objective test of efficiency.
2. Consequently the 'political market' has a strong inherent tendency towards expansion. The steady growth of government expenditure since 1945 is attributed to the self-interest of the principal political actors. It led to the 'overload' problems of the 1970s whereby governments were besieged and overwhelmed by the weight of interests embedded in the political and bureaucratic structure (Rose, 1980).

These descriptions of the political process can be seen to be at any rate overdrawn and exaggerated. They do not conform to the evidence about actual behaviour uncovered in the last chapter. Public choice theorists themselves often present their propositions as 'ideal models' or constructs rather than literal descriptions. Still the construction of an ideology does not deal in refinements but in general images and beliefs. The self-interest assumption, for example, may be much too narrow (see further, Chapter 8), yet it has enough plausibility in common experience to pass muster without close examination. Also the allegedly 'scientific' methodology of public choice thought adds to its credibility among otherwise educated individuals. Thus this highly critical picture of the political process can be influential without necessarily being fully believed or altogether consistent with the original theories.

Critical theories of the political process underlie or reinforce normative theories of public choice such as Riker's very limited view of the scope for democracy and Buchanan's constitutionalism. Whilst public choice concedes to government a vital duty to maintain social order, its attitude towards the value of democracy is sometimes more ambivalent because of the wide scope for self-seeking action under conditions of majority rule. Buchanan, for example, suggests that 'governmental forms that explicitly limit the range of politicization, even if the choices made within that range are non-democratic' may well be preferable to the unlimited sway of a procedural democracy (Buchanan, 1986, p. 254). The ideology of public choice more usually accepts the intrinsic value of democracy (as indeed does Buchanan), but leaves a question mark over how fully democratic choice has to be respected if it blocks reforms in the balance between state and market.

The above conclusions would not be acceptable to those public choice writers who accept that political preferences express different and equally legitimate values from those which can be realised through a market system; or indeed from those alternative interpretations of rational choice, introduced in Chapter 1, which turn this methodology against the market system itself. However for mainstream public choice the market is the benchmark which reveals the distortions of politics. By contrast with the very weak nature of political choice over public goods, the market is an efficient allocator of resources between competing wants. The market is driven by the profit motive not to waste resources upon particularist favours. Economic incentives and competition sustain the efficiency of firms in the market and weed out poor performers, whereas a public bureaucracy never (or hardly ever) dies. Thus public choice theory coalesces with market theory to produce a powerful ideology.

Government by the market

The first objective of this new ideology has been to slim the state and to liberate market forces in a variety of ways, such as deregulation and through monetary and fiscal policy. The second objective has been to import market concepts and incentives into the operations of government itself. Public choice theory has contributions to offer towards both the nature and justification of these goals and the possible political strategies for achieving them. The history of attempts to achieve these goals analysed in the next three chapters follows three main themes.

Slimming the state entails measures to reduce the relative size and growth of public expenditure and to cut down the range of functions that government performs. On a public choice analysis, these aims involve inevitable confrontation with the various interests contributing to the growth of government. Consequently political entrepreneurs are needed who can harness 'latent interests' (such as those of taxpayers and consumers) to overcome opposition and who can wean public opinion to a radically different view of the responsibilities of government. Specific tactics can be suggested for placating and neutralising obstructive interests. It is a basic and often repeated tenet of public choice ideology that a slimmer state is bound to be also a more impartial one, once the pressures of interests embedded in its structure have been removed.

Privatisation is a basic means both of slimming the state and of increasing the competitive influence of market forces within government. The former policy requires the wholesale transfer of functions and assets to the private sector, the latter involves contracting out the provision of public services. Privatisation may be pursued for pragmatic, tactical or systemic purposes, although the reasons often overlap. A pragmatic approach is concerned only with the relative efficiency of public or private service delivery in achieving given ends. This is the usual, traditional approach of economists and administrators. A tactical approach uses privatisation to pursue specific political or economic goals such as pleasing the party faithful or raising funds quickly to reduce a budget deficit. A systemic approach aims at making a 'regime change' which will shift the whole system towards a market economy and away from reliance upon government (Henig *et al.*, 1988; Feigenbaum and Henig, 1992).

The pragmatic reasons for privatisation hinge upon comparison of the likely performance of publicly and privately run services. This comparison is simplest for commercial and technical services where costs are important and goals or standards are fairly easy to specify. In the old American saying there is no Republican or Democratic way of disposing of garbage, and equally it matters little whether the garbage is handled by public employees or private contractors provided appropriate standards are maintained. However even the simpler cases can involve such matters as effects on wages, the reliability of contractors and the possibility of a private monopoly emerging. Another branch of economic thought, transaction cost analysis, suggests that the case for privatisation must take account of the possible 'opportunism' of private operators and hazards to the core functions and responsibilities of the public agency (Williamson, 1975, 1985) – considerations which tell against, for example, the privatisation of fire services or prisons. Thus a pragmatic approach to privatisation, while moderate and sensible in principle, is also somewhat open-ended and cannot determine such political issues as the desirable reserve powers of government or the significance of equity and social objectives.

The new ideology utilises these pragmatic reasons for privatisation but inclines towards a 'systemic' belief in the intrinsic superiority of private provision. The 'efficiency' argument is used to stress cost comparisons and service to consumers and to underplay questions about equity, social policy and basic responsibilities of government. Enough zeal for privatisation can also overcome economic arguments such as the need for competition. Moreover, once privatisation is on the agenda and has been made respectable, it may also be pursued for tactical reasons, which will sometimes have little or no theoretical justification but may offer a successful way of pursuing political objectives – for example, privatisation can produce funds for tax cuts (see next chapter).

Restructuring government entails measures to refashion the operations of government along market lines. This objective can be pursued in a number of ways.

1. All public agencies should keep accurate and full accounts, including the cost of services supplied by other public agencies. Budgets should be expressed in 'output' not just 'input' terms, for example, the costs (and where possible the benefits) of each public service should be accurately measured. These accounts should be 'transparent', for example publicly known and open to criticism. All agencies should seek ways of containing costs and being 'cost-effective'. Perverse inducements to spend money, such as the rule that agencies must surrender any unspent money at the end of each financial year, should be replaced by rational incentives for economy and efficiency. These injunctions are relatively uncontroversial, command wide political support and have an established history of such innovations as output budgeting and cost–benefit analysis. The chief and very large problem concerns measurement or evaluation of the benefits of public services, on which there is often a wide divergence of opinion between the opponents and supporters of some piece of public expenditure.

2. Competition is highly desirable, wherever possible, over the delivery of public services. This dictum replicates the central role of competition within efficient markets. Its justification is the lowering of costs and the improvement of service to the ultimate consumers. Ideally the competition should occur between public and private providers; failing that, an internal market should be established within government. The most appropriate units for competition are small ones such as individual schools, hospitals or housing associations. This stress

upon micro-institutions corresponds to the place of small firms in fully competitive markets. Competition can be promoted by voucher schemes which enable individual consumers to choose their preferred service provider; but failing the use of vouchers (for equity or political reasons) competition can still be achieved by allocation of public funds according to the 'revealed preferences' of consumers, for example their free choice of provider. There are limits to the doctrine of competition: it cannot be directly applied to the wide field of public regulation, although different authorities (such as states in a Federation) can have freedom to experiment with different regulations; or to 'pure public goods' which are not individually supplied, although allocations of public funds can be based upon the number of people who use some public facility such as a national park.

3. Bureaucratic efficiency should be promoted by economic incentives, including less use of seniority rules, a wider spread of pay differentials, merit or performance pay for individual achievement, and so on. These proposals would move bureaucracy closer to the methods of market firms. As happens also with market firms, but may be more necessary within government, performance pay can sometimes be treated as a collective award for team work rather than being assigned to individuals. The rewards of bureaucrats should also, as in the market, be related to competitive performance in satisfying consumers or increasing cost-effectiveness.

4. The distribution of costs and benefits within government should be moved closer to the market model. This can lead to the proposition that taxation should be proportionate not progressive, because it ought not to interfere with the efficient (and supposedly fair) allocation of market income according to the skills and endowments of each individual. Similarly, when practicable, consumers should be expected to pay at least some and in suitable cases all of the cost of a public service ('user pay' principle). Full cost recovery suggests the desirability of privatisation save where special considerations apply. Partial cost recovery induces responsible (meaning market-oriented) consumer behaviour save where overruled by clear considerations of equity. Welfare provision for the needy should be separately funded and should not interfere with a market-oriented treatment of public services in general. These proposals differ from the previous ones in being much more strongly ideological and in using market outcomes as an appropriate basis for allocating public costs.

Contrary currents

The above agenda covers what is often termed the 'new institutional economics'. Its proposals range from pragmatic arguments for improving the efficiency of government for meeting public purposes (whatever these may be) to ideological arguments for reducing government to a sort of pale auxiliary of the market system. It is important to realise that some of these devices are warmly endorsed by enthusiasts for better public administration. For example, the authors of *Reinventing Government* demonstrate that public purposes can often be achieved more effectively and economically through a relaxation of bureaucratic rules, decentralising authority to micro-institutions, introducing some measure of internal competition and attending to the needs of different publics instead of offering uniform services (Osborne and Gaebler, 1992). However the aim of these proposals is essentially different from the more ideological interpretations of this agenda. Their concept of internal competition is set within an intended framework of equitable public rules and democratic co-ordination; and the advocacy of governmental 'entrepreneurship' and administrative flexibility in order to cope with a great variety of social problems is very different from the public choice stress upon restricting the role of government and controlling bureaucracy more closely.

An example of the ideological use of internal competition is a short and frequently quoted article by Charles Tiebout (1956). Tiebout argues that the existence of a large number of independent local governments within a metropolitan area enables its citizens to 'vote with their feet' by moving to the local area which best supplies their preferred package of taxes and services. However it is obvious (and is indeed the case in large American cities) that this kind of competition enables rich citizens to congregate in low-tax, well serviced areas and poor ones to suffer the reverse situation; and this result is compounded by the greater immobility of poor citizens and their stronger dependence upon public services. The effect is that the unequal distribution of market wealth is not modified but is compounded in the allocation of public costs and services. On the other hand competition between public authorities *can* be designed within more equitable rules, although the task is made harder by the frequent association of competition with a market-based concept of equity (see further, Chapters 5 and 6).

These goals are also somewhat differently treated by public choice and market theories. Public choice analysis can suggest both desirable goals and, utilising its own critical analysis of political behaviour, strategies for attaining them. Contradiction can result; for example, the creation of a more impartial state is a favourite public choice goal, but the tactics suggested for slimming the state involves a manipulation of interests which vitiates the goal. Market theories advocate the promotion of a competitive economy, but the requirement of competitiveness may be dropped or relaxed in the political pursuit of privatisation.

Other interpretations of a 'rational actor' methodology point in quite different directions from market ideology. The alternative theories discussed briefly in Chapter 1 stress the restrictive conditions under which most individual choices are made, the inequalities of resources and power which occurs in both the market and political systems, and the strong possibilities open to governments for manipulating individual preferences.

These conclusions, however valid, do not contribute to the creation of a dominant ideology in the way that 'mainstream' public choice does. The theory that an individual's preferences are strongly shaped by her economic and social situation is more realistic than the economic assumption that her preferences are autonomous, but it does not have the same emotive appeal. The concept of free individuals engaging in mutually beneficial trade has always been basic to market ideology. It celebrates the ideas of individual choice and personal responsibility for results. To carry these notions into politics and to show that they work much less well there has been the distinctive contribution of public choice thought towards the design of a new and strengthened market-oriented ideology. This new ideology overshadows, politically if not objectively, alternative versions of public choice which offer relevant criticisms of its beliefs but no equally potent set of new ideas.

Transmission by think tank

The new ideology has been effectively transmitted through a growing number of strongly right-wing 'think tanks'. The growth of think tanks is a post-1945 phenomenon, helped initially by the interest of governments and charitable foundations in seeking new answers to policy problems. Although all social inquiry involves some value assumptions, earlier independent think tanks like the Rand Corporation or the Urban Institute in the USA were more technocratic than ideological. They avoided political partisanship in their search for technical or adminis- trative solutions of policy problems. The Brookings Institute in Washington drew on the experience of Federal politicians and administrators, especially Democrats, but its outputs were scholarly and well reasoned policy studies.

The strongly ideological think tank emerged in the 1970s when political consensus collapsed in English-speaking countries (in Germany, by contrast think tanks remain embedded in a policy consensus: *The Economist*, 25 May 1991). Leading the field were right-wing think tanks dedicated to destroying the Keynesian– welfare state consensus and substituting new market and anti-government doctrine. These bodies provided a vital arena for fusing academic theories with practical policies and for spreading the new gospel among politicians, officials, academics and the media.

In America leading right-wing think tanks included the American Enterprise Institute, the Heritage Foundation, the Manhattan Institute of Policy Research and the Hoover Institute, but there were many others. In Britain the Institute of Economic Affairs was the more intellectual wing of the new movement (its publications include contributions by public choice theorists such as Buchanan and Niskanen) and the Centre for Policy Studies was more politically oriented. The Adam Smith Institute put out ideas which might surprise anyone who has actually read Smith. In Australia, by 1990, there were four or five leading right-wing think tanks. In New Zealand the Business Roundtable and in Canada the Fraser Institute excelled mainly in the venom which they directed against government spending and controls.

A vital factor in the growth and influence of these bodies was the plentiful finance provided by big business either directly or through foundations set up from private fortunes. Bodies such as the American Enterprise Institute and the Heritage Foundation got support from many of Fortune's list of the top 500 US companies. The Heritage Foundation, started on money from a brewing company and drawing on a foundation based on an oil and gas fortune and 87 of the top 500 companies (with a boast that it could get many more), had a budget of over five billion dollars by 1981. In the other countries links with business finance were equally close and helpful.

Influence on government

Two examples can be given of the influence of these think tanks upon government. The Heritage Foundation has specialised in detailed, closely argued policy proposals. When President Reagan took office, twenty of the Foundations 'staffers' joined his Administration and he was greeted with a twenty volume, 3 000-page report entitled 'Mandate for Leadership', filled with detailed recommendations for cutting down government and boosting defence (the report was also boiled down into a best-selling paperback: *New Republic*, 12 December 1980). Four years later the Foundation could boast that 61 per cent of its proposals had been implemented in a relationship described elsewhere as 'incestuous', and a new 'Mandate' was issued for Reagan's second term with 1 300 specific proposals (*The Nation*, 22 December 1984). The Foundation's claims to influence are certainly overdone and some of its proposals – for example, the dismantling of social security and medicare in favour of private individual accounts – were too extreme to get far; but it blazed the new ideological trail effectively. Equally effective were the Foundation's wide contacts and linkages – for example it enlisted 1 000 scholars into its academic network.

In Britain the Centre for Policy Studies, founded in 1974 by Sir Keith Joseph and Margaret Thatcher, was said by the latter to have 'provided inspiration for many of our policies', including (she continued) policies initially regarded as impractical but now 'universally accepted' (Haas and Knox, 1991, p. ix)! The Centre allows its authors to pursue their own ideas and arguments and some have been critical of the Conservative Government but its aim is 'to form policies designed to be tomorrow's engines of capitalism, of freedom and of enterprise'. It keeps close contacts with Conservative politicians, top officials, academics and the media (ibid., p. xii). However the Centre may possibly be too closely aligned with Thatcherite beliefs to survive as a policy powerhouse after her departure.

In Australia and New Zealand, the linkages between think tanks and right-wing politicians are extremely close. In his review of Australian think tanks, Marsh concludes that the 'neo-liberal' ones, although their expenditure is relatively small, have had a very substantial policy impact, quite as significant as that of the issue movements and major interest groups (Marsh, 1991, p. 30). A bizarre development was that one of the seven federally funded 'centres of excellence' (and the only one in the social sciences) – the Monash University Centre of Policy Studies – became so overtly right-wing as to advise the Liberal Opposition and business groups on tax policy. After a critical review of the Centre's work by an academic committee the Federal Government in 1987 withdrew funding.

A natural response to these developments has been the emergence of new left-wing think tanks, such as the Progressive Policy Institute and the Economic Policy Institute in the USA, the Institute of Public Policy Research in Britain and the Evatt Foundation in Australia. These bodies have been thrown on the defensive by the cutting edge of the new ideology. They cannot call in the same way on the financial resources of big business, and they are fewer in number. They are also caught between defending the paradigm of the Keynesian welfare state and creating a new paradigm. This latter effort may eventually bear fruit, but in the meantime some left-wing think tanks have bowed somewhat under the widely disseminated influence of the new ideology.

The erosion of moderation

One aspect of ideological zeal is the pressure to erode or abolish earlier governmental bodies which attempted to build policy consensus with the aid of expert advice. A body such as the Scientific Council for Public Policy in the Netherlands harnessed the policy advice of a wide range of academic and other experts (Baehr, 1981). The Economic Council of Canada sought to build consensus and educate public opinion about national economic policies. In Britain the National Economic Development Council (originally a Conservative innovation) brought together government and the two sides of industry and fathered a large number (thirty-five) of sectoral committees bringing expert thought to bear on the problems of particular industries.

Radical right-wing governments are inclined to see such bodies as 'corporatist' manifestations of a mistaken search for policy agreement. In Britain the NEDC and its various offshoots were gradually eliminated, despite the opposition in some cases of the Confederation of British Industry which valued their expert advice. The zeal for partisan policies led to attacks upon the Economic Council of Canada on the grounds that the private sector could do its job (*Globe and Mail*, 28 October 1987) and in Australia the role of the Economic Planning Advisory Council was scaled down in 1992.

Bureaucracies have become increasingly dominated by 'economic rationalists', wedded to pro-market and restrictive governmental policies. In some cases this occurs through stronger political control of senior appointments, in others it is due to the conversion of bureaucrats to the new way of thinking; often both factors apply. In New Zealand the Treasury is run by public choice disciples (see Chapter 6). In Australia, Michael Pusey has analysed the qualifications, values and attitudes of the Canberra bureaucracy. A high proportion of officials in the three central agencies (Treasury, Finance, Prime Minister and Cabinet) have economic or business degrees (72 per cent), espouse economic rationalist values and have established a strong ascendancy (both administrative and intellectual) over the service departments who espouse different values (Pusey, 1991).

The American or British bureaucracies are too large and diverse for similar generalisations to be possible. While there has been a swing towards the new ideology, especially in top, politically sensitive positions, many public servants have good reasons to remain faithful to earlier values which stressed the positive opportunities for good government, careful attention to equity in administration, and balance and moderation in policy advice. These values have taken a hammering from the exponents of the new ideology, which is reflected in a narrower and more strongly partisan approach to policy decisions. As a result a valuable range of expert advice, from within as well as from outside the bureaucracy, has been squeezed out or discounted.

Right-wing think tanks often promote extreme policy proposals in order to reverse the existing consensus, for instance by arguing that equal pay and anti-discrimination laws to protect women abrogate property rights and contradict women's genetic inheritance (Quest, 1992) or through the Heritage Foundation's wish to dismantle social security in America. Their frequent concern is that political leaders should press on with the creation of a new order and not collapse back into consensus politics. Accordingly they sometimes urge politicians not to worry about their popularity; for example, the Business Roundtable in New Zealand urged the National Government in 1992 to privatise all eighteen state-owned public enterprises quickly, regardless of the poor state of the economy and of the government's own standing. Naturally such proposals often fail, but they show the somewhat undemocratic momentum of the pressures for radical change.

Ideas into action

It is a long haul from academic theories to actual public policies. The academic ideas become simplified, exaggerated or diluted along the way. Modern partisan think tanks provide an important link in this development. The 'policy intellectuals' in the think tanks, the private offices of ministers and the large policy staffs which serve President and Congress adapt the original ideas to what they see as political opportunities. The media are enlisted to spread the ideas in the form of simple, often dogmatic assumptions. Bureaucracies are permeated with new policy directions and axioms. A new ideology is created for political consumption.

Keynesian economics and concepts of the welfare state were earlier transmitted in a similar manner, although with less use of think tanks and on a broader surge of popular opinion. The reasons which influence the political acceptability of different ideologies will be further considered in the last chapter. This brief review is intended only to give some indication of the way new beliefs about government and markets have been spread and packaged for political application – an enterprise now to be considered.

4
Slimming the State

Leadership and ideology

Strong political leadership is essential to change the balance between state and market and to remake the character of the state. This is a task for political entrepreneurs, whose possible role was briefly considered in the last chapter. These entrepreneurs need to invoke some concept of a general interest to oppose prevailing special interests; to harness 'latent interests' to overcome the roadblocks of entrenched organisations; and to persuade their own party and supporters to eschew 'consensus politics' in favour of radical measures and a bold confrontation of opponents.

The election of the Thatcher Conservative Government in Britain in 1979 and of President Reagan in the USA in 1980 brought to power political leaders who were committed in principle to pursuing radical change of this kind. Political leaders in most Western countries at this time were moving in the same direction of government retrenchment and market liberalisation (France, with the election of President Mitterrand in 1981, was a clear exception, but conformed to the trend after Mitterrand was confronted by a right-wing National Assembly in 1986). This new political direction was pursued even by the Labour governments of Australia and New Zealand. However, with the possible curious exception of New Zealand, Britain and the USA offered the strongest and most committed examples of this new form of *pro market* political entrepreneurship. Since Reagan was re-elected for a second term in 1984 and Thatcher survived for eleven years as the longest-serving British Prime Minister this century, the 1980s in these two countries offer a laboratory for testing the results of this brand of political entrepreneurship.

The new ideology

Numerous books have been written about the ideology of the 'New Right' (in 1987, three books containing this title appeared in

Britain; see Barry, Green, King) and about the policies of Thatcher and Reagan. It is not our purpose to cover the same ground as these accounts. The objective of this chapter is to examine how far these political leaders put into practice, wittingly or not, public choice theories and what the results suggest about those theories themselves. While some of the history may be familiar, the perspective is different.

Admittedly politicians cannot be expected to model their behaviour upon academic theories of any kind. Even in the case of an influential body of thought such as public choice, there is a threefold dilution of ideas from academic writing to think-tank tracts to the arguments and beliefs of politicians themselves. Despite this inevitable dilution of ideas, the new political leaders in Britain and America did quite self-consciously justify their policies with theories about state and market derived from the public choice school and from market theorists such as Hayek and Friedman. This was truer of Margaret Thatcher and some of her ministerial colleagues, especially her intellectual guru Sir Keith Joseph, than of Ronald Reagan and his associates, some of whose intellectual beliefs were too shallow to be debited to any respectable theorist.

Not only strong leadership but a powerful ideology seem to be necessary for achieving any major structural change. Political ideology can be conceived as a more or less coherent set of values, beliefs and attitudes which govern an individual's perceptions of the relations between state and society. Mrs Thatcher certainly possessed an ideology which she applied with an almost messianic belief in her own role as a political saviour. She continually affirmed that her policies were based upon her own political convictions. Sir Keith Joseph enunciated theories about the value of individual self-reliance and the errors of egalitarianism with the energy of a convert who had once helped to promote the growth of state welfare. President Reagan, according to David Stockman (1986, p. 9), 'had a sense of ultimate values and a feel for long-term directions, but he had no blueprint for radical governance'. Stockman claims that he could have provided the latter requirement.

Reversing beliefs

Moreover the only way to beat an existing ideology is with a stronger one. The ideology of the 'Keyresian welfare state' dominated Western politics up to the late 1970s. It stressed the beneficent properties of the state in extending social welfare and combating market failures with selective interventions. It did not repudiate the capitalist system, but it looked to a balanced partnership between state and market for achieving economic growth, maintaining full employment and distributing the fruits of growth equitably. This dominant ideology was embraced, with some differences, by parties of the Right as well as the Left. In Britain, Prime Minister Macmillan upheld the virtues of the 'middle way' and R. A. Butler, the Chancellor of the Exchequer, declared that the Conservatives had never been a party of laissez-faire and supported positive government planning (Hoover and Plant, 1989, pp. 138–40). In the USA, President Nixon and Republicans in Congress had contributed strongly to the steady expansion of the welfare state.

To overthrow such beliefs was a formidable task. It was necessary to argue that state regulation and aid were destroying the essence of an 'enterprise culture', which had to be rehabilitated by the restoration of weighty incentives for entrepreneurs. Conversely it was necessary to rebut the concept of 'social justice' as an illusory ideal which triggered an endless growth of the state and led to wasteful schemes of redistribution to placate particular interests (see *Equality*, 1979, by Keith Joseph and Anthony Sumption). It was necessary too to combat the middle-class guilt complex about the problems of the poor, which Minogue (1987) ridiculed as an unwarranted form of sickly compassion. These beliefs were often represented in terms of a strong individualism which allowed little for the role of intermediate bodies or the facts of modern economic organisation.

There seems little evidence of broad-based popular support for this new ideology, but it could act as an intellectual counter to faltering beliefs in the Keynesian welfare state. The initial victories of Thatcher and Reagan can be plausibly explained by the apparent failures of their predecessors to manage the requirements of the previous political consensus. The emergence of strong 'stagflation' in the 1970s, combined with the sharp squeeze on take-home pay caused by lower economic growth and rising public spending (Rose and Peters, 1978), had already led to measures of government retrenchment and breaks with Keynesian policies. In Britain, Prime Minister Callaghan declared that it was no longer possible to 'spend our way out of unemployment' and, with the introduction of cash limits on public expenditure,

Tony Crosland declared 'the party over'. President Carter also moved uncertainly in the direction of retrenchment and market liberalisation. However these leaders did not believe in the new ideology; they were still believers in state planning, as shown for example in Carter's ambitious energy policy. This situation helped leaders who genuinely believed in the need for change and had alternative ideas and proposals to offer. Thus conviction politics showed its force, albeit at the cost of substituting a much simplified view of state and society for the more complex view of reality held by the previous leaders.

The new ideology of individualism was mixed with a strong strain of social conservatism over such issues as drugs, crime, abortion, sexual behaviour and religious observance. These attitudes were particularly pronounced among the 'moral majority' in the USA who constituted some of Reagan's most vociferous supporters, and to some extent were shared by Reagan himself. They were more muted in Britain, although Mrs Thatcher was fond of extolling family values and virtues, and of attacking local Labour councils rash enough to promote the rights of lesbians and gays. The appeal to familial, patriotic and religious values had particular salience in countries suffering relative economic decline. Britain, as the pioneer of modern capitalism, and the USA, as for long now its most powerful and successful exponent, might both be persuaded to re-embrace the social values once associated with a prosperous and industrious society.

Unfortunately for such hopes social and economic conditions had changed drastically by the 1980s. The increasing mobility of the population, a trend necessarily encouraged by the advocates of free markets, militated against family stability. So did the rising unemployment and dependency which resulted from new market disciplines and the reduction of state supports. The sexual mores and religious beliefs of the population had also moved too far away from 'Victorian values' for reversal to be practicable. The one traditional value which both Reagan and Thatcher tapped successfully was patriotic nationalism. Reagan's exhortation for Americans to 'walk tall' in the world, and his determination to build enough military power to protect American interests everywhere, were a popular antidote to the humiliation inflicted by the Vietnam War. Mrs Thatcher got her political bonus from the victory in the unforeseen, unexpected and unnecessary Falklands conflict.

Because social conservatism could not turn the clock back, it easily degenerated into a hostile intolerance of ethnic minorities and sexual nonconformists. But in any case, as an effective ideology, it was a weak and inconsistent partner to liberal individualism, which showed greater coherence and relevance for ongoing political issues. Indeed the two philosophies were at many points in conflict. Social conservatism might be thought of as a balancing factor against the impersonal discipline of the market system, but the dominant direction of market reform was likely to reduce its credibility and appeal.

Institutional factors in leadership

In considering the entrepreneurial role of the Thatcher and Reagan administrations, it is important to recognise the very different institutional conditions under which they operated. Victory in the House of Commons provides a determined British government with a very free mandate, provided party discipline and loyalty can be maintained. It faces no constitutional barriers save for the possible delaying tactics of the House of Lords, and it has complete legislative power over lesser elected bodies such as the local authorities.

Margaret Thatcher herself was an unusually active and energetic Prime Minister, being more like 'the chief executive of a very large corporation with a hand-picked board of directors' (Pliatzky, 1989, p. 12) than the chairman of a formally equal group of Cabinet ministers. For party reasons she had to include in the Cabinet a number of moderate ministers, but she skilfully achieved the successive resignations or dismissals of these Tory 'wets', causing one of them (Norman St John Stevas) to observe that 'convinced of her own rectitude, she has tended to reduce the Cabinet to subservience' (Hennessy, 1987, p. 56), although even so moderate ministers still resurfaced in Cabinet. She did not much increase her personal staff, which was miniscule by White House standards, but she used to the full the prime ministerial tactic of getting decisions made by small *ad hoc* groups rather than in full Cabinet. Right up to her departure she commanded the strong powers and loyalty which a Conservative Leader enjoys in Britain. The extent of her domination can be seen from the fact that the most troublesome opposition to the government's legislation came from the weak but Conservative-dominated House of Lords.

By contrast any President of the USA is 'a chief but not an executive' (Rose, 1988). His legislation depends upon Congressional approval, and his initiatives are hampered by both the separation of powers and the constitutional rights of the American states. He sits at the top of a sprawling executive branch, headed by short-term and often inexperienced political executives, and supported by a large personal staff and an institutionalised Presidential Office, which speaks in his name but which has grown beyond the supervisory capacity of even a competent chief administrator. Thus the President has to operate largely through setting the general climate of opinion and establishing key priorities, through appointing like-minded individuals to his own staff and as Secretaries of State, and through wooing Congress, including especially but not solely the members of his own party.

Reagan played a strong initial role in climate-setting and establishing key priorities. However he was 'more at home as a communicator than as a chief executive' (Rose, 1988). His presidential style was to 'go public' over the heads of the politicians in order to achieve his policies (Kernell, 1986, p. 110) and this populist approach helped him initially. However he was a poor executive and administrator. His nonchalant and detached attitudes, including a tendency to fall asleep at Cabinet meetings, made him ill-equipped to push through a positive or coherent programme. He let his appointees resolve conflicts themselves and settle the details of policy, which left considerable independence to key individuals but meant that outstanding issues were often not resolved (Pfiffner, 1988). He was increasingly ineffective and inattentive in his dealings with Congress. Thus Reagan's leadership role gradually declined and became dissipated, despite his skill as a popular communicator.

Mobilising interests

Political entrepreneurs bent on slimming the state will try to harness latent generalised interests to oppose the entrenched interests of existing pressure groups. The most obvious 'latent interests' for this purpose appear to be those of taxpayers and consumers who, on the chosen theory, had to carry the cost of the many concessions made to special interests during the long postwar period of government expansion. On examination this tempting thesis becomes problematic. In both cases, interests are differentiated between different classes and groups so that, for example, the distribution of taxation is as much or more a controversial issue as the right level of taxation. The actual gains and losses from cuts in expenditure vary widely among individuals, social classes and occupational groups.

Inflation and unemployment

The median voter occupies in theory the 'saddle-point' in public opinion that reflects the preferred balance between levels of taxation and expenditure on public services. Similarly the voter balances his dislike of inflation as a consumer against his dislike of unemployment as a worker. The second equation, unlike the first, is lopsided because all voters are consumers, whereas it takes a very severe depression to put more than one in six people out of work. On the other hand, unemployment is a much more serious personal deprivation (emotionally and morally as well as materially) than the impact of even a quite high rate of inflation. Not only the self-interested fear of joining their ranks but altruism or empathy influences voters' dislike of unemployment.

Most studies of political opinion find that voters had greater aversion to unemployment than to inflation during the thirty or so years after World War Two. This attitude is sometimes credited to memories of the 'Great Depression' of the 1930s which would eventually grow weaker. The objective of maintaining full employment was embodied in post-war legislation in both the USA and Britain, and throughout this period unemployment was in fact at very low levels in most European countries, but rather higher in North America. Any small increase in unemployment set the political alarm bells ringing.

The task of changing public perceptions about the causes of unemployment and inflation was helped by the simultaneous growth of both in the 1970s, especially in Britain, and by the conversion of even Labour leaders to the view that there was no easy cure for unemployment. In the USA, this task was helped by a stronger cultural distaste for inflation and by less belief in the beneficence of government intervention. It also seems that growing fear or dislike of inflation is powered by popular misunderstanding of its actual effects; for example, many people view increases in take-home pay as 'eroded' by inflation without appreciating that their pay would have increased much less (or not at all) in its absence (Barry, 1985).

'By the mid-1970s public opinion in most advanced countries had shifted from unemployment aversion to inflation aversion' (Lindberg and Maier, 1985, p. 35). Opinion had also shifted in favour of tax reduction rather than further expansion of public services. These shifts of opinion seem in retrospect to have been somewhat marginal, but were encouraged by the new ideological claims that unemployment could not be cured only by governments, but only through the free movement of wages and prices, whereas government itself was said to be the main cause of inflation, which could be cured by a radical infusion of monetary discipline. This dramatically changed version of the powers and limitations of government was a vital ideological tool, although its acceptability to public opinion was always very doubtful.

The concept of a 'general interest' dearest to the new entrepreneurs was the restoration of a prosperous market economy. Such an economy would restimulate the lagging rate of economic growth and broaden the freedom of choice of market consumers. To achieve this result it was thought essential to reduce the 'unproductive' share of public expenditure which was seen as 'crowding out' productive private investment (Bacon and Eltis, 1976). The benefits of a larger, freer and more competitive market economy would, it was claimed, 'trickle down' to all members of society, including the poor and (eventually perhaps) the unemployed. Everyone would eventually benefit. There was, however, no disguising the fact that the degree of benefit (or perhaps loss) would depend upon the individual's position within the market economy. Even if the vision held, the transitional stage would be painful for many.

Thatcher's strategy

In his book *Micropolitics* (1988) Madsen Pirie, President of the Adam Smith Institute and a Thatcher adviser, used public choice theory to outline a strategy for slimming the public sector by successively buying off opposing interests where necessary, and by creating new interests that would be supportive of this basic goal. These tactics would include:

1. *Privatisation*: offer good redundancy payments and generous share offers to workers in the nationalised industries; offer inducements to management to go private.
2. *Housing*: sell public housing to tenants on very favourable terms and create a new grateful class of owner-occupiers.

3. *Health and education*: offer tax concessions for private schemes, create competition within the public services.
4. *Other public services*: promote subcontracting to private firms.

These tactics were those used by the Thatcher Government, particularly in the successful development of its privatisation programme (see below). However, these tactics could not avoid confrontation with many strong groups working in the public sector.

The Thatcher Government therefore adopted a strong ideology of distrust of organised interest groups in general. Following the familiar public choice theme, it blamed these groups for the growth of public expenditure and inflation. It engaged in successive confrontations with public service providers – with the civil service unions, blue-collar workers in local and central government, teachers, welfare workers and even with the powerful British Medical Association over the introduction of economic competition into the National Health Service. It passed (but did not always enforce) strong measures for curbing the trade unions, such as the outlawing of secondary picketing and the requirement of a secret ballot for strike action. Its bloodiest but eventually successful confrontation came over the miners' strike in the nationalised coal industry. Although the government mainly won these conflicts, the power of opposing interests in some cases showed a remarkable resilience.

The government's hostility to established interests extended beyond the public sector and the unions. It tussled with solicitors and, much more gingerly, with barristers over legal monopolies. It cut down customary practices of consultation with professional and voluntary bodies, such as the Royal Town Planning Institute and the Town and Country Planning Association. Voluntary bodies were regarded as just other pressure groups. Even the Confederation of British Industry, a natural ally of Conservatives (though less favoured than the City's financial institutions) complained of inadequate consultation. The Church of England, once described as the 'Tory party at prayer', was strongly attacked by some ministers as 'Marxist' because of the plea of a Church Commission for more government aid for the urban poor.

These assertions of government authority are seen by some writers as resting upon an ideology of the 'strong state' which accords with traditional conservative beliefs (Gamble, 1988). However the radical policies pursued by the Thatcher Government were quite contrary to the traditional conservative respect for established interests and social consensus. Strong government was wanted to try to bring about a basic change of regime. From that perspective the role of the 'strong state' for achieving change bears a mild resemblance to the theory of the 'dictatorship of the proletariat', and could cause the same cynicism as to whether the projected task will ever be completed. Certainly Mrs Thatcher did not seek or wish a dictatorship, but she did believe that public opinion would eventually endorse her strong use of public authority to effect basic changes even when these changes, as with the poll tax, were extremely unpopular at the time.

Reagan's strategy

In the USA there was no possibility of a similar coherent strategy for confronting interest groups or reasserting government authority. In the first place, there was no long list of nationalised industries to be tamed or privatised. There were, it is true, a number of regulatory bodies whose activities were perceived as blocking the goal of market liberalisation, but the Carter Administration had already struck the first blow here by abolishing the Civil Aeronautics Board. Trade unions, as in Britain, were a force to be opposed, but trade unionism was weak and was further eroded through the effects of monetarism and unemployment without the need for direct confrontation. The Federal health programmes were channelled largely through private doctors and hospitals, and education was under the control of the individual states and local governments. Privatisation and decentralisation were deep-rooted features of the American system, and Reagan's declared policy was to extend these principles further. He did not face the numerous direct conflicts that Thatcher did with public service providers.

His policies did encounter the opposition of powerful interest groups, but their main home was Congress. David Stockman, Reagan's Budget Director, had a highly critical 'public choice' view of the way in which political coalitions in Congress had built up a great pile of subsidies to special interests; but to overcome these interests a Congressional majority had to be assembled. The Administration's struggles to establish such a coalition initially won some success but soon faltered badly. Stockman found that he could not count upon Reagan's full support for confronting major interests.

Reagan and many of his political appointees directed their main hostility against the Federal bureaucracy. 'Bureau-bashing' was a sporadic and emotional pastime which had serious effects upon public service morale, and which was supported by painful changes in the pay, promotion and discretion of officials. However this guerilla warfare did not involve major confrontations, nor did it reflect any coherent strategy or goals.

There was a paradox in Reagan's position which was absent in Thatcher's case. Reagan presented himself as the sworn foe of 'big government', yet he was the chief of the government which he criticised. The capacity of Reagan to distance himself from his own bureaucracy was thus a unique feature of the American system. An American President has increasingly come to depend and rely upon the support of public opinion for maintaining his own prestige, overcoming internal opposition and influencing Congress. Reagan carried this process a lot further by staying aloof from administrative and Congressional conflicts, and presenting himself as a sort of supreme tribune of the people. This attitude is inconsistent with any effective ideology of strong government. Thatcher, while very critical of the bureaucracy and intervening in top appointments, could rely upon the strong traditional ethos of the civil service (contrary to a frequent public choice assumption) faithfully to serve the government of the day. A 'distancing' approach would have been quite inconsistent with the claim of leading a strong, decisive government.

This chapter will review policies of the two governments for controlling public expenditure, altering the costs and benefits of public services and changing expectations about the role of government. Because it was so comprehensive, the Thatcher Government's programme of privatisation will be considered in some detail before we move to some conclusions about the influence and relevance of public choice theories.

The failed politics of expenditure control

The Thatcher and Reagan Governments both set out to curb inflation and to reduce public expenditure, although President Reagan had the additional contrary goal of boosting defence. Their declared policies for public finance were otherwise identical; to reduce both public spending and taxes and to balance the budget. However their priorities and tactics differed markedly, as the result of institutional and personal factors. While the Thatcher Government followed what might be called 'the politics of persistence', Reagan pursued 'the politics of impulse'. Although some parts may be familiar, it is worth summarising these two histories before drawing conclusions.

The politics of persistence

The Thatcher Government set out its policies in its 'medium term financial strategy' (MTFS). Basically the MTFS aimed to rein in inflation through strict monetary controls and to cut public expenditure in real terms through reductions in the public sector borrowing requirement (PSBR). The government's aims were immediately blown off course by severe world-wide recession, intensified in Britain by monetarist policies. Because of a reduced national product, existing commitments and the costs of unemployment, public expenditure rose to its highest ever level as a proportion of GDP (46.75 per cent in 1982–3). The 1981 budget was the critical point for government policy. The Confederation of British Industry, dismayed by the rapid decline of manufacturing industry, called for a boost to the severely depressed economy and was supported by a number of moderate and alarmed ministers. Thatcher and her supporters, giving complete priority to the fight against inflation, persuaded the Cabinet to authorise the largest ever annual tax increase made in Britain.

The next period saw some resumption of economic growth (which only returned to the pre-Thatcher base in 1983 and then grew at about the Organisation for Economic Co-operation and Development (OECD) average for the major seven industrial countries), a sharp decline in inflation by 1983 (which then moved somewhat above the OECD average), but continuing heavy unemployment of over three million right up to 1986. The government vigorously pursued selective public expenditure cuts and privatisation, but, except in the case of public housing, it took care before the 1983 election to reject any intention of making a major assault on the welfare state. After discovering the impracticability of its original goals without such an assault, and after learning from experience the imperfections of monetary controls, it modified its targets. Monetarism, once pursued with 'an almost Khomeini-like fanaticism', by adherents 'who could not see the connection between high interest rates and a crippling exchange rate', was turned into a guide and auxiliary to economic policy instead of being a ruling principle (Pliatzky, 1989, pp. 117–142). The public expenditure goal was changed to freezing its total in real terms (1984) and later to allowing an annual 1.5 per cent increase (1988). Public expenditure actually increased annually by 1.6 per cent between 1983 and 1987, compared with 4.4 per cent in the previous four years.

By the 1987 election, the third phase of government policy had begun. The aim now was no longer to reduce or even necessarily to stabilise public expenditure in real terms, but to control it in such a way that the larger share of any annual increase in economic growth would go into take-home pay. Helped by the proceeds of North Sea oil and by the rather absurd counting of privatisation proceeds as 'negative public expenditure', the PSBR requirement for 1987–8 had at last become zero (actually a £3.5 billion surplus if privatisation is included and a £1.6 billion requirement if, as the Treasury preferred, it was not). This situation at last enabled Nigel Lawson, the Chancellor of the Exchequer, to make some substantial tax cuts in his 1988 budget. The standard rate of income tax had already been cut from 33 per cent to 30 (1979), 29 (1986) and 27 (1987 election year) and now came down to 25, while the top rate, which had been cut from 83 per cent to 60 in 1979, now came down to 40. These successive tax reductions, which strongly favoured those in the top bands, had over the years been more than offset by large increases in national insurance contributions and indirect taxes. Lawson's budget, initially welcomed in the City, was soon followed by a return to inflationary trends and balance of payments deficits, leading one expert observer to conclude that after nine years of Thatcherism Britain was back with its traditional economic problems (Pliatzky, 1989, p. 155).

The Conservative Government had finally reached a situation where the share of public expenditure in GDP had returned to the same level as when it took office nine years previously, while the share of taxation remained slightly higher. What had been achieved, with the help of windfall oil revenues and privatisation proceeds, was an actual budgetary surplus (although if these two factors are excluded, the PSBR would only have fallen from £9.8 billion in 1978–9 to £6.3 billion in 1987–8, after being higher in all the intervening years).

The politics of impulse

Reagan's 'politics of impulse' followed a quite different course. The aim of reducing inflation was almost (but not quite) as salient for the US Administration as for the British Conservatives, but this task was the responsibility of the formally independent Federal Reserve Board, which had in fact already launched a monetarist policy in 1979. Reagan's most urgent priorities were to reduce taxation and to boost defence, and his largest policy impact as President was made immediately in his first year.

His big tax reduction proposals worried members of Congress, who feared their effects upon expenditure claims (or, as public choice writers would put it, upon their powers of patronage), but the Administration succeeded in putting together a conservative coalition of Republicans and 'boll weevils' (southern Democrats), which legislated an effective 23 per cent reduction in income tax spread over three years (Reagan had wanted 30 per cent). However the price of Congressional support was a set of new tax exemptions and concessions – 'politicians' ornaments' as Stockman called them – which increased further the prospective loss of public revenue.

Reagan requested a massive real increase of 10 per cent a year in Defence expenditure. Director of the Budget Stockman rashly agreed some tentative figures with Secretary of Defence Weinberger, which assumed that this big increase would come on top of a 3 per cent annual increase already mandated by the Carter Administration. Upon realising the size of the increase, Stockman sought arbitration from the President, but in a rather comic scene Weinberger won the day with a cartoon showing an American soldier as either a giant or a midget. The quick defence build-up gave the Pentagon an open-ended shopping list for a few years.

Stockman set out to cut public expenditure drastically. After a Congressional struggle and some trimming of the Administration's proposals, he achieved initial cuts worth $25 billion a year from a variety of mainly small programmes, including food stamps, welfare entitlements, job training and housing subsidies. These reductions cut especially into the 'great society' programmes of the Kennedy–Johnson period and the entitlements of the 'working poor' and unemployed. Stockman saw these cuts as merely a prelude to an assault upon the big outlays such as social security, medicare and veterans' benefits, which went to most of the population and cost $250 billion annually –

half the domestic budget. This intended blitzkrieg never materialised. Reagan backed off and referred the future of social security to a politically balanced commission of inquiry. Although some cuts were eventually introduced by the 1983 Social Security Act, Stockman mainly had to be content with finding sundry small 'cats and dogs' to sacrifice. He estimated the eventual impact of the Reagan 'revolution' on the American welfare state as a cut of $52 billion or 9 per cent, if compared with the continuation of the policies which the Administration inherited (1986 figures, Stockman, 1986, p. 401).

The problem of a looming budget deficit was theoretically met by a 'rosy scenario' or official budget forecast produced in 1981. This scenario made quite unrealistic forecasts about the growth of GDP and the level of inflation. In fact GDP stagnated and inflation fell fast under the impact of the world recession and the Federal Reserve Board's monetary policy, reducing the anticipated tax revenues. Equally or more serious, the supply-side theory of the buoyant effects of tax cuts upon the economy failed to work.

Reagan and his fellow believers had seriously expected that the tax cuts would virtually pay for themselves by stimulating private enterprise. Their pet theory of the 'Laffer curve' claimed that beyond a certain point higher taxes brought in lower total revenue through destroying work incentives. At some tax point – perhaps 70 per cent – the theory might be true, at any rate in the individualist culture of the USA, although even at this level the prevalence of tax evasion was a stumbling block for the theory. But in any event the theory became arithmetically absurd when applied to a marginal tax rate of about 33 per cent, where a tax reduction of 8 points would require increased earnings of 25 per cent for revenue to break even. The Laffer curve simply failed to deliver.

As these facts became apparent, though not to the President himself, Reagan was reluctantly compelled to agree to several tax increases and eventually to some cuts in the defence build-up. Even so the budget deficit climbed to over $200 billion by 1985 compared with the small surplus intended by the 'rosy scenario', and in five Reagan years a trillion dollars were added to the national debt, as much as in all the previous half-century. By 1986 public expenditure had climbed to 24 per cent of GNP, compared with 20 per cent in 1979; but tax revenue at only 19 per cent left a budget deficit equal to $226 billion or 5 per cent of GNP.

This situation meant that the second period of Reagan's presidency (1984–8) saw desperate efforts by Congress to reduce the budget deficit. The situation seemed so intractable that Congress bound itself by an Act (the Emergency Deficit Control Act of 1985) to follow a compulsory programme of deficit reduction to a target of nil by 1991. As White and Wildavsky (1989) argue, this attempt to force future budget decisions represented an abnegation by Congress of responsible decision-making and a guarantee of annual budget crises. The Act was doubtfully constitutional, and the empowerment of the Controller-General of Congress to monitor the reduction programme was struck down by the Supreme Court, and his responsibility transferred to the Director of the Budget. Various evasions were used to break the Act's timetable, and in 1990 the budget crisis brought Washington to a standstill.

The failure of expenditure control

What does this history tell us about the policies of Thatcher and Reagan? The outcomes were in one sense strikingly different. The Thatcherites gave complete priority to the goal of beating inflation, even at the cost of heavy unemployment and high taxation. The Reaganites went for quick tax reductions at the cost of a large eventual deficit. Reagan's policies were partially justified by White and Wildavsky (1989, pp. 330–45) on the grounds that it was necessary to reduce the tax burden in the USA to its more 'normal' level of just under 20 per cent of GDP; yet this course was only reasonable if public expenditure growth could also be decisively stopped (which they admit was impossible) and in any case tax levels in the USA were already among the lowest in OECD Countries.

Reagan's 'politics of impulse' produced a situation where public expenditure went up substantially as a proportion of GDP, but the tax take fell. The enormous budget deficit contrasted with Reagan's declared aim of balancing the budget within three years. His policies amounted to a military-led Keynesianism, which proved compatible with both a reduction in the inflation rate and (after the initial recession) only a moderate level of unemployment. These gains were paid for by a large deficit in the balance of payments, which sustained American prosperity by a transfer of assets to other countries.

Reagan, ever the optimist, claimed an 80 per cent success rating for his five policies of tax cuts, defence build-up, monetarism, deregulation and public expenditure control; but the success of monetarism was dubious and the first two goals were easy to achieve if one did not bother about the fifth. Stockman gave a harsher verdict. The Reagan revolution 'ended up as an unintended exercise in free lunch economics', it was not 'a good try that failed' but a 'radical, imprudent and arrogant' disaster (Stockman, 1986, pp. 8–9).

In terms of their original goals, the story is one of unmitigated failure in both cases, though greater in Reagan's case than in Thatcher's. The Thatcher Government failed to reduce the share that either public expenditure or taxation took from GNP. It did achieve by much patience a balanced budget or (if capital expenditure is excluded) a substantial surplus on current account; but this result was only possible because of windfall profits from privatisation and North Sea oil.

At the overall level three main factors account for the failures of public expenditure control.

1. The poor performance throughout much of this period of both national economies, worse in Britain's case than America's, created extra burdens for public expenditure and blocked its reduction as a share of national product. Both economies did resume an upward growth, but at a lower rate than in the despised 1960s and 1970s. This indifferent performance also seemed to refute the large claims made for supply-side economics. Letting the market rip, and in the US case reducing taxation, simply did not produce the anticipated benefits, let alone any trickle-down effects to lower income groups. It could be argued that supply-side measures would eventually have an impact; for example, manufacturing productivity in Britain grew faster after 1985, but from a heavily depleted manufacturing base which naturally helped productivity gains among the surviving industries. The trade surplus in manufacturing goods which Thatcher inherited was turned into a deficit by the time she left office, adding greatly thereby to Britain's chronic balance of payments problem.
2. Both governments had their own spending priorities. Both were in fact already committed by their predecessors to an annual 3 per cent defence build-up, which Reagan amplified greatly but which the Thatcher Government terminated after the intended period. The Conservatives in Britain were committed to spending more on law and order, and started with a big increase in police pay. The process of modernising and 'fattening up' the nationalised industries for privatisation was also costly, and the government incurred emer-

gency expenditure upon the Falklands War and the miners' strike (cost £2 billion). In the USA, the national debt, which had doubled by 1986, was itself a major cause of increased expenditure.

3. The costs of the welfare state grew through unemployment (although entitlements were cut back), job training (a large programme in Britain to cope with the massive unemployment, but severely cut in the USA), and a rise in the number of pensioners. Costs also rose in labour-intensive social services at a faster rate than in the private sector. Thus, if draconian measures were ruled out, the cost of the main social services was bound to rise even if many auxiliary services were cut or eliminated. The attack on 'fraud and waste', a favourite theme of Reagan's, failed to achieve the expected savings. Either there was not nearly so much 'fat' in government as public choice theorists supposed, or it was successfully hidden by clever bureaucrats.

This third and major policy failure could either be attributed, in public choice style, to the effective opposition of interest groups and bureaucrats, or it could be traced to the necessary responsibilities of modern government backed by public opinion. Either way, the Reagan and Thatcher efforts were in their own terms a failure at the 'macro' level of public finance. This outcome does not mean, however, that their reforming zeal had only minor effects upon the functioning of government or upon its distribution of costs and benefits among the population. The effects were substantial at this 'micro' level.

Winners and losers

There is some tendency to judge the size of the state too much in terms of public expenditure totals. In Britain and America during the 1980s shifts in the distribution of both public expenditure and taxation, combined with economic policies intended to create an 'enterprise culture', had a considerable social and political impact. A series of piecemeal, pragmatic measures, justified by arguments of economy and efficiency, were gradually changing the parameters of state action and challenging established expectations about the role of government.

The effects of tax changes

For political as well as economic reasons, both governments were committed to and both eventually achieved substantial reductions in the level of direct taxation. These gains were paid for partly by the elimination of tax concessions and exemptions, but mainly by increases in social security contributions and (especially in Britain) in indirect taxation. The stress placed upon restoring strong economic incentives was used to justify giving much the largest gains to high-income taxpayers, although the incentive argument actually applied more logically to the poorest taxpayers, whose earnings were close to the level of eligibility for welfare. However Reagan followed the strange course, in terms of his own espousal of family values, of actually eliminating the proportion of earnings which a welfare recipient was entitled to retain without losing benefit. Glazer (1988, pp. 44–6) is inclined to justify this change on the grounds that it stressed the moral obligation to work and seemed anyhow to have little effect on workforce participation, but the proportion working among single mothers with children under five had already risen rapidly by 1980 to over 50 per cent. It was a curious doctrine to stress the need for very large work incentives for the rich and deny incentives for the poor.

In Britain the tax structure became distinctly more regressive. It has been estimated that two-thirds of all the cuts in direct taxation went to the top 20 per cent of taxpayers (20 per cent to the top 1 per cent), whereas the poorest six million taxpayers together gained only 8 per cent of the benefit (Hoover and Plant, 1989, p. 266). Treasury estimates show that a taxpayer on average earnings with two children paid 40.5 per cent of his gross income in 1988–9 compared with 38.5 per cent ten years earlier, whereas a rich person on five times' average earnings had benefited to the extent of 15 per cent of his gross income (Pliatzky, 1989, pp. 145–9). The 1988 Budget was especially inegalitarian, conceding 47 per cent of its tax cuts to the top 10 per cent of the population (whereas the lower half of the population got a mere 17 per cent) and simultaneously initiating the replacement of local property tax with a 'community charge' (poll tax) of a flat rate per adult, so that the proverbial duke in his mansion paid the same local tax as the dustman in his council flat.

In the USA the poorest taxpayers did not share the benefits of Reagan's initial tax cuts. On the contrary, a family on the poverty line paid 1.3 per cent of their income in direct taxes in 1975, 5.5 per cent in 1980, and 10.4 per cent in 1986. Explanations were the failure to raise exemption limits in line with inflation, and increased social security contributions (Gottschalk, 1988, pp. 70–2). However by 1988 the same family was only paying 2.2

per cent as a result of the Tax Reform Act of 1986. This Act was primarily concerned with replacing various tax concessions with a further reduction in direct taxation to stimulate incentives, but this time Congressional pressure sufficed to reverse the Administration's previous discrimination against low-income taxpayers.

Shifts in public expenditure

Sectoral changes within public expenditure were substantial in both countries. In the USA, the higher costs of defence and the national debt together absorbed the whole increase in public expenditure up to 1986. As there were increases in social security, due to more old people and a faster rise in cost-of-living entitlements than in GDP, and also in medicare, due to rises in medical costs and technology, the whole burden of retrenchment fell upon numerous smaller programmes. Agriculture suffered little because of its political influence. Major cuts were made in Federal grants to the states and local governments. The 'Great Society' programmes for job training and placement, and for providing educational opportunities for poor children, were drastically cut. Housing and public transport subsidies were reduced. The sectors which suffered most when compared with previous policies and entitlements were the 'Great Society' grants and services (−25 per cent); transportation, public works and economic subsidies (−16 per cent); and the means-tested safety net (−10 per cent) (Stockman, 1986, p. 401).

In the UK in the period 1978–9 to 1985–6 the major increases were for agriculture (62.6 per cent, largely the result of EEC policies); the Home Office (40.7 per cent, largely reflecting the law and order commitment); social security (33.7); and defence (29.8 per cent). The largest increase (employment, 67.2 per cent) and the growth in social security reflected the pressures created by more than three million unemployed, but cuts were made in unemployment benefit and eligibility. The largest cuts were in housing (59.0 per cent) and trade and industry (56.0 per cent), the former due to sharp reductions in public housing subsidies and starts, the latter due to the phasing out of support for 'lame duck' industries and for regional development (Hoover and Plant, 1989, p. 163). Public transport subsidies were also cut and bus services deregulated.

In America particularly the severest losses fell on those around or below the poverty level. Welfare cuts were justified on the old

Poor Law argument of 'less eligibility', meaning that welfare payments ought not to exceed minimum wages or they would undercut the incentive to work. But more pragmatic considerations were also relevant. The poor and the unemployed had relatively weak political muscle, and cuts had to be made somewhere. Stockman declared that his aim was to attack 'weak claims not weak claimants', but admitted that in the outcome it was the weak claimants who suffered most.

The growth of poverty

However the worst effects upon poverty resulted from economic policies. In Britain the legislative curbs placed upon trade union rights and activities contributed to a fall in total membership (from 13 500 000 in 1979 to 10 700 000 in 1985; Hoover and Plant, 1989, p. 181) and by 1992 only 38 per cent of the labour force was unionised as against 53 per cent in 1979; but the trade union movement was not broken and remained strong in some manufacturing industries and the public sector. In the USA trade unionism, already weak, declined further in the hostile environment to a mere 18 per cent of the working population.

More significant than the assault upon trade unionism was the decline of manufacturing employment, especially in Britain, and the switch of some of the labour force into low-paid service jobs. These developments could be seen and portrayed as an inevitable market result of a post-industrial economy. Actually this result was far from inevitable (see Chapter 7). In Britain the process was impelled by the removal of industrial subsidies – except for those public enterprises being 'fattened up' for privatisation – and by the rundown of public investment in the depressed industrial regions. In the USA by 1986 the proportion of low-paid 'junk jobs' in food, cleaning and waiting was 7.8 per cent of the labour force, and the ratio of low-quality to high-quality jobs was much higher in the USA than in Germany and Sweden (Esping-Andersen, 1990, tables on pp. 205–7). In both countries minimum wage legislation was eroded.

In Britain the number of recipients of supplementary benefit is a fair test of welfare dependency. This number grew from three to five million between 1978 and 1987, while inclusion of the dependants of these recipients could swell the total to almost a sixth of the population. The level of support in real terms was almost identical between 1978 and 1987, but increases in average real incomes meant there had been an increase in *relative* poverty, the welfare cheque now covering 53 instead of 61 per cent of average disposable income per head (Hoover and Plant, 1989, 264–5). While the principle of giving everyone protection against severe poverty was maintained in Britain, it began to fray at the edges. In 1986 many of the discretionary allowances which formed part of supplementary benefit were replaced by a system of emergency assistance payable from a fixed and relatively small 'social fund'. The innovation of the 'social fund' only scraped through the Conservative-dominated House of Lords through the shameful whipping up of 'backwoods peers' who normally never attend (Deakin, 1987).

It is hard to give comparable figures for the USA, because of different reactions by the states to Federal cuts in entitlements for AFDC (aid for families with dependent children), food stamps and unemployment benefit. For example, almost half the unemployed became ineligible for benefit. Congressional budget data suggest that in Reagan's first term the numbers living below the official poverty line increased from 26 to 35 millions (Piven and Cloward, 1988, pp. 75–6); and that the value of AFDC benefit and food stamps for a family of four fell from 70.6 per cent to 63.9 per cent of the poverty threshold (Gottschalk, 1988, p. 70). 'American society has become meaner and harsher for those whose lives were mean and harsh to begin with' (Piven and Cloward, 1988, p. 75).

Economic policies caused a re-emergence of traditional concentrations of poverty. Policies of Federal aid to depressed cities and regions in America, and of help for the old industrial areas of England, were victims of the market doctrine of moving towards a more 'level playing field' of competition between regions. In Britain some regional development subsidies were available from the European community, but the government insisted that any such aid to local governments should be deducted from their entitlements to national financial grants. The 1930s dichotomy of a depressed industrial North and a prosperous South (though with substantial pockets of poverty also) re-emerged in the 1980s. The attempted government answer in both countries was the use of urban development grants to trigger off private investment in the depressed cities. The results were some attractive tourist facilities and festivals, but little impact upon the numbers of unemployed.

Housing policies in Britain were particularly crucial, because of the heavy dependence of a third or more of the population upon local government rented housing. The sale of one million 'council houses' to their occupiers removed 15 per cent of the local stock of rented housing, including many of the better properties. Simultaneously the government severely restricted the new building which local councils could undertake and switched funds for non-profit housing to housing co-operatives. The co-operatives could not take up the slack and the government made no provision for unemployed workers heading south to high-cost housing areas in the search for jobs who swelled the ranks of the homeless. Annual additions to the non-profit housing stock in the 1980s averaged under a third of those in the 1970s. By 1990 the official number of homeless totalled 170 000, and the government – alarmed by, if nothing else, the image presented to tourists – required all available non-profit housing to be allocated to the relief of homelessness. In the USA homelessness also increased substantially to a nightly figure of at least 300 000 (Butler, 1990, p. 3), although some reports give a much higher estimate.

Impacts on public opinion

How did public opinion react to this growth of poverty and dependency? A cynical view, drawing support from public choice theory, might hold that so long as a large majority of the population had jobs and some rising prosperity, the government need not worry about the plight of an impoverished 'underclass', even if it amounted to a sixth of the nation. This possibility would be strengthened to the extent that the public was really persuaded that unemployment and poverty were not basically the government's fault. Moreover, if many in the 'underclass' shared the same opinion, this argument would be further helped; and it does seem that many among the poor did blame themselves for their poverty rather than the government, especially in the USA (Glazer, 1988, pp. 159–61), or had reverted to a deferential and acquiescent attitude towards the decisions of those in authority, especially in the UK.

As the 1980s progressed some social surveys found that public opinion was again changing over the government's appropriate role. In 1983 more people in Britain believed that 'government can't do much to create prosperity' and that 'in difficult economic times, government should be tough rather than caring' than held the opposite view; but two years later the balance was reversed, especially on the second issue (Kavanagh, 1987, p. 206). In the USA Congressional majorities had been found initially to support the Administration's cuts in means-tested welfare programmes. Congressional opinion gradually swung back. The 1986 Tax Reform Act included measures for relieving the plainly inequitable tax burden on the poor. The provisions of the Emergency Deficit Control Act (1985) reflected a changing set of political priorities. Thus no less than 60 per cent of Federal expenditure, including social security and nearly all welfare schemes, was excluded from the draconian annual cuts required by the Act, putting still greater pressure on the remaining expenditure, half of which represented defence (White and Wildavsky, 1989, pp. 453–7). The priority which defence had enjoyed over welfare in the early Reagan years was thereby partly reversed but budgetary problems left little scope for welfare improvements without a redistribution of existing entitlements.

What does this section tell us about the goal of slimming the state? From that standpoint the largest gain (if it could be sustained) was the apparent reduction of government's responsibility for maintaining a high level of employment and adequate living standards for all citizens. Simultaneously the stress upon the need for public economy and cuts in taxation might strengthen the appeal of privatised forms of welfare targeting among some traditional supporters of the 'welfare state'.

The successful politics of privatisation

The simplest way to slim the state is to sell off public assets to private investors. This meaning of 'privatisation' needs to be distinguished from the use of private contractors to perform functions for which government continues to take financial and political responsibility. The latter process (discussed in the next chapter) is more easily reversible than the actual shedding of assets and functions.

In the 1980s there began a process described by Letwin (1988) as 'privatising the world'. Governments in numerous countries started to dispose of nationalised industries, public utilities, government-owned companies, land and other assets which they had usually acquired over a long period. The assets and activities thus discarded were generally of a basically commercial character, even if subsidised, and thus did not involve the political trauma which would accompany the shedding of such social functions as education or health, although these also were long-term targets of the more enthusiastic proponents of privatisation.

The Thatcher Government's programme of privatisation started earlier and became larger than that of any other government. It served as something of a model to be copied elsewhere. Britain had earlier, under the 1945–51 Labour Government, gone in for a large programme of nationalisation, including gas, electricity, coal, steel, railways, civil aviation, the Bank of England and the public development of numerous new towns. Nationalisation like privatisation had a distinctive ideology, based in the former case upon Labour's belief that the state should own the 'commanding heights of the economy' and that basic industries and utilities should serve public not private purposes. However technical arguments about the advantages of integration and economies of scale, based on a series of expert reports, offered rationalist backing for these measures. Subsequently, and especially during the 1970s, the range of public ownership became greatly extended through government rescues of 'lame duck' firms such as Rolls-Royce and British Leyland, and of the shipbuilding and aircraft manufacturing industries.

During the 1980s the government managed to sell off all but a few of these numerous public corporations and companies, and to extend its sales to other public bodies such as the water boards which had been publicly owned for a much longer time. In 1980 the extent of public ownership of eleven major industries and utilities was greater in Britain (scoring nine out of eleven) than in any other developed country save Austria (Veljanovski, 1987, p. 50). (The USA by contrast scored only one.) By the end of the decade all these industries had been sold off except for postal services, railways and the strife-torn coal mines, and even coal and railways were due for privatisation by 1992. The programme of disposals started slowly and pragmatically, then took off to the point where sales of at least £5 billion a year were being realised in the late 1980s, until more than twenty major privatisations and a host of smaller ones had taken place with net proceeds estimated as £42 billion (Pint, 1990, pp. 279–81).

Political goals of privatisation

The economic rationale for privatisation is clear: it aims at competitive efficiency. However political goals are different from economic theories. This point is explicitly recognised by the proponents of privatisation. Thus Veljanovski, who became research director of the Institute of Economic Affairs (a right-wing think tank) explicitly follows a public choice approach in declaring:

> Politicians are self-interested individuals. They maximise returns just like the businessman. But obviously the constraints differ from those in the market place . . . The political pay-offs from privatisation are the ones which will be the dominant influence on privatisation.
>
> (Veljanovski, *Selling the State: Privatisation in Britain*, Weidenfeld and Nicolson, 1987, p. 19).

In similar vein, Oliver Letwin (1988), one of Mrs Thatcher's advisers, stressed the political goals of the programme. These goals developed pragmatically as the programme grew. They included securing public revenues to reduce public borrowing and attracting small shareholders so as to build up 'popular capitalism'. These two goals conflicted to some extent, for concessions to small shareholders meant a lower sale price, and also conflicted with the basic theory of promoting economic competition, for selling a public corporation as a monopoly increased its market value. A yet further goal, given the failures of expenditure control, was to offer an alternative area of achievement to the Conservative Party faithful. Hence a trade-off was necessary between diverse political goals, often at th expense of 'economic rationalism'.

The tactics of privatisation were also very significant. It was important that the sale of each public body should be well prepared and executed successfully, even if this meant a lower price than might be secured through a more speculative procedure. It was important too that the new companies should have reasonably good economic prospects, so as to please new shareholders and demonstrate the policy's success. It was necessary to try to assuage the fears and answer the objections of many critics and doubters, including leading Conservatives such as ex-premiers Edward Heath and Lord Stockton (Harold Macmillan), the latter seeing the process as a desperate expedient of 'selling off the family silver'. Most important of all, perhaps, it was necessary to co-opt or neutralise established interests who might otherwise block or hold up the sales.

The process of privatisation was in fact very skilfully engineered. A number of subsidised industries had to be turned around so that they could be sold as profitable concerns, which involved substantial investment and the elimination of redundant workers. Paradoxically the Thatcher Government demonstrated that public enterprises could be run efficiently and at a profit. British Steel, for example, shed 35 per cent of its workforce within a few years (Letwin, 1988, p. 72), and became a profitable instead of a subsidised concern. Previous 'lame ducks' such as British Leyland and Rolls-Royce were also successfully fattened up for sale. However considerable restructuring and writing off of debt was necessary to lubricate the eventual sales.

Placating interests

The government set out to make the process acceptable and indeed palatable to the nationalised industries. Although some trade union opposition surfaced, it was disarmed by the fact that major redundancies had been carried out before privatisation, and by generous offers of shares in the new companies. In some cases too, such as British Gas, consumers were offered shares on favourable terms. The boards of the public corporations had the incentive of being able to raise new capital on the stock exchange, but a more direct and tempting incentive was the freedom to raise their own salaries substantially to what proved in practice to be up to three or more times their previous levels.

Most fundamental of all, it was decided that some of the largest public corporations would retain most or all of their monopoly status. British Gas was sold as a single unit, so was British Airways. The monopolistic status of British Airways, based upon its possession of negotiated overseas routes and its dominant base at Heathrow, was actually significantly enhanced, because the government ignored the advice of its regulatory agency (the Civil Aviation Authority) that no real competition would exist unless some of BA's protected routes were transferred to its minor rival, British Caledonian. As predicted, BA soon swallowed up the latter, without government objection (Baldwin, 1990). British Telecom was saddled with only one minor competitor (Mercury), although others may be added later. Later the Central Electricity Generating Board was sold as two units, but its unprofitable nuclear power plants were retained as a government responsibility. The regional electricity boards and the various water boards were inevitably sold as local monopolies.

Economic critics pointed out that these decisions destroyed the declared goal of promoting market competition. For example, in an *Economic Journal* article, Kay and Thompson (1986) declared that 'Economic efficiency – which is the most important of these goals – and the most difficult to obtain has systematically been subordinated to other goals'. However political considerations prevailed. Monopoly sales would maximise proceeds and satisfy or appease the staffs of the industries. In addition of course the same technical arguments which had helped nationalisation in the first place could again be trotted out (more weakly this time); and there were also considerations of speed and administrative convenience.

Naturally the City of London warmly welcomed the process, which meant excellent business for financial consultants, bankers, stockbrokers, underwriters and advertisers. Often the same city firm acted in several capacities. No evidence has been produced of bribery and collusion, but certainly these participants were treated generously, helped along by the government's concern to ensure that the flotations were successful. In the case of British Gas, for example, advertising (the famous 'Ask Sid' poster) cost £29 million and underwriting cost £70 million. The underwriting was unnecessary as the shares were subscribed for more than twice over and commanded an immediate premium of 20 per cent, leaving the government with an estimated loss from underpricing of a further £500 million (Veljanovski, 1987, pp. 108–9, 94–5).

The government attracted criticism for the persistent under-pricing of its asset sales. The giant British Telecom sale was more underpriced than British Gas, being oversubscribed five times and trading at a premium of 86 per cent after one day; British Airways was oversubscribed nine times for a premium of 68 per cent. With a few exceptions, the extent of oversubscription for public sales (a few public companies were sold by tender) varied between twice and an exceptional 34 times for Associated British Ports (Veljanovski, 1987, p. 94; Pint, 1990, p. 280). Intentionally or not, these results seemed an easy way to popularise British capitalism, but in a sense the aim backfired. Many of the new shareholders took their quick gains and pulled out, so that within a few years the number of shareholders in the privatised companies fell sharply – by about a third in the case of British Telecom and British Gas, and by over a half in British Airways (Pint, 1990, p. 281). Although the number of shareholders in

Britain increased substantially (from estimates of two million in 1979 to 12 million in 1989), most held only a few shares. The beneficiaries from the government's generous disposals were overwhelmingly financial institutions and major investors, British or foreign. The Kuwaiti Investment Office, for example, was the largest purchaser of BP shares.

Thus it seemed as if the Conservatives had managed to achieve maximum political success from selling off a large chunk of the British state. There was something for everyone in the process. The managers of the transferred industries had the prospect of higher salaries and greater freedom of operation, without (in several big cases) losing any of their monopoly privileges. Many employees and members of the public had acquired a few shares on very generous terms. The City of London had had a bonanza, which also helped the substantial growth of its capital market in the 1980s and the boom in financial services and salaries. Public housing tenants were offered highly generous discounts (up to 50 per cent of market price) to help and encourage them to buy their houses from their owners, the local government councils. Taxpayers got the benefit of large financial receipts, which were used for writing off debt and eventually reducing taxes; and the argument that the proceeds might have been larger was unlikely to worry many. The Conservative zealots were gratified by the scale and momentum of the government's programme. Economic rationalists might not be satisfied with the programme, but from a cruder ideological viewpoint – one which Mrs Thatcher herself held – *any* switch from public to private enterprise was bound to be an improvement.

Long-term effects

The privatisation programme looked like a genuine success story; but was it really so in the longer term? James Buchanan, the apostle of public choice, has stressed the tendency of politicians to seek quick gains at the expense of eventual larger costs. Certainly Mrs Thatcher and her colleagues did not think they were acting in this way, their ideology being too strong for such a gloomy hypothesis; and if they did, it would be future governments who would reap the whirlwind. Nonetheless the longer-term effects of privatisation need to be explored, and to do this we will concentrate on three aspects of the programme's consequences: the continuing problem of monopoly, the effects on public investment and finally the political impact.

The monopoly problem

Intelligent exponents of privatisation, such as Letwin and Veljanovski, recognise that it is mistaken to assume that a private monopoly will necessarily perform better than a public one. Privatisation changes but does not abolish the necessary role of the state. Instead of the government having direct responsibility for the performance of a major public utility such as gas, electricity or water, it now has to establish an effective system of regulation to prevent the private abuse of monopoly powers. Since the opportunities for breaking up monopolies were not taken, the need for regulation was still stronger. Indeed American experience suggests that private monopolies in water distribution, and still more so in electricity distribution, are actually *less* efficient than public monopolies (Donahue, 1989, pp. 73–8). This evidence, which links well with the opposition of public opinion to these particular privatisations, was apparently disregarded by a government which was usually partial to American precedents.

Mindful of the extent to which American regulatory agencies, with their strong discretionary powers, had been 'captured' by the firms they were supposed to be regulating, the British government opted to introduce a leaner but more emphatic form of regulation for the privatised monopolies. In the first place, the licences of the new companies include some social obligations; for example, British Telecom (BT) is obliged to maintain rural phone boxes and to provide special phones for the semi-deaf. In several cases these licences restrict the volume of shares that can be held by any one owner or by foreign nationals. The government is vested with a 'golden share' which can be used only to block changes in the licence conditions.

In the second place, small regulatory agencies were created – known as OFTEL (for British Telecom) and OFGAS (for British Gas) – to monitor prices and performance. Prices were controlled by a formula, $RPI-X$, which limits the average permitted price increase to the level of inflation less an amount fixed to induce greater efficiency. In the case of water the issue of pollution proved strong enough (especially given the EEC's censures on Britain's water quality) for a stronger regulatory agency, the National Rivers Authority, to be established, and the new water companies were permitted substantial annual price increases on condition of abating pollution.

As Letwin (1988, pp. 28–32) says, a major argument for privatisation is the effect upon the government system itself. Ministers had a heavy task supervising the work of numerous public corporations, and bureaucrats in the 'sponsoring' departments may have been too sympathetic to the claims of their industry. (This sympathy perhaps also showed up in the privatisation of monopolies as single units.) Ministers also in practice often used their controls over the nationalised industries to promote government policies over prices and wages, to the detriment of their efficient functioning. Moreover the assumption that government cannot go bankrupt stimulated pay demands within the industries and led to large public subsidies. So privatisation is claimed to take a large load off the back of government and free ministers for better things.

However, if regulation is to be at all effective, some of this load returns by the back door. Ministers still have the ultimate responsibility for deciding what price increases to concede to privatised monopolies; whether to use their 'golden share' to block a foreign investor; whether to intervene to protect a major British supplier such as the coal industry; whether to act upon a recommendation of the Monopolies and Mergers Commission which sits on top of the small regulatory agencies. Also there are cases where perhaps a minister ought to intervene, but cannot easily do so under the new dispensation. For example, it is hardly consistent with environmental policy that British Gas should have the maximum economic incentive to sell as much gas as possible, rather than to promote fuel conservation. Of course, if environmental concerns grow, this sort of situation could be tackled by an amendment to the Act; but then the same sort of 'vested interest' which occurred before is now still more strongly placed to block reform.

Ministers no doubt hope that such interventions can be kept to a bare minimum. However without strong political backing, it is difficult to see the regulatory agencies working effectively. They have tiny staffs and small salaries compared with the enormous firms they are controlling (OFTEL is actually financed by a levy on BT); they depend on their industries for most of their facts; they cannot intervene in detailed pricing arrangements; and they cannot, as the Director of OFTEL told a Commons committee, intervene for social purposes unless these are stipulated in the firms' licence (Wiltshire, 1987, pp. 83–4). The same Director, Professor Carsberg, drew favourable publicity when he refused to sanction BT's price increase until it mended the numerous public phone boxes that were out of order. Facing the Goliath of BT, Carsberg described himself as 'David with a machine gun', but after the initial enthusiasm has waned it will be difficult for these small detached agencies to avoid either ineffectiveness or capture by Goliath.

Private monopolies may possibly achieve greater efficiency than public ones (the evidence is by no means certain), but against this they have a much stronger incentive to exploit their consumers. The final sanction which the market offers and government does not – a successful takeover bid – is not really available against a giant undertaking in which government holds a 'golden share'. The water companies have a special vulnerability to criticism over pollution, big price increases and the declaration of good profits under conditions of drought and water restrictions in 1990. In fact the privatised utilities soon found themselves at least as unpopular and criticised as their predecessors, some of the strongest complaints coming from erstwhile Thatcher aides such as Ferdinand Mount (Letwin, 1988, p. 46).

Conservatives may see the greatest gain from these privatisations as the 'depoliticisation' of industrial relations and the reduction of union power. This is indeed a likely result. Paradoxically it was the extent of labour unrest which led earlier to the nationalisation of the coal mines and to a reduced level of industrial turbulence – at least until the miners' ill-starred confrontation with the Thatcher Government. The strongest criticism of the creation of private monopolies for basic services like water and electricity is that it reverts to a situation which had worked badly in the past.

Effects on investment

Privatisation entailed a substantial loss of the state's stock of capital. It is true that some of the public industries sold had at one time been heavily subsidised. (Subsidies in 1978 were £2.5 billion.) The nationalised industries had for a long time been set financial targets by the Treasury, but some yielded only a low return on capital. The Thatcher Government, however, set stiffer financial targets and with debt write-offs and other adjustments all the organisations sold were profitable going concerns.

The proceeds were used to reduce the size of public sector borrowing (PSBR), which made no distinction between capital and current requirements. Unlike the situation in Germany, where a balanced budget for current expenditure was constitutionally required but did not include capital investment, capital receipts in Britain were not separately treated as a source for reinvestment. This arrangement matched the ideological assumption that public investment was somehow less 'productive' than private, or that political behaviour was too short-sighted to reinvest wisely. Brittan (1984) argued that the effect of privatisation proceeds was merely 'cosmetic', a strange way to speak of such enormous sums; if true, it would imply that the government was giving away most of its assets for next to nothing. Still more curiously Pliatzky, an ex-head of the Treasury, in his otherwise perceptive book nowhere discusses the criteria for public investment.

As a consequence the British government disinvested heavily during the 1980s. The economy drive resulted in much bigger cuts in capital than in current public expenditure; yet much public infrastructure, such as the railways, water and sewerage, was in urgent need of renewal, and public services such as education and health had huge backlogs over buildings and equipment. The 1980s were an ideal time for a large programme of public investment, given not only the massive realisation of public assets and the pool of unemployed labour, but also the exceptional (and probably temporary) profits to the Treasury from North Sea oil. The earlier argument for cutting public investment so as not to 'crowd out' private investment (Bacon and Eltis, 1976), lost its justification in a recession, as these critics themselves later agreed. The opportunity was simply not taken, and Lawson's vaunted budget surplus and tax cuts of 1988 rode on the back of massive public disinvestment. Privatisation was handled more far-sightedly in France, where the basic law required all the proceeds to be reinvested or used for debt reduction (Letwin, 1988, 69–70).

The sale of public housing offers a more direct example of the long-term pain caused by the treatment of privatisation proceeds. The proceeds were paid to the local government councils, as legal owners of the houses, but these councils were denied by the government the right to reinvest more than 20 per cent of the proceeds in any one year. Since in Britain public housing accounts for most of the rented sector, and since the councils had lost most of their better properties, the inevitable result was a severe shortage of affordable rental housing, especially in the south of England. The logical and equitable course of reinvestment in local housing was blocked off.

Political impact

How popular actually was the privatisation programme? Studies of public opinion suggest that by 1980 there was more enthusiasm for some privatisation than for *more* nationalisation, but that the largest block of opinion still favoured the status quo (Heath *et al.*, 1985, p. 132). The supporters of privatisation increased during the early Thatcher period, but, when it came to the privatisation of particular major utilities, the position was reversed. Rather more people opposed than favoured the privatisation of British Telecom and British Gas, and large majorities were opposed to the privatisation of electricity and water. These facts support the conclusion of McAllister and Studlar (1989) that privatisation, like nationalisation at an earlier time, reflected a movement of élite, not popular or median opinion.

Letwin (1988, p. 72) regards the political future of privatisation as having been secured by 'creating a great interest group (of new shareholders) in its favour'. The case is doubtful, however. In 1987, 68 per cent of the population owned no shares, and those that owned any appreciable number were in the higher income groups (McAllister and Studlar, 1989, p. 166). With one or two notable exceptions, such as the National Freight Corporation which was the subject of a very successful but unique workers' buy-out, employee ownership in the new companies did not exceed 5 per cent of total shares (Wiltshire, 1981, p. 115). It is questionable whether the ownership of a few shares will count for more in an individual's political attitude than his or her perception of the performance of privatised industries.

The case is different with the million households who bought their council houses. This outcome is certainly irreversible. Housing status is also a more potent predictor of political attitudes, if only a partial one. This source of Conservative support is matched by the contrary opinion of those left dependent upon the much reduced resources of public housing, but the former effect is more likely to influence marginal voters.

A success story?

To conclude, the British privatisation of public industries can be counted a political success which overcame or bribed the potential sources of opposition and built up a momentum which gladdened the heart of the Tory faithful. Indeed the programme did much to strengthen the position of the Thatcherites within the often divided counsels of their party. It can also be seen as a product of élite rather than popular opinion, since public opinion was at best only mildly supportive and hostile over particular cases. However the programme did recruit new interests, such as the favoured shareholders and home-owners, who could be expected to support the new privatised system and (hopefully perhaps) the party which had engineered it.

The programme's longer-term impact looks much less rosy. Ministers were relieved of supervisory responsibilities which they had not discharged very well, but the new private monopolies produce equal problems of inadequate accountability and regulation. It is uncertain whether consumers will ultimately benefit from the change of ownership, and some social and environmental goals will suffer. Taxpayers lost out through the serious underpricing of their assets and the loss of future profitable revenue, while the benefits of the proceeds went overwhelmingly to the richest taxpayers. Alternative devices for remedying the defects of nationalisation were simply not considered. It was a very doctrinaire programme.

Although Britain provides the largest example of this form of privatisation, similar exercises were starting up all over the world during the 1980s. There is no space to review these many developments here, but it is worth noting that they were often driven by two considerations. One was the purely pragmatic case for raising revenue to cover rising levels of public expenditure or debt. The other factor was the fashionable tide of the new ideology, which assumed – almost as an act of faith – that privatisation would prove superior to public enterprise, so that it was pressed upon dependent or debt-ridden countries as a partial solution to their problems. These two factors were linked to the globalisation of markets and the volatility of financial capital, which piled up huge imbalances in national debts and balances of payment.

Reversing public choice theory?

The evidence in this chapter about Reagan's and Thatcher's efforts to slim the state is limited. Further evidence will emerge in the next two chapters. However enough has been said already to suggest some conclusions about public choice theories, and these conclusions will be further supported by the evidence about public goods and bureaucracy still to be considered.

The influence of the political market

The most publicised version of public choice theory stresses the expansionist character of the political market, fuelled by the self-interest of organised groups and bureaucrats and by their coalitions with politicians. It was the declared aim of the new political leaders and their supporters to break these entrenched interests and to establish a purged and slimmer, but more objective and impartial state. But is this happening? And if it is not, does the fault lie in the leaders' policies or in defects in the theory itself?

At first sight the evidence may seem somewhat ambivalent. After all Reagan and Thatcher (especially Reagan) were singularly unsuccessful in their aim of reducing public expenditure, either in real terms or as a proportion of GDP. The Thatcher Government with much persistence held the line but no more on the second test, while the Reagan Administration comprehensively failed both tests. This result seems to support the expansionist tendencies of the political market. However, as the earlier analysis showed, these results were due to failures of economic growth, intrinsic features of public services and the initial costs of defence build-up. The intrinsic tendency of welfare costs, whoever pays for them, to rise faster than GDP at any time and certainly in a recession does not seem to have been appreciated by these conservative governments and for some critics constitutes a 'crisis in the welfare state' (see next chapter); but in any event this factor is not evidence for the irresistible pressure of interest groups or bureaucracy.

Against this background, both governments could and did make substantial cuts in public services, without thereby being able to reduce the share of the public sector in the total economy.

In doing so, they successfully overcame the resistance of bureaucrats, public service unions and interest groups to a perhaps surprising degree. In both countries there were substantial cuts in the size of the bureaucracy, a decoupling of its pay linkages with the private sector and attacks on public service leave and retirement entitlements. While some part of these reductions was cosmetic, their impact was substantial enough to make a crude expansionist theory of bureaucracy look simple-minded (see further in Chapter 6).

The Thatcher Government privatised one industry after another without being thwarted by the strong public service unions in those industries. In the USA there were few Federal industries or utilities to privatise – although Reagan did dispose of the public railroad CONRAIL – but deregulation was forced upon some large industries in the face of strongly entrenched interests. Following the deregulation of the airlines, the trucking industry was liberalised despite strong opposition from both the carriers, united in the American Trucking Association, and the powerful Teamster's Union. Still more strikingly the opposition of the giant AT&T (American Telephone and Telegraph) failed to stop the deregulation of telecommunications (Derthick and Quirk, 1985). However these cases are viewed by Derthick and Quirk not as products of Reaganite ideology, but as a victory for political consensus on reforms 'whose time had come' against the particularist interests strongly fixed within the regulatory agencies. At least these examples suggest that the attack on special interests has in a few cases been turned against powerful private corporations (although there are no similar examples from Britain).

The opposition of voluntary organisations and cause groups did not prevent, although it occasionally modified, some severe cuts in welfare entitlements and services available to the poor and unemployed in both countries. The one major form of opposition which did check the plans of the political leaders was the perceived popularity of universalist social services. However this check was administered less by entrenched interests than by electoral considerations based upon the evidence of opinion polls. The median voter theory is a factor which no elected government can afford to ignore for long, though a determined government with a supportive press may have considerable success in manipulating opinion to accept gradual changes in the structure and financing of the social services.

This analysis need not deny that the 'political market', interpreted as self-interested coalitions of special interests and politicians, played a significant part in the long period of government growth, without being the only cause of this process. However, to the extent that public choice theory can explain politics plausibly, it must surely accept that 'slimming the state' can be just as much (or more) an exercise in political exploitation and favouritism as can the process of expansion.

The political gains from shrinking government

Western states had by 1980 built up an enormous stock of assets, resources and legal powers which could, if the will was there, be thrown into reverse. Under favourable circumstances, it may in fact be a lot easier to make quick political profits out of running down the state than out of the incremental process of building it up. For all their rhetoric of substituting general for particularist interests, this is just what the Thatcher and the Reagan Governments seem to have done – and to have partly paid for by the public choice recipe of 'quick benefits, deferred costs'.

As already described, the Thatcher programme of privatisation was in fact deliberately based upon a strategy of bribing affected interests into acquiescence or support. Managers, workers (to some extent) and potential shareholders were all offered varying financial inducements – very strong ones in some cases – to 'go private'. This strategy might be defended as offering necessary but temporary inducements to bring about a worthwhile reform. However, some of the effects will be long-lasting. As Pint (1990) concludes, the beneficiaries are once again special interests – the managers (especially of the new private monopolies), the shareholders (mainly large institutions) and the new home-owners not, as a rule anyhow, the general interests of consumers or taxpayers. The public choice theory of the primacy of special over general interests was thereby demonstrated by the very apostles who set out to disprove it.

An expansion of the market sector, as it now operates, offers huge rewards for merchant bankers, stockbrokers, insurance salesmen, financial consultants and advertisers. Anti-union policies and a large pool of unemployed have helped private firms to lower wages or to employ non-union or part-time labour. Doubtless some of these economic interests expected to get

eventual benefits from the plentiful funding which they provided
for right-wing think tanks and forums. Government leaders, at
any rate in Britain, seem to have kept clear of direct inducements
from business and financial interests; but the same cannot be said
for some of their supporters or for the process of implementation,
where politicians and officials were thrust into close relationships
with business beneficiaries. The ideological commitment of these
leaders in itself produced a favourable attitude to the claims of
the market sector.

Both governments piled up heavy burdens on the future.
Reagan's big tax concessions, coupled with his defence build-
up, have created a formidable problem of Federal debt (which
increased three times during his incumbency), while his policies
contributed considerably to the amazing transformation of the
USA from the leading creditor to the largest debtor nation. The
decline of UK manufacturing capacity and Lawson's eventual tax
concessions left the country by the end of the decade with its
highest ever annual deficits on current account. More fundamentally, from the standpoint of running down the state, the Thatcher
Government failed to use the proceeds of privatisation or North
Sea oil either to stimulate manufacturing or to invest in the
capital-starved public services and urban infrastructure. Instead
public investment declined both absolutely (for a time) and as a
proportion of public expenditure.

These policies will leave future governments with weakened
resources for tackling backlogs in the public services. From a
right-wing standpoint, this outcome has compensations. It will be
harder to restart the engine of public investment or fill up holes in
the welfare system. A more cynical view is that the US deficit was
intended to torpedo welfare policy for two generations.

Paradoxes of performance

How then are we to evaluate the performance of these anti-state
and pro-market political entrepreneurs? Here a seeming paradox
appears. On most tests of economic and social welfare they failed
badly, yet politically they won considerable success. Reagan won
a second term and was succeeded by another conservative
although less extreme Republican in the shape of George Bush,
while Thatcher lasted for the record twentieth-century period of
eleven years and her Conservative successor, John Major,
unexpectedly remains Prime Minister after the 1992 election.

Most governments in the post-war period have ultimately been judged upon such criteria as economic growth, standards of living, employment and inflation. Economic growth in both countries was lower than in the despised 1970s, but that was true for OECD countries as a whole. Britain's economic growth in the Thatcher years (1980–88) averaged 2.0 per cent, America's at 2.5 was the same as the OECD average. Unemployment in this period averaged 10.0 per cent in the UK and 7.5 in the USA, compared with the OECD average of 6.7. Figures for inflation give a more favourable impression, since the high 1979 figures in both countries had fallen a long way by 1988, although still above the OECD average (Mishra, 1990, Appendix B, Tables 1–3, pp. 125–7). In Britain, real incomes (as measured by the Family Expenditure Survey) grew between 1979 and 1987 by as much as 50 per cent for the top 10 per cent of households, grew more modestly (in descending order) for the next 40 per cent, were roughly static for the next 40 per cent, and declined for the bottom 10 per cent. In the USA the pattern of change was not dissimilar. The quality of many public services clearly declined. These are hardly figures to enthuse a political advocate.

Reagan was and Thatcher tried to be a 'populist' leader. Vice-President Mondale had earlier said, 'I don't believe it is possible to run for President without the capacity to build confidence and communications every night' (Rose, 1988, p. 118). Reagan concentrated on his image and was obsessed with popular appeal (*New Yorker*, 1989). Thatcher claimed to have a special rapport with the British people, continually exhorting them to follow her principles. However neither leader scored well on popularity. Reagan was personally popular but his highest rating (68 per cent after his early escape from assassination) was well below that of President Truman (87 per cent) or Johnson (80 per cent), while like other Presidents he suffered heavy downswings, falling to 35 per cent after the 1982 recession and 40 per cent after the Iran–Contra scandal (Rose, 1988, 270). Thatcher's highest popularity rating was 59 per cent and her average rating was the lowest of any Prime Minister since 1955 (Kavanagh, 1987, p. 270). Neither were her policies popular, anyhow for long. Throughout the entire Thatcher period a large balance of opinion favoured better public services plus higher taxes, rather than the reverse policy which Thatcher was energetically pursuing (Kavanagh, 1987, pp. 296, 294). In America, on the other hand, Reagan's policies for reducing taxes by slimming government were certainly popular, although by 1984 only 20 per cent favoured further cuts in domestic programmes and 27 per cent wanted increases (Piven and Cloward, 1988, pp. 88–9). However this finding may reflect a well-known public ambivalence which dislikes service cuts but wants tax cuts still more.

Sources of political success

How then did these leaders achieve their political success? Under the British electoral system the Conservatives profited enormously from a divided Opposition which resulted from conflict and demoralisation within the Labour Party and the consequent and perhaps temporary growth of a strong third party. This situation enabled the Conservatives to win four elections running on a minority of the popular vote, although both the other main parties were strongly opposed to Thatcherism. In the USA, the electorate split its attitudes towards the Congress and the Presidency. Republican Presidents achieved a successful identification with populist attitudes of nationalism or xenophobia and of opposition to taxation and bureaucracy, while Congress with generally Democratic majorities represented more diverse interests.

An important factor in Thatcher's success, and to a lesser extent Reagan's, was the unpopularity of trade unions who were held responsible for the damaging strikes in the 1978–9 'winter of discontent'. Equally much of the actual if not always avowed appeal of privatisation was based upon the restrictive practices of public service unions, which influenced (tacitly if not openly) even the Labour Governments in the Antipodes. A further factor here was the tensions within the labour force caused by Labour's 'social contract' of the 1970s. Many trade unionists themselves voted for Thatcher or Reagan, and one result of their policies was to restore wage differentials. The results of these assaults upon trade unionism hardly support Olson's (1982) public choice thesis that the main obstacle to economic growth in the UK and USA is the well-entrenched power of particularist interests, especially perhaps trade unions. Sharp reductions in the size and influence of trade unionism did not produce any surge of economic growth.

Contrary to public choice theory, the evidence suggests that a major factor in political success is the ability to create a dominant ideology. There is no doubt that, in English-speaking countries especially, market ideology became the conventional wisdom of the 1980s. This ideology was popularised through a compliant media dominated by a few extremely right-wing proprietors. This ideology spread even to the Labour Governments of Australia and New Zealand, leading in Australia to comprehensive financial deregulation and the beginnings of privatisation, and in New Zealand to an extraordinary programme (for a Labour Government) of wholesale privatisation, deregulation and tax concessions for the rich. This New Zealand experience, followed by major cuts in social services made by the successor National Government, represent a most curious transportation of popularised versions of public choice theory and market ideology (Boston *et al.*, 1991).

It does not follow that a popular majority, save possibly in the USA, believed this ideology – it was too contrary to their actual experience – but they were bound to be influenced by it in the temporary absence of any effective alternative body of beliefs. Moreover history suggests that policy failures take time to shake an ideology once it has become enshrined as the conventional wisdom. Thatcher rammed this argument home with her continual theme of TINA – 'there is no alternative (but mine)'. Her combative approach, a sharp break with the 'gentlemanly' traditions of British politics, appropriately breached by a lady, helped the ascendancy of the Thatcherites within the Conservative Party and for a time dominated political discourse.

Changing the political map?

Have the Thatcher and Reagan policies altered the political map more permanently? On one view they have done so by creating and favouring interests implicated in the market order and the private sector, thereby deflating support for government provision. For example, one study estimates that the combined electoral impact of the Thatcher Government's subsidised promotion of home ownership and wider share ownership is worth a 2.5 per cent vote swing to the Conservatives, after allowing for counter-effects of occupation and trade union membership (McAllister and Studler, 1989, pp. 170–4). Of course very many people have been severely hurt by these leaders' policies, especially the unemployed, the poor, those in the housing rental market (still nearly 40 per cent of households in Britain), and those heavily dependent on public services. However these groups are much less organised or influential than the favoured interests and therefore (so it is often said) will be unable to upset a tolerably satisfied or acquiescent majority. After all a majority (just a bare one in Britain) did improve their living standards during the 1980s, helped in Britain's case by a strong pound floating on North Sea oil, thus supporting the thesis (introduced in Chapter 2) of a winning distributional coalition of the rich and the middle classes. However the support of that majority seems to depend crucially upon popular beliefs about what governments can and should do; and it is on this point that these political leaders achieved their greatest if perhaps temporary success.

This chapter may seem to support some of the more cynical versions of public choice theory. Theories of self-interested coalitions between political leaders and favoured interests acquire new salience in the context of privatisation and redistribution of income. So too does the hypothesis that politicians will pay for quick political benefits with deferred costs. Thatcher and Reagan might be claimed as good students of public choice theory, in the sense not of creating a less flawed political order but of organising, if only temporarily, winning coalitions based upon rational egoism.

Political calculation cannot explain all aspects of these leaders' behaviour. Ideological beliefs in both camps can be seen to have had an independent effect. They governed the attempted policies of 'even-handed justice' and the eventual resignation of David Stockman. They led Reagan into a misplaced trust in the efficacy of the Laffer curve. Ideological zeal led Thatcher to espouse policies, such as the local poll tax, which in no sense were politically rational and which contributed greatly to her sudden downfall. The emotionally demagogic attitudes of both leaders – Reagan never tired of castigating bureaucrats and 'welfare scoundrels' and Thatcher attacked trade unions and spendthrift or 'looney' local governments – represent a darker side of politics which rational choice theory also cannot explain, yet what these leaders believed and did cannot be taken as typical of the whole of politics. Other motives, beliefs and forms of leadership have a relevance and potentiality which have still to be considered. The public choice theories which influenced these leaders may eventually be seen as explaining some often prevalent *pathologies* of politics rather than providing an adequate description.

5
Privatising Welfare

This chapter deals with policies to change the institutions of the modern welfare state through increasing the role and participation of the private sector, 'empowering consumers' and promoting competition within the governmental system. These policies are strongly driven by the ideological goal of changing the balance between state and market in the crucial and once impregnable citadel of state welfare provision, although they also involve measures which can be claimed to represent improvements in public service. The chapter starts and ends with the political basis of the welfare state and includes examples of policy changes in the provision and delivery of personal social services, housing, education, health and social security.

The politics of welfare

The 'welfare state' as it is often understood comprises certain basic services – principally social security, health, education and to some extent housing and transport – which should be made available to all citizens. Its auxiliary elements comprise specialised social services for the handicapped, mentally ill, children, old people and the destitute (although in a comprehensive welfare system, there should be rather few and usually temporary members of the last category).

However an adequate concept of the welfare state also includes economic rights, such as adequate opportunities for employment, minimum wages, protection in the workplace, paid holidays and so on. One of the founders of welfare state theory, T. H. Marshall (1963) coupled these economic rights with social rights to constitute the distinctive character of modern citizenship. This combination was equally crucial to Beveridge's master design for the post-war British welfare state, which was premised upon the maintenance of full employment. Without supportive economic policies, universalist welfare schemes are unlikely to be fully realised or practicable because too many people will slip below the poverty line as a result of unemployment or low wages and become dependent upon means-tested assistance. If there is little difference between the welfare payment and the going wage, individuals will fall into the 'poverty trap' and have little incentive or opportunity to extricate themselves.

Many trade unions were initially sceptical of state welfare schemes, regarding them as a sop or diversion from their major goal of economic advancement. In Australia, for example, a 'workers' welfare state' was built up on the basis of compulsory wage arbitration based upon the right of the worker to a decent standard of living for himself and family. Social welfare was a secondary consideration, except for old age pensions which were means-tested (Castles, 1985). Social and economic change in Australia (as elsewhere) have made so much reliance on wage arbitration unrealistic, although still a vital factor in the welfare system. Thus the 'Keynesian welfare state' is a correct description of the necessary interdependence of economic and social policies.

Finally, in the modern world, one can further add the concept of 'environmental welfare', which refers to such goals as the reduction of pollution and the planning of cities so as to create an attractive environment and improved access to work or other facilities for all citizens. W. A. Robson (1976) stressed environmental goals within his earlier definition of the welfare state, and today many more people see 'the environment' as a critical and often missing element in the provision of welfare.

The growth of state welfare

How are we to explain the growth of state welfare services? One straightforward explanation is that this growth was a response to popular, majority wishes. There are some simple reasons for this preference. As a society grows richer, individuals will spend less of their income on basic needs like food and more on such purposes as education, health and personal security, while increasing life expectancy adds to these demands. If people believe that the state can provide these goods more efficiently and comprehensively than the market, they will support a rapid growth of public social services in a time of growing affluence such as that from 1945 to 1970. In support of the preference for public provision, it can be pointed out that historically the voluntary sector was associated with the stigma of charity for the 'deserving poor' and anyhow could not operate upon anything like the required scale. In historical perspective too, the market sector was ill-equipped to offer many of the required services to the general population; and where, as in the UK and USA, large insurance companies offered rudimentary coverage to the poor – for example, burial insurance so that an individual could avoid the disgrace of a pauper's grave – the service was marred by high overheads and frequent individual defaults. Moreover private insurers have difficulty in coping with the long lead times of pension payments and are reluctant to take on 'bad risks' for health and other forms of lifetime protection.

Goodin and Dryzek argue that in many European countries the demand for comprehensive state welfare was based quite rationally upon a preference for 'risk-avoidance' which was nourished by wartime conditions (Goodin and Dryzek, 1987, pp. 37–76). One may doubt this explanation, since the growth of state welfare has longer and deeper roots than wartime experience. However it is the case that a comprehensive pooling of risks, mixed with the prospect of impartial and efficient administration by government, made state social security attractive. The same concept of risk-pooling had obvious relevance to the appeal of the British national health service, since this scheme equalised risks not only between rich and poor, but also between the healthy and the sick. Given the high costs of serious illness (much higher today), a rational individual might well welcome the prospect of comprehensive risk-pooling within a single scheme, and even the healthy might accept the plan not only as a form of insurance but as a reasonable repayment for their own good fortune.

This populist interpretation of the growth of state welfare is inadequate and naive as a full description of political history. Welfare states developed at different paces and in different ways (Ashford, 1986), yet political support for the growth of state welfare grew everywhere until the 1970s. The rise of state welfare is often associated with left-wing parties and governments, and it is the case that such parties have been much more likely to *initiate* welfare schemes (Goodin and Le Grand, 1987, p. 220), but the big growth of state welfare after 1945 was carried forward by governments of both Left and Right. This very fact might seem to support the populist hypothesis.

Peter Baldwin's study of the class basis of the welfare state strongly supports this 'populist' conclusion. He plays down the influence of labour movements and parties, stressing instead the role of bourgeois and rural interests in creating the Scandinavian welfare states and the pivotal role of middle-class support everywhere in Europe. The consensus 'that evolved around welfare policy during the immediate post-war years was the outcome of a sense of social solidarity heightened by an awareness that risk and class are only partially correlated, that all potentially stand to gain from redistribution, that even the bourgeoisie has had much to win from a correctly crafted welfare state' (Baldwin, 1990, p. 28).

However a 'convergence hypothesis' does overlook one significant difference between welfare state regimes. In Scandinavia the successful alliance between left-wing parties, trade unions and sometimes farmers produced corporatist arrangements, which managed to combine a high level of state welfare with effective policies for employment and adequate minimum wages. In the UK and USA post-1945 governments were also committed to full employment (more weakly in the American case), but there was no effective integration of social and economic policies. In the USA state welfare did grow rapidly, starting with social security under President F. D. Roosevelt, and extending to health insurance for the aged and the poor (Medicare and Medicaid) under Presidents Kennedy and Johnson. American state welfare was more selective and less comprehensive than elsewhere, and was powerfully fuelled by electoral politics which stimulated generous extensions of welfare benefits under President Nixon (Esping-Andersen, 1990, pp. 174–5); but these welfare goals were divorced from economic policies and (as the 1980s were to show) wage and employment goals commanded no equivalent support and conflicted with the strong ideology of economic individualism. Thus American history does endorse a populist interpretation of the growth of the welfare state, but only in its social welfare aspect.

This hypothesis of a rational, popular demand for the growth of state welfare seems completely at odds with some public choice theories yet it accords with one basic *normative* criterion of public choice, namely that public policies ought to mirror (as far as is technically possible) the aggregated preferences of individual citizens. This strange discrepancy may be due to the fact that some public choice writers have been so obsessed with the assumed impotence or stupidity of the electorate that they have missed the contrary evidence in favour of rational electoral choice. However the popularity of state welfare hinged upon a tacit or explicit alliance between the interests of the middle and working classes, and a question for the future is whether this alliance still holds and can continue to be supported by Baldwin's 'sense of social solidarity'.

The assault on state welfare

If we have gone some way to explain the growth of welfare states, how are we to explain the malaise which has affected these states during recent decades? 'Crisis' may be too strong a term for this reaction, but the existence of considerable disillusion with the welfare state is undeniable, and applies not only to the UK and USA but also if more moderately to the more developed welfare states of continental Europe. In accepting the term 'crisis', it is argued that three separate if related criticisms have gained currency about the performance of welfare states.

Rising costs

The most obvious criticism is the rising cost of state welfare as a proportion of national income during a period of relative economic stagnation. According to Rose (1986, p. 29), public expenditure in seven OECD countries grew by averages of 5.5 per cent (1952–60), 7.2 per cent (1961–72) and 5.8 per cent (1973–82). However the 'front-end load', meaning the proportion of economic growth absorbed by public expenditure, grew from 28 per cent in the first period to 47 per cent in the second and 147 per cent in the third – a result which meant that the real value of take-home pay was actually declining under the pressure of government commitments. Given the fact that many continental countries are bigger welfare spenders than Britain or the USA, it may seem surprising that the taxpayers' revolt should have surfaced more strongly in those two countries. However Britain had in the last period the highest front-end loading (222 per cent) save for Sweden, while the USA (85 per cent) is known to be politically very sensitive to rising taxation.

Perhaps too much should not be made of these particular figures. The actual and prospective cost of the welfare state is a much disputed subject. However the financial viability of state welfare has become threatened by the onset of global capitalism, deindustrialisation and unemployment. The abandonment of the economic elements of welfare goals in the UK and USA inevitably places a heavy strain upon welfare services. Even in Scandinavia the changed economic circumstances have made the maintenance of integrated welfare goals much harder to sustain.

Technocracy

The second criticism is that public services have become rigid, remote and unresponsive to the wishes and problems of their clients. There is a curious element in this criticism, since what were once seen as distinctive virtues of bureaucracy, namely its impersonal rules and uniform administration, are now portrayed as 'dehumanising'; but it is true that long years of expansion had increased the power of the public service providers and professionals without improving their weak accountability to their actual clients. This situation could be defended on the grounds that in most social services, especially health and the care of dependent groups, the professional providers are the best judges of the needs of their clients, and anyhow are subject to the oversight of politicians.

Sometimes clients' wishes and tastes should be a major factor in the design of a public service. One bad example of 'technocracy' was the high-rise public housing which many governments, national or local, built in profusion during the 1950s and 1960s. The causes of this policy were complex (Dunleavy, 1981) and included the simple wish to take advantage of new building techniques to satisfy large pent-up demands, but there was little or no consultation with the intended clients about their preferred form or style of housing. The result was a large accumulation of unpopular, costly and sometimes unsafe public housing, much of which had to be demolished or extensively rehabilitated within a short period.

Disillusion with public administration also surfaced in the critical 'access' literature analysing the problems of clients in their encounters with bureaucracy (Schaffer and Lamb, 1979). Much of this literature was primarily concerned with third world countries and reflected conditions of political manipulation and administrative corruption. In Western countries long queues for services are not necessarily the fault of officials but arise from lack of funding. However the isolation of clients tends to grow under the increasing complexity of administrative rules designed to prevent fraud, ensure uniformity of treatment or preserve the principle of formal accountability. It was also argued that 'throwing money' at a service like education had not in fact produced a more educated population or prevented a considerable amount or even growth of illiteracy. In the USA a one-time liberal like Nathan Glazer (1988) reached the conclusion that the 'great society' programmes to increase educational and job opportunities for the poor had quite failed to deliver results.

Inequalities

A third criticism is that the 'welfare state' has failed in its presumed objective of achieving greater equality. Le Grand (1982) contended that in the UK the middle-class were gaining much more than the working class from public social services and subsidies. Health service benefits were said to be tilted towards the middle class by virtue of their greater knowledge and resourcefulness. Education benefits were mildly redistributive for primary and secondary stages, because of some private schooling, but this effect was heavily reversed by middle class domination of free university and tertiary education. Transport subsidies were also skewed towards the middle class because they mainly helped white-collar rail commuting. Subsidies for public housing amounted to much less per capita than the value of mortgage tax relief and other concessions to owner-occupiers. Only the personal social services which benefited disadvantaged groups were definitely redistributive. In the USA 'Director's Law' claims that the public budget benefits the middle mass at the expense of the very rich and the very poor (Stigler, 1970). However later evidence has questioned Le Grand's analysis, and it must also be remembered that services such as health and education need primarily to be judged by need or capacity, not income redistribution, even though redistribution will be the likely result if the service is working properly.

In any case Le Grand and other critics were careful to state that their analysis did not amount to an argument against the continuation of public services. So long as the tax system remains even moderately progressive, it will more than compensate for some differential use of these services by the middle classes. Moreover social security is redistributive, although in varying degrees. Also the poor would suffer if they did not have access to services of reasonable quality. The total system of state welfare has been shown to be mildly redistributive in Britain and the USA, and much more strongly so in other European countries

(Ringen, 1987). These important reservations have not prevented the spread of the idea, even among some of its erstwhile supporters, that the welfare state has a cloven hoof.

Alternatives to state welfare

These criticisms of the welfare state gladdened the hearts of its increasingly vociferous opponents. Each criticism elicited from them an appropriate response and remedy. The rising cost of state welfare should be met by resolute cuts and economies, thus freeing more resources for 'productive' enterprises. The claimed inefficiency and 'unresponsiveness' of state services should be met partly by an infusion of market concepts and disciplines into the public sector, and partly by shedding some of its load to the private sector. The inegalitarian aspects of state services were seen as an argument for concentrating state support upon the needy while reducing or abolishing other services. However the last argument – given its redistributive implication – was watered down by the proposition that the quest for greater equality was anyhow an illusory and illegitimate use of public powers, and should be replaced by the historically earlier concept of a minimal safety net for those in poverty or distress.

This reform programme reflected a very different ideology from that of the architects of state welfare who had once thought they were building a durable edifice. However its supporters were placed intellectually on the defensive, and instead of proposing their own remedies tended simply to resist change. Thus the thesis of 'populist' support for state welfare has become open to challenge. It can be argued that socio-economic change is shifting the distribution of interests, and that a 'cleavage' may be opening up between the interests which defend and oppose state welfare. How far this belief is true will be tested in this chapter's conclusions.

The remainder of this chapter deals with the impact of market theories and techniques upon the welfare state. First we examine the impact of market theories upon the delivery of welfare services in the USA. Next comes the important new theme of 'empowering consumers' by establishing markets or quasi-markets for the supply of basic social services. A review of developments in social security leads on to conclusions about theories of the welfare state under changing political and economic conditions.

Privatising service delivery

The concept of 'privatisation' now carries a heavy ideological load. The sale of state enterprises and other assets, which was discussed in the last chapter, is a fairly straightforward example of privatisation. It does not cover the many forms and meanings of the word or encounter the complex political problems associated with the 'privatisation' of state welfare. Moreover privatisation is bound up with other issues about public services.

Methods of privatisation

The provision of welfare can be regarded as a complex mixture of contributions from four sources: government, market, voluntary organisations and individual households (Rose, 1986). The advocates of slimming the state put a good deal of theoretical stress upon the contributions to welfare that should be derived from the last two sources – from voluntary bodies as representing a desirable form of charity to the disadvantaged, and from households as representing a proper exercise of personal responsibility and foresight. Some erstwhile supporters of the welfare state share this position (Glazer, 1988), while Donnison (1984) and others see voluntary and community organisations as desirable alternatives to the overcentralisation and bureaucratisation of state welfare. The obvious limitations to these arguments is that voluntary bodies, unless heavily subsidised by the state, lack the resources to make more than a minor contribution to the modern 'welfare mix', while individual households have become too fragmented and mobile to resume in more than limited ways their historical role as carers for the sick, handicapped and aged.

The simplest way for the state to privatise welfare is to shed some of its functions and simply leave the other sources of welfare to fill the gap if they can. However such a policy is too draconian to seem politically feasible except for a few marginal services. The more usual course is one of 'benefit erosion' through tightening conditions for eligibility, reducing benefits or imposing user charges. Such devices are logically independent of the uses of privatisation, but have accompanied its use in the UK and USA during the 1980s. Some forms of privatisation, on the other hand, *could* be used to improve the distribution of welfare (O'Higgins, 1989), although O'Higgins concedes that, in these two countries, they have generally been employed in a reverse direction. Thus the coupling of privatisation with state welfare cuts has given the concept a powerful ideological image which obscures any beneficial contributions that the process might make to the welfare system. Paul Starr concedes the possibility of such beneficial uses but concludes that basically privatisation is a political movement and ideology which 'needs to be understood as a fundamental reordering of claims in a society and in the extreme case as 'an instrument of class politics'' (Starr, 1989, pp. 42–3).

The privatisation of services can take four forms along a descending scale of the state's own concern with the outcome:

1. 'Contracting out' means that the state hires private providers to deliver some service but retains full financial and political responsibility for the outcome.
2. Under the agency approach the state gives grants to or contracts with private bodies to perform some function, but retains responsibility for setting and monitoring standards of performance.
3. A third possibility is for the state to mandate agents, usually employers, to provide some service with or without compensation. This method shifts the 'welfare burden' away from the state, but does not necessarily reduce its costs to society. The state still has some responsibility for the outcome.
4. A fourth approach is to offer subsidies or tax incentives to the consumers or producers of some service, but the state has only an indirect responsibility for the outcomes.

Contracting out welfare

This section is mainly concerned with government contracts under the first two headings, especially in the USA where the process has gone much further than elsewhere. 'Contracting out' started as a pragmatic process of saving money in the operation of primarily technical services, such as refuse collection, street cleaning and sewage disposal. If there is a standardised product and effective competition among contractors, there are often but not always efficiency gains (Fisk *et al.*, 1978; Walsh, 1989, pp. 42–8; Ascher, 1987, pp. 14–18). However in the US Federal Government, the process has developed to the point where half the total expenditure on the provision of services is purchased from the private sector (Donahue, 1989, p. 34). Besides the strength of market ideology, this policy was influenced by the political case for reducing or disguising the extent of public employment.

Privatisation in the USA covers an increasing range of core governmental functions, such as the vetting and payment of social security claims, the management of prisons and other institutions and the redesign of public programmes. Reagan vigorously accelerated this process by strengthening the existing Presidential directive in favour of contracting out whenever it was feasible and economical to do so. Many of these uses of privatisation raise broader considerations of equity and policy than technical comparisons of service costs and efficiency.

Originally many state and local governments gave modest grants to help voluntary welfare organisations without bothering much about how the money was spent. This is still the practice in many countries. However in the USA the formal contracting out of welfare services has grown rapidly in recent decades. It has been stimulated by cuts in Federal grants to the states, which have influenced some states such as Massachusetts towards a greater but much more regulated use of non-profit bodies for service delivery (the term 'non-profit' has a more rigorous legal definition than 'voluntary'). The result has been a veritable explosion of the voluntary sector. In Massachusetts, 7 per cent of the 1988 budget went on purchasing from over 1 200 contractors such services as family counselling, the rehabilitation of alcoholics, day care and the teaching of English, and altogether 200 types of social service were covered by contracts. Over four million people work nationwide for non-profit health, social and legal organisations, mainly with the help of government funding (Lipsky and Rathgeb-Smith, 1990, pp. 8, 10).

The massive use of contracting introduces a new type of relationship between governments and private organisations, which changes the behaviour of both parties, increases their interdependency and blurs the traditional distinctions between them. This new regime has some obvious advantages to both parties. For government there may be not only financial savings but in the USA particularly the political advantage of utilising and working with the widely respected voluntary sector. For non-profit bodies there is the substantial support and scope for expansion provided by government funds which far exceeds the likely scope of voluntary donations. One analyst (Salamon, 1986) estimates that 58 per cent of the non-profit sector's spending on social services was financed by government, while voluntary donations – even with the help of tax relief – came to only 30 per cent.

America has a wealth of local community organisations, which are often dedicated to particular local goals or ethnic concerns and which utilise volunteer or low-paid workers. Government contracts bring new requirements of equity, efficiency and economy. The ethnic, local or other special priorities of voluntary bodies are changed by rules of eligibility, equal treatment for like cases and cost controls; sometimes new professional staff must be appointed, in many other cases staff complements have to be cut.

While such controls are often imperfectly administered and applied, they do affect the freedom of voluntary bodies to pursue their distinctive missions in their own way. The result has been a considerable bureaucratisation of non-profit organisations, with successful ones tending to expand, lose some of their local roots, and sometimes engage also in commercial activities to finance expansion. Non-profits have pioneered *ad hoc* remedies for growing social problems, such as refuges for battered wives, shelter for the homeless and care for AIDS victims, but as state support for these purposes is sought and sometimes obtained, more routinised and regulated forms of treatment are required. This process simply repeats the old story of voluntary concern leading on to more uniform state provision, but now on a basis which co-opts the voluntary organisations into the service of the state. It is hoped that the result might be a mixture of public equity and efficiency rules with voluntary initiative and discretion, but some of the vitality, enthusiasm and local roots of the voluntary sector is being lost.

Effects on government responsibilities

Governments for their part have difficulties over protecting their statutory responsibilities in regard to contracted out services. For example, the assessment of complaints about child abuse is contracted out in Massachusetts, but the decisions have to be made by the state government. Commercial contractors for social services pose this problem more acutely, since for financial reasons they tend to skimp tough individual cases requiring time and trouble (Gurin, 1989). The privatised detention centres run by the Corrections Corporation of America are 10 per cent cheaper than conventional prisons, but provide less in the way of job training or specialised services like psychiatry (Bendick, 1989).

Government faces a most difficult task over monitoring the quality of personal social services, often including those which it supplies itself. For example regulation of nursing homes in America and Britain has mainly been concerned with physical standards, which are easy to measure, not with personal care and relationships (Day, 1988). Contracting out adds to this problem, since at least in theory public institutions are subject to some political control and scope for complaints. In Australia the main requirement seems to be a closer and more sensitive monitoring of institutional care, whether it is publicly or privately provided (Braithwaite *et al.* 1992).

In both America and Britain, and indeed elsewhere, governments have sought to 'deinstitutionalise' the care of the mentally ill, the chronically sick and the aged, and transfer responsibility to local community services and individual families. This exercise in cost-cutting can in this case claim some support from professional opinion, provided good local services are made available to handicapped individuals and their families. However in both countries the policy has moved much faster, for economy reasons, than the provision of community support. In Britain the transfer of responsibilities was first delayed by the government's reluctance to entrust local government with any major new tasks and, when it found no alternative, by inadequate funding. In America the provision of local or voluntary care is full of gaps, and the closure of mental institutions has contributed greatly to the growth of homelessness and vagrancy (Levine, 1985). In Canada it is now recognised that the shift to community care has definite merits in many individual cases, but has been oversold as a general policy.

Contracting out welfare in the USA has favoured commercial providers as much as voluntary organisations. Two-thirds of the costs of nursing homes are paid for from public funds, mainly Medicaid, but over 80 per cent of the homes are operated for profit (Gilbert, 1983). Similarly Medicaid funds have supported the rapid expansion of commercial hospital chains. In terms of quality, non-profit bodies have the advantages of stronger local roots, a better outreach to ethnic minorities, and the absence of commercial incentives to cut corners; by contrast abuses in commercial homes have been documented in such studies as *Tender Loving Greed* and they seem to attract more complaints than voluntary homes (Bendick, 1989). However commercial providers seem better at realising economies of scale and management, and at producing a more standardised type of service – hence the expansion of commercial chains of hospitals, nursing homes and child care centres which are the new beneficiaries of public finance. In Britain on the other hand a study of residential homes for old people found that the commercial homes not only had a cost advantage over local government homes, but often had the benefit of close attention from hard-working individual proprietors (Judge and Knapp, 1985).

Other policies of the Reagan Administration were to favour subsidies to producers or taxpayers in preference to state responsibility for a service. Job training was transferred from public agencies whose main emphasis was on placement within the public service to business councils who concentrate upon finding private sector jobs. The Federal grant to providers of child care for low-income families was cut, and the attempt to regulate standards abandoned, but tax credits were introduced for child care expenditures on a tapered basis up to a maximum income of $28 000. In this case total Federal costs almost doubled between 1980 and 1986, and helped to finance a big expansion of commercial child care centres, but the distribution of Federal support was shifted away from the growing army of poor working mothers (Kammerman and Kahn, 1989b).

In Britain the Thatcher Government promoted contracting out with an increasing use of compulsion, but it did not initially attempt an American-style transformation of welfare services. Its directive to hospital authorities to put their cleaning, laundry and catering services out to tender might seem a fairly mild exercise in technical efficiency. However Kate Ascher's (1987) study concludes that the policy had an adverse effect upon the morale and operations of the hospital services. This was because the providing bodies were not always allowed to reach their own decisions between in-house and commercial provision, or to allow for the indirect contributions which their existing staff made to the welfare of patients and the ethos of team work. In one case a hospital was required to allocate a contract to a supplier whose tender was higher than that of the in-house team, although a National Audit Office (1987) study did estimate that tendering had produced a modest annual saving of £86 million.

Local governments were initially cajoled and eventually coerced into putting a wide variety of mainly more technical services out to tender. Here the initial results were not so adverse

because the locally elected councils were at least more independent bodies than the local agents of the national health service,
and could exercise more discretion. Also the evidence supports
the familiar finding that competition will have a stimulating
effect upon the efficiency of any monopoly provider (Walsh,
1989; Fisk *et al.*, 1978). However the more dogmatic requirements
of the Local Government Act of 1988 led to large contractors
(often European or American rather than British) undercutting
the in-house tenders in order to dominate the market, and
produced much redundancy and loss of morale among the
direct labour force. The contractors often had superior technology and sometimes produced impressive results, but tended to
pay lower wages and use more part-time staff. There were also
some difficult problems over the design and monitoring of
contracts, and some bad examples of default over the quality of
services.

How successful are welfare contracts?

This brief review suggests three conclusions. First the public
choice theory that market competition for welfare contracts will
improve the quality of services gets little support from the
evidence. The range of adequate service providers is limited,
and unlike their costs the quality of their performance cannot be
closely controlled or easily evaluated. The contracting relationship is much more a political and administrative one of mutual
dependence than one of promoting economic competition
(Lipsky and Rathgeb-Smith, 1990, p. 23). This conclusion applies
to contracts with both non-profit and for-profit organisations, but
in the latter case financial motivations combine with government's search for economies to make improvements in quality
hard to achieve.

The outcomes of contracting are much more complex than any
simple calculation of possible financial savings. 'Transaction cost
analysis', which shares the individualist assumptions of public
choice theory, concludes that contracting out may not be suitable
or desirable where there is uncertainty about future needs, lack of
clear and visible standards of performance and little or only
temporary competition among contractors. These conditions
encourage opportunism among contractors and reduce the
capacity of government to control the quality of services
(Williamson, 1975). On the other hand contracting out can serve

as a useful counter or stimulus to public service staffs suspected of serious inefficiencies.

Secondly any positive advantages from privatising welfare have been clouded by their association with the ideological assault on the welfare state. The Thatcher policies were motivated primarily by hostility to public service unions and the wish to cut government spending. The replacement of state provision by tax subsidies, for example for child care in the USA, has reduced the access of the poor to welfare services. The cost savings from contracting have been gained through reduction in wages and more use of female part-time labour. Moreover, whatever the merits of voluntary bodies, they simply cannot cope with sudden cuts in statutory benefits. In Wellington, New Zealand, for example, the demand for soup kitchens and food parcels provided by the Salvation Army and other voluntary bodies increased more than sevenfold after the 1991 cuts in welfare benefits.

Thirdly there is increased blurring of roles between public, commercial and non-profit service providers (Rein, 1989). Up to a point this mixture of provision may in itself be beneficial. Voluntary bodies (if their contribution is not too diluted by bureaucratisation) bring a special value to welfare provision and their increased use has many merits, but it does entail extensive subsidisation and complex administration. A greater use of voluntary bodies may also strengthen public support for helping the poor, but it may also undercut the case for comprehensive welfare services. Commercial providers may sometimes offer as good or better services as public providers, but effective monitoring of the quality of welfare care is very difficult.

A basic problem with the privatisation of service delivery is the difficulty of sustaining 'the capacity of government to perform well its roles in policy planning, financing, monitoring and regulating' the services in question (Gurin, 1989, pp. 203–4). This is a crucial matter where questions of equity and individual rights are concerned, as is the case with many welfare services. The extreme case perhaps is that of privatised prisons. A study of commercially operated prisons, county jails and juvenile detention centres in America finds that they are tolerably well run within existing constraints, but notes that there is not, nor likely to be, effective competition among contractors or much scope for entrepreneurship outside the bulk provision of food and equipment. However the potential dangers to the public interest are considerable. The contractor effectively controls prison discipline and opportunities for parole, and there is the political danger that the problems of overcrowding and other aspects of the 'punishment industry' will be shuffled out of sight into the private sector (Donahue, 1989, pp. 150–78). Operating prisons for profit could also undermine the civic roots of criminal law and lead to costly litigation. Government cannot safely or equitably entrust its responsibility for judicial offenders to commercial enterprise, and the case of the sick, the old, children and the mentally ill poses a similar if less extreme need for effective public accountability.

Empowering consumers

A basic goal of public choice writers is to 'empower consumers' by giving them a wider choice of services. The intention is to stimulate competition and to reduce the power of bureaucrats to act as 'gatekeepers', controlling the allocation of services in a paternalistic or authoritarian manner. Public providers would no longer have a monopoly position, but would have to compete for clients with each other and preferably with private providers as well (Ostrom, 1973).

The capacity of consumers to be 'empowered' varies greatly with the 'market' in question. Generally consumers of housing have a good idea of the type and location of housing they would like, subject to their income. Parents of children are in a weaker position (although it could be improved) because in private as much as in state schools teachers have the capacity (and some would say the right) to determine the content and style of education. Consumers' information and capacity to control outcomes are still weaker in the case of health services. Efforts to extend or establish markets in these three arenas will be considered in turn.

Extending the housing market

Traditionally the main method of improving the housing of low-income groups has been through public or co-operative housing projects. However in the USA a Federal-financed system of housing vouchers has also operated since the 1970s. An eligible recipient gets a voucher equal to the difference between 25 per cent (now 30 per cent) of family income and the average rent of adequate housing. The family chooses its own accommodation in the private housing market and is free to spend more or less than the assumed 30 per cent of its income for housing. Thus the voucher functions as a low-income subsidy within a private, competitive housing market.

A favourite theme of right-wing think tanks such as the Heritage Foundation is that the Department of Housing and Urban Development (HUD) should cease financing public housing projects and mortgage insurance for low-income families – activities already reduced during the Reagan years – and rely exclusively upon a fuller use of housing vouchers (Butler, 1990, pp. 1–68). They argue that public projects are expensive, carry a social stigma and do not always target the poorest groups. By contrast vouchers respect freedom of individual choice and cost less than half as much as public housing for every family assisted. The bureaucracy in HUD and its coalition of interests are claimed to block this desirable reform which would also serve to cut back the costs and influence of bureaucracy.

These arguments have clearly more weight in relation to housing than to other social services. All the same they overlook the other side of the urban scene in America. There is a severe shortage of affordable housing for the poor in American cities. Indeed the same critics concede that before vouchers were introduced many poor families were paying 50 per cent of their income upon housing and the assumed payment of 30 per cent (under the voucher scheme) is still a substantial burden upon poor families. Pilot studies suggest that vouchers have helped many recipients to repair or improve their homes but do not stimulate the production of new housing. The market in housing for the poor is affected by the same 'ghetto' conditions which stigmatise public housing projects. Moreover middle-class suburbanites have had the benefit of Federal mortgage insurance which HUD has been striving (with limited success) to extend to poorer families. It seems clear that more positive measures than housing vouchers will be needed to improve the housing conditions of America's poor, such as more and better non-profit housing projects and local schemes of environmental improvement.

In Britain, with its large public housing sector, 'empowering consumers' has taken the reverse form of the massive sale of public rented houses to their tenants, and the creation of a 'quasi-market' within the public sector by promoting co-operative housing associations and by strengthening the rights of local council tenants, including encouragement to transfer to a housing association or individual landlord. Contrary to government expectations, council tenants generally seem to prefer the devil they know to the uncertain prospects of a different landlord (Spencer, 1989), although many local governments spurred by the threat of sanctions are now promoting their own housing co-operatives.

A major change has been the conversion of the 'producer' subsidies for local government housing into 'consumer' subsidies in the form of a means-tested housing allowance as part of the national system of social security. This support to low-income families is much more comprehensive and generous than the American voucher project, but simultaneously the supply of new affordable housing has fallen drastically, leaving increasing numbers in sub-standard accommodation. The British changes would make more sense in the context of an increased supply of affordable housing to rent.

School choice plans

There has been much advocacy by think tanks of the use of vouchers to widen educational choice. An education voucher could take a variety of forms. At its broadest it would enable a parent to purchase a given amount of education at any school, public or private. Those who chose to purchase more expensive private education – or more expensive state schools if such were allowed to exist and to charge differential fees – would pay the extra cost. In this form the system could be seen as inegalitarian, since it would subsidise private education and enable some pupils to go to the best state schools for a probably small extra cost. However the scheme could be made as egalitarian as its framers wished. Vouchers could be means-tested and rich parents issued with small or nil vouchers (thus requiring them to pay for public education if they chose that option). More mildly, vouchers could be taxable, reducing their advantage to rich parents, or poorer parents could be issued with higher vouchers to compensate for their children's disadvantages (Blaug, 1984).

In the USA the Federal administration did an evaluation of school voucher plans and tried a pilot demonstration at Alum Rock. The idea did not take off but instead at least a dozen states have developed 'school choice plans'. One goal is to widen parents' ability to select the school of their choice. The other goal is to offer more variety of educational programmes geared to the pupil's specific needs. This is done either by offering funds to local school districts to provide more variety of courses or by establishing regional 'magnet' schools with special facilities (for example there are over 40 speciality state schools in Milwaukee).

The most successful scheme is Minnesota's, where the state permits parents to send their children to a school in a different district provided the racial balance is not upset. Although rather few parents utilise this provision, public opinion has responded favourably to the existence of this option which by 1989 was supported by 60 per cent of both parents and teachers. The Minnesota plan does not remove the co-ordinating authority of the school districts and has not led to any school closures (Osborne and Gaebler, 1992, pp. 96–101). In Minnesota too the state pays most of the cost of public education; in the more usual situation of local financing a loss of pupils to other schools could damage the viability of the local school system. In fact there is considerable anxiety among educationists about the effects of school choice upon disadvantaged schools, especially in the big cities (Rinehart and Lee, 1991).

President Reagan regarded school choice as a panacea for educational problems. He tried but failed to get Congress to legislate to allow parents to opt out of school taxation and choose a private school instead. Advocates of private education argue that the public system is too costly and has a religious (pro-Protestant) bias (Lieberman, 1989). They contend that parents should be free to choose a school which teaches values they believe in. However the public system has the merit of promoting civic and socially egalitarian values even though these have been eroded in the big cities by residential segregation.

This erosion would be taken further by the expansion of private schooling. Private education is of very variable quality, from the prestigious east coast establishments to highly idiosyncratic schools. It seems that many private schools are in any case not keen to participate in a comprehensive plan, because they would be exposed to state regulation and might come under pressure to raise their often lower wages. A voucher or choice scheme which included private schools would be likely to run into the same problems of cost escalation, weak accountability and unequal access which afflict the American health system.

State school systems such as Minnesota's have shown considerable initiative over broadening the range and variety of educational courses. Parental choice plans have also contributed to this
result when kept within limits and accompanied by measures to
improve the opportunities of poorer pupils – a task which
requires skilful counselling of parents and attention to remedial
education.

Parental choice in Britain

Despite strong advocacy from the Institute of Economic Affairs,
the Thatcher Government did not introduce a voucher scheme.
They may have been swayed by the consideration that a scheme
which included private schools would seem too inegalitarian,
and that their goals for state schools could be achieved without
the complications of a voucher scheme. Instead the government
legislated in 1988 to give greater autonomy and financial
responsibility to the governors of individual schools, who in
future would include representatives of parents. Moreover the
governors, provided they have the support of 20 per cent of
parents in a secret ballot, can withdraw from the control of the
local education authority and become an independent state-
supported school subject to the guidance of the central ministry. Simultaneously parents have been given the right to send
their children to any school within the area of the local education
authority, subject to the availability of a place. The right of the
local governments who provide the education service to allocate
pupils between schools so as to preserve neighbourhood schooling or to balance supply and demand has been abrogated or
diminished (Ranson and Thomas, 1989).

What is the effect of these provisions? Increasing numbers of
schools are taking the option of achieving independent status.
The process of letting successful state schools expand, while
others decline or are abolished, is bound to be a slow one.
Favoured schools should raise their educational standards, but
declining schools will attract less good teachers and suffer from
low morale and expectations. 'Middle-class welfare' will be
accentuated, with the more informed and resourceful pupils
tending to monopolise the better schools. This tendency will be
accentuated by the more favourable financial terms offered to
opted out schools and also to the new business-sponsored city
technology colleges.

A study of three local government areas in Scotland, where the new system was introduced earlier, confirms these expectations. In two of the areas school accommodation was too scarce (as yet) to allow much freedom of parental choice, but in the third one the schools in disadvantaged urban areas were losing not only pupils but also teachers and resources. The same study confirmed the tendency towards still greater social polarisation, but noted also the inadequate information available to parents for making an effective choice of school (Adley *et al.*, 1990).

A deliberate aim of the new legislation is to weaken the educational powers of local government, while strengthening those of central government. Simultaneously with the other changes, the government is introducing a national curriculum, covering programmes of study for each 'foundation' subject, to be taught in all state schools and to be the basis for testing pupils at ages 7, 11, 14 and 16. The rationale for this national curriculum is the perceived decline in educational standards and literacy, but even if (as seems to be the case) the curriculum is fairly liberally designed, it is bound to inhibit educational variety and experiment and to exalt the importance of frequent, standardised tests. The government's statement that 'parents will be able to judge their children's progress against agreed national targets for attainment' (Department of Education and Science, 1987) suggests a very paternalistic view of 'consumers' choice'. Parents will have a choice only within the government's view of what constitutes a good education, and local government policies will be replaced by the uniform edicts of a more powerful master.

The Education Act of 1988 does introduce a quasi-market into the state system. Local governments are required to allocate funding to individual schools largely on the basis of numbers, although account can be taken of special needs including (if the minister does not overrule it) educational disadvantage. If the funds and the will are there, this provision can help schools in poor areas, and some local councils are doing so on a generous basis. However one effect of these reforms is likely to be a return to the stratified system of public education which existed in Britain before the advent of comprehensive schools. Parental involvement, although valuable, is a secondary feature. The re-establishment of better quality state schools is actually more likely to check than to stimulate the demand for private education. Conversely the hope that competition between schools will raise standards all round cannot succeed unless

Britain's low educational budget (by international standards) is substantially increased and equitably distributed.

The public health market

Health services offer the most intractable arena for 'empowering' consumers. The incidence of ill-health varies widely and unpredictably; costs of treatment can be extremely high; patients have to trust to expert advice and have little control over outcomes; and the evidence suggests that they have a weak capacity to influence the costs of treatment (Barr, 1987, pp. 293–6). For these reasons private health insurance is costly and discriminatory according to age and condition unless closely controlled. All countries make extensive use of publicly funded health insurance or provision, but with significant differences over organisation and the role of the market sector.

If one identifies the adequacy or quality of health care with actual expenditure, then the USA should have a superb health service. For example, a 1989 survey gives total expenditure per head on health services as $1 926 in the USA, $1 370 in Canada and $701 in Britain, equal respectively to 11.1, 8.5 and 6.2 per cent of GDP. As Rose points out, health expenditure in the USA is so considerable that, even though the public sector accounts for less of it than the private sector, the former still exceeds total British expenditure per head of the population. However Rose's apparent conclusion that these figures are an index of health welfare hardly stands up to the evidence (Rose, 1986).

The same three-country survey found that on six tests of popular satisfaction with health services, the American system was regarded as much the worst. The Canadian system was voted as best on all tests, with the British system intermediate. Satisfaction with the health system was 56 per cent in Canada, 27 in Britain, 10 in the USA; satisfaction with health care services gave figures of 67, 39, 35; and the need for a complete change was supported by only 5 per cent in Canada, 17 in Britain and 29 in the USA (Blendon and Taylor, 1989). Moreover, despite its high expenditure, the American system had only slightly more physicians per 1 000 population and a lower pharmaceutical expenditure per head (at purchasing power parities) than the Canadian and showed lower levels of life expectancy and higher levels of infant and prenatal mortality than both the Canadian and British systems (for details see *Health Affairs*, 10.3, 1991, pp. 22–38).

What explains these surprising results? One principal factor is that the British and Canadian health schemes provide universal coverage of a mainly free service, whereas in the USA there are an estimated 37 million Americans without any health coverage. Medicare provides health benefits for the aged and Medicaid for those on welfare; employers have tax inducements to provide health insurance, but many low-paid workers and their families are not covered. Because of the complexity of the system, administrative costs are also much higher in the USA than in the other two countries.

Secondly the cost of medical treatment is much higher in America. Although attempts are being made to control the costs of the publicly financed programmes, they have had an inflationary effect upon what is in any case a large, insulated and high-priced system of private practice, backed by powerful medical organisations. Even the funds for Medicaid are being drained by the requirements of middle-class citizens driven into poverty by the costs of medical treatment (Butler, 1990, pp. 197–228). Visitors to America have become aware that their survival from an accident depends crucially upon possessing an expensive insurance policy.

Comparative performance

In Britain the national health service is almost wholly financed from national taxation and subject to strict budgetary limits. The system has worked, according to Klein (1989), through a sort of 'Faustian bargain' between the government and the medical profession. In return for budgetary stringency, doctors have had clinical freedom to determine the medical needs and priorities of their patients. An ethos of social restraint has prevailed: doctors' salaries are only two and a half times average earnings compared with five times larger in America, and patients accept delays (up to a point) in return for free and fair treatment. Naturally enough the medical profession has frequently criticised the shortage of funds, but its professional rights and tenures have been very well protected until recently.

In Canada the cost of national health insurance is shared between the Federal and Provincial governments. Federal grants initially matched the Provincial contribution (with separate treatment for Quebec), but in 1977 this open-ended commitment led the Federal government to put its funding on a per capita basis which was frozen in the 1990 budget. Simultaneously the cost of the service was rising rapidly, which put a heavy burden upon Provincial governments which control the budgets of hospitals (usually non-profit corporations) and the fees of physicians. The Federal government requires that the service be free, comprehensive, non-discriminatory and publicly controlled (Brown, 1983). The Canada Health Act of 1984 disallowed extra charges being made by doctors and hospital user fees, thus securing a free and universal service, but pressures for economy measures or extra sources of finance are growing.

A historical survey of health services in four countries (Britain, France, Sweden and USA) concludes that centralised control over the funding, prices and personnel of the medical system has been positively associated with improvements in the cost-effectiveness or 'social efficiency' of treatment and with greater equality of access to services, but shows a negative relationship to the diffusion of high-technology innovations (Hollingsworth *et al.*, 1990). The USA has the most advanced hospitals in the world for those who can afford them, although commercial motivations in situations of consumer ignorance can also lead to the oversupply of medical operations and drugs.

Advocates of privatisation or more competition have difficulties in applying their ideas to health services. In the USA the dominant pressure for reform is actually towards fuller coverage by existing public schemes or the introduction of a new one. In countries with stronger public systems, the favoured argument is to reduce the load on public finance by encouraging private health insurance. Australia, for example, has alternated politically between favouring public and private health insurance. The present dominant system of Medicare is a public one, but private insurance plays a supplementary role on the controlled basis that rates must not vary with age or vulnerability (and a public agency participates in private insurance to monitor the system). The Opposition would offer tax concessions for private insurance and compel richer individuals to take it out. However private insurers are still less capable than governments of controlling escalating medical costs, as their support for a public inquiry into the high costs of private hospitals and consultants in Britain shows (*Observer*, 13 September 1992). In Canada, private insurance is tightly restricted to prevent it undercutting the price control of the public system.

The superior performance of the Canadian system over the British has been due to more generous funding, but economic and political pressures are eroding this advantage. Consequently, as in Britain, queues for some operations have been growing. The popularity of both systems depends crucially upon their appeal as a basically satisfactory service. Since there is little evidence that user fees or shifts to private insurance will improve the overall quality of health care, it is natural for reformers to seek internal economies and efficiencies. In Britain critics advanced the familiar argument about the entrenched position of public providers. The guaranteed rights to practice and basic income of general practitioners, the long-term contracts of hospital consultants and the existence of a strongly unionised workforce were claimed to produce a lack of incentive to cut costs or improve service (Enthoven, 1991). In Canada, experts have stressed the amount of health expenditure which achieves little result and the need to involve providers in new, more flexible patterns of service delivery (*Financial Post*, 6 April 1992).

Organising a health market

The national health service is or was until recently the most popular British institution next to the monarchy. This situation posed an awkward problem for the Thatcherite ideologues who believed, as an article of faith, in the superior efficiency of the private sector. Two early steps were to offer minor tax concessions for private health insurance (later extended to much more generous rebates for medical care of the aged) and to permit NHS consultants to carry out private practice.

However private medicine remained a dwarf compared with the giant public health service and was in fact strongly integrated with and dependent upon the public service. The private sector was mainly concerned with by-passing the queues for public treatment of some forms of elective surgery, and offering its customers extra amenities and choice of timing over hospital stays. Privately insured patients still used NHS doctors and made more than one-half of their hospital stays and four-fifths of their outpatient attendances under the NHS. Private insurance 'offers treatment to improve the quality of life for people of working age rather than coping with life-threatening conditions for the population as a whole' (Day and Klein, 1989, p. 14). The modest growth of private insurance enabled its recipients to shop in or out of the public service to suit their needs and timetables, and to many Conservatives this represented a wholly beneficial way of reducing NHS queues for elective surgery; but in terms of the basic health criterion of need it was much less satisfactory than allocating more resources for the direct reduction of NHS queues.

The government's initial recipe for the NHS was a strong infusion of managerial philosophy and increased cost-efficiency. Output measurements and targets were introduced for various types of treatment; general practitioners were subjected to medical audits and limited in the range and cost of their drug prescriptions. These efforts reduced the wide variation of medical costs within the NHS, but did not please the doctors who lost some of their autonomy. Nor did they solve the problem of underfunding. In the 1980s the government maintained NHS financing in line with inflation, but refused to supply the small extra funding previously agreed to cope with new demands and technologies. A storm of criticism from the medical profession, backed by a parliamentary committee, eventually, in 1988, persuaded the government, very reluctantly, to make up this backlog of £1.8 billion a year.

Thus by 1989 the government had resolved, rather desperately, upon pursuing its goals through the device of an internal competitive market within the health service itself. The market was to be quickly introduced, starting within two years, but only its framework was lightly sketched, leaving many issues for settlement by regulation and negotiation (Department of Health, 1989). At the time of writing (1992), the effects and the future of this 'internal market' are not clear, yet the subject is important enough for some comments to be risked.

This internal market has two elements. First the district health authorities, instead of providing services directly, purchase them from either public or private hospitals (thus extending the market into the private sector). In exchange, approved NHS hospitals achieve the status of independent public trusts, which enables them to determine their own salaries and conditions of work and to set their own prices. Their assets will be capitalised as debt paying interest to the government and profits will be available to expand the hospital's activities. Secondly family doctors with large practices of more than 7000 patients can become 'budget holders', meaning that they are allocated a total sum, based on the NHS system of a fixed annual fee for every client, and are free to supply or purchase the specialised treatment required for their patients from the most efficient source.

The 'health market' being ushered in is a curious one. It is a partial market, although the government is now encouraging all hospitals and most family practitioners to achieve independent status. It is primarily a 'managerial market', since the 'consumers' have no direct part in its operations except through their choice of family doctor. The competitive relations between the district health authorities and the hospitals seem from the client's viewpoint to be artificial, since the former bodies are wholly appointed from the centre, not elected (and do not any longer even have local government representatives), while health administrators can and do play musical chairs between the competing levels of health administration.

There is doubt as to how much effective competition between hospitals will eventually emerge. Many local hospitals have a virtual monopoly over some forms of treatment, while hospitals are quite likely, tacitly or otherwise, to restrain price competition for services. One possible result is that, as in America, the competition will concentrate on fringe benefits and amenities. A more serious possibility is that independent hospitals using their new freedoms will bid up salaries and prices, causing administrators to seek economies by cutting the quality of care. This seems to have been the outcome of competitive bidding and poor regulation in the USA (Maynard, 1989, pp. 22–3). The government itself seems uncertain as to how far it means to stimulate genuine competition, for example by insisting upon open contracts, and how far it means to control competition so as to prevent abuses or defend existing interests.

On the other hand the experiment of enabling larger medical practices to provide or buy a range of specialised services for their patients does seem to be working quite well. It is achieving a more efficient and economical balance between primary and secondary health care. Similar policies are being tried in Canada, and have been pioneered in the USA by health maintenance organisations which cover all medical needs of a patient for a fixed annual sum, using a variety of facilities. In the American context this is a relatively efficient form of market choice, because the functions of provider and insurer are combined, but poor or vulnerable individuals are unlikely to qualify (Barr, 1987, pp. 335–7). In the British context of free service and the well-established status of family practitioners, this approach may enable consumers to choose between medical practices offering a wide range of health care (Klein, 1991, p. 83).

The converse danger is that the internal market will undermine the whole ethos of the NHS with a creeping process of privatisation. New money may be attracted into private medicine instead of being injected into the national service. Doctors and some hospitals may themselves encourage their more affluent patients to switch to private practice for some purposes so as to protect their NHS budgets. The new distribution of NHS funds takes no account of the lighter load which the service carries in more affluent areas through the greater use of private medicine (Maynard, p. 27). The very stress on economic competition may itself undermine the distinctive egalitarian ethos of the NHS. Those who see the internal health market as an attempted 'privatisation by stealth' (or by default) have some cause for worry. On the worst prognosis the NHS will be formally maintained, but 'all the dynamism and resources will be directed to the opted-out sector . . . . [which will be] increasingly motivated to attract non-NHS money from private patients' (Williams, 1989, p. 7).

The scope of state welfare

As noted earlier public choice theorists are undecided as to whether public goods are likely to be over- or undersupplied. The latter view stresses that there is an unmet demand for many forms of welfare owing to public fiscal constraints and bureaucratic inflexibility. Thus Arthur Seldon of the Institute of Economic Affairs argues that consumers 'are increasingly able to pay for, and will therefore demand, better education, medicine, housing and pensions than the state supplies, and that suppliers are increasingly able to provide alternatives in the market' (Seldon, 1981). This approach leads to the now familiar argument that state welfare schemes should be cut down and private provision helped and encouraged for those who can afford it.

The scope of state welfare is often presented as a political choice between 'universalist' and 'particularist' forms of provision. Universalism means that basic welfare services are provided free or heavily subsidised, for all citizens as a right of citizenship. Particularist schemes are supposed to be aimed at vulnerable and disadvantaged groups. This dichotomy gives a misleading analysis of the evolution of welfare systems. Universalist schemes are widely supplemented by private provision, and particularist schemes are often used to support not the poor but the affluent.

Universalist schemes, especially social security and comprehensive health insurance or provision, serve two functions and respond to two different motivations. One function is to provide protection against the vicissitudes of the individual's life cycle, such as giving birth, rearing a family, falling sick, becoming unemployed, getting old and even getting buried. These events entail some or complete interruption of an individual or family's earning power, they cannot be closely foreseen and some of them involve either very long time spans (provision for old age), very heavy expenses (health hazards) or the quick impact of external events (unemployment). Hence the popularity of all-in schemes of state welfare which at least reduce these life hazards, provide a sense of security and have the further advantage of relatively cheap and efficient (because comprehensive) administration.

Universalist schemes also as a rule have some redistributive effect, taking from the rich and giving to the poor. However the political support for this purpose is more problematic, because it seems to require feelings of altruism or social solidarity, or a moral belief in equality. It cannot be presented as a purely self-interested form of mutual insurance, although some degree of redistribution can ride on the back, so to speak, of collective insurance against individual life hazards.

Welfare states differ considerably in the weight placed upon these two functions and motivations. Sweden has a system of comprehensive cash benefits and free welfare services which is strongly redistributive; for example, since 1946 it has paid universal flat-rate pensions without regard to previous earnings, although in 1959 these were supplemented by earnings-related pensions qualified by extra compensation for those on low incomes (Allardt, 1986). Many other European countries have features of the Swedish system, such as generous levels of sickness or unemployment benefit and old age pensions. Germany has a strong welfare system but not much of a redistributive one, since most benefits are paid and partly financed by employers and are related to previous contributions. Germany has been described as a social state but not a welfare one, whose politics revolve around 'status preservation' (Zapf, 1986).

Britain has a comprehensive system of social security, but its basis of flat-rate contributions and benefits accompanied by a low level of entitlements means that its redistributive effect depends entirely upon a large system of means-tested supplementary benefits. This redistributive effect has been offset by the substantial tax concessions offered for private pension plans. Whilst supplementary allowances kept the flavour of means-tested charity, subsidised private pensions were presented as an entirely respectable form of self-help.

The American social security system is more generous in some ways than the British. Both contributions and benefits are earnings-related, proportionately in the case of contributions but weighted towards low incomes in the case of pensions. Social security has in fact had a much stronger impact upon the relief of poverty than the numerous means-tested programmes; for example in 1982, 33.8 per cent of the poor were raised above the poverty line by social insurance payments, compared with only 3.8 per cent by public assistance money. The low incidence of poverty among the old is due to social security pensions and Medicare which have created a 'large segment of the population that is growing in size and electoral importance' (Hanson, 1987, pp. 174–5). By contrast, only about a third of the unemployed receive social security benefits, owing to tough eligibility conditions and a six-month limit on benefit.

Nibbling at social security

Universalist schemes have been squeezed between two political pressures. It is claimed that they cannot adequately meet, nor should they, the needs of the more affluent groups, but it is also claimed that the state cannot afford the rising cost of present schemes, especially given the growing numbers and longevity of old people. An answer is then sought in reducing the coverage and level of state provision, while stimulating private provision.

In Britain the inadequacy of its basic state pension led in 1975 to the introduction with bipartisan support of a supplementary earnings pension scheme (SERPS), related to the individual's earnings and covering all employees not provided for by an equivalent or better private pension plan, the latter group being allowed to 'contract out' of the state scheme with the incentive of a state guarantee of the value of their pension. 'The vast private pension industry was given the largest boost in its history . . . as the price eventually paid for the guarantee of an earnings-related pension for all at work' (Abel-Smith, 1984, p. 173). On this concession the Thatcher Government could build further.

The government wanted to abolish SERPS, subject to a requirement that all employees should be covered by private pension plans with a minimum contribution of 4 per cent of earnings, contributed equally by employer and worker. Initial financial savings from the abolition of SERPS would be small, but the idea accorded with Thatcherite ideology. However the proposal met strong opposition from some surprising quarters, such as the Confederation of British Industry and the National Association of Pensions Funds, who argued that administrative costs would be increased by a multiplicity of private plans, and that a 4 per cent annual contribution could not yield an adequate pension on an actuarial basis. The government finally compromised by reducing the value of SERPS pensions while encouraging private pensions by an initial five-years subsidy of 2 per cent of earnings to be paid out of the national insurance fund. This way of strengthening private and cutting public provision clearly had adverse redistributive effects, although the reverse approach of strengthening SERPS would have been equally practicable (O'Higgins, 1989).

The American debate over social security was equally dominated by pressure for cost-cutting, given the yawning budget deficit. This pressure was intensified by the fact that the social security 'trust fund' was running down, although in a sense this fund was a mirage. In effect the government acquired a large surplus from early contributions to social security and had to pay out increasing amounts as the population aged (White and Wildavsky, 1989, p. 316). However the idea that social security was simply an insurance system, not a form of welfare, played a large part in its popular support.

Much of the argument turned upon the issue of intergenerational equity. Social security pensions could be taken on favourable terms at age 62, they were index-linked to consumer prices (which were rising faster than wages) and benefits had been raised by previous administrations to the point where they covered an average 51 per cent of final year earnings – although benefits were much higher than this in many European countries where tax protests were much less in evidence. Whereas there were 3.2 workers to each pensioner in 1982, it was argued that the ratio would be only two to one by 2035, entailing an increase in the taxation of earnings from 12.00 to 16.80 per cent (Peterson, 1988). Peterson, a previous Secretary of Commerce, argued that the rights of pensioners could not be maintained without gross injustice to younger generations of workers, and pointed out that only 3 per cent of old people were below the poverty line compared with 16.1 per cent of children under age six (ibid, p. 100).

President Reagan, however, had early abandoned any frontal attack upon the popular social security system. The Social Security Act of 1983 was eventually engineered through Congressional compromises which White and Wildavsky (1989, pp. 310–30) regard as a 'triumph of governance'. Certainly the Act did not include the penal provisions of the British 'reform' and was on balance mildly redistributive. Congress took the comfortable course of satisfying the demand for a better actuarial balance by postponing the pain – and the savings – well into the next century. The standard retirement age was to be raised to 66 in the year 2004 and to 67 in 2022 – almost forty years away! Immediate savings were made by taxing part of the benefit of higher-income pensioners (a redistributive gain), by relating indexing in certain circumstances to wages instead of prices, and by bringing future Federal employees into the scheme which produced a short-run actuarial gain and savings in the existing more generous level of public service pensions. The intergenerational injustice was hardly resolved, but budgetary and actuarial norms were appeased.

These attempted reforms of social security were largely motivated by cost-cutting considerations. Their limited impact showed the weight of support behind state provision, which in the USA was reinforced by the increasingly organised weight of 'grey power'. However the British changes did reduce both the coverage and redistributive value of state provision, and they occurred without the comprehensive review which many critics were urging.

Public or private pensions?

The case for universalist social security is that it is a more efficient and equitable form of provision than reliance on private insurance. Its limitation is that flat-rate benefits are bound to be too low to satisfy many people on above-average earnings. However this problem can be overcome by adding an earnings-related supplement, as in Sweden and Britain, or by varying contributions and benefits, as in America. Thus a social security scheme can be made as comprehensive, flexible and egalitarian as its framers choose. The trouble with actual social security schemes such as the British and American is that they have become too small or insufficiently egalitarian to offer the basic rights which the system promises. This situation opens the political argument for more use of private pensions.

Since 1945 in Britain and the USA the private pension industry has expanded rapidly in tandem with the growth of social security systems. However the multiplicity of private schemes and the actuarial problems of long lead-times (especially under inflation) mean that private schemes are less economically efficient than an all-in scheme. Moreover the private pension industry is in many ways parasitical upon state schemes. It builds on their back to offer supplementary pensions. More than this, it requires and utilises tax breaks, subsidies or government guarantees in order to grow on a financially viable basis. The argument that private insurance deserves state support as a means of supplementing inadequate state schemes has no justification. The revenue thereby lost would be spent more efficiently and equitably upon improving the state system.

An economic argument for supporting private occupational schemes is that they will boost savings. This is a correct argument for a country like Australia where there are only means-tested welfare benefits paid out of current taxation; but the increasing vulnerability of Australian workers to international competition is a strong argument for introducing a comprehensive social security system there. The stock of national savings is increased just as effectively through social security contributions. Extra private insurance for those who can afford it is beneficial, but not if it interferes with the scope and adequacy of the state system.

Welfare and political change

It is necessary to consider how far the policies discussed in this chapter are changing the political basis of the welfare state. Can the welfare state still be afforded? Is state welfare being undermined by new social cleavages? How does the welfare system respond to economic change?

Can the welfare state be afforded?

In principle the answer is clearly yes. The level of social benefits in any society must necessarily vary with its prosperity as well as with the normative weight placed upon basic needs. Whatever the verdict on these issues, comprehensive schemes of state welfare still offer the most equitable and cost-efficient form of provision. The alternative of leaving the market to cater for the needs of the affluent and designing public schemes for the remainder of the population increases total expenditure upon basic needs. The earlier analysis of the American health system is an extreme example of this point. Equally private insurance is frequently impracticable or very expensive in actuarial terms unless bolstered by generous state guarantees or tax concessions. Directing welfare services to the poor is ethically superior to subsidising middle-class welfare, but inferior to comprehensive schemes which are equitably financed and distributed.

These contentions can be challenged on two grounds. One is the public choice argument that politicians will inevitably inflate expenditure and produce large budgetary deficits. However it seems more plausible that public education and health services will be *underfunded* in terms of their social and economic benefits. The large American budgetary deficit was due to a mix of military expenditure and tax cuts accompanied by cuts in social welfare. The intergenerational injustice which is said to be occurring in America (and perhaps elsewhere) is due less to excessive state support for the aged than to quite inadequate funds to cope with child poverty and neglect. The case for taking social security 'off-budget' and putting it on a strictly actuarial basis fails anyhow because its annual income and expenditure cannot be separated from macro-economic management, as even some critics of government spending agree (Butler, 1990, pp. 71–82). The insurance basis of social security can be no more than a useful fiction. It is too pessimistic to assume that any political foresight about future commitments is impossible, a viewpoint that is also contradicted by recent changes in American social security.

The real threat to comprehensive state welfare comes from the political pressures to cut taxation. Think tanks have been active in suggesting means to this end, for example by the state replacing social security with a small universal 'social dividend' and leaving all further welfare provision to voluntary bodies or private insurance (Davies, 1991). The widely argued case for a proportionate (and low) income tax returns to an aggressive economic individualism which accepts market allocations of income as a fair basis for the distribution of taxation. Successive dents in the system of progressive taxation, which has been the ethical basis of state welfare for the last century, are bound eventually to make comprehensive state schemes fiscally unworkable, although there is no evidence that public opinion wants this development.

Quality of state welfare

The above analysis does not deal with the quality of state welfare services. Public choice theory has especially attacked what is claimed to be the insulated status, lack of incentives and self-seeking behaviour of public service providers. These criticisms are sometimes a plausible argument for introducing competition into a public service, but restrictive practices are not confined to the public services. Governments are logical when they use the same market tests to condemn the behaviour of private professions such as lawyers, doctors and architects, but they have not pursued this quarry far. In fact the 1980s saw a large increase in the numbers and incomes of professional groups within the market sector (but often delivering services to government). As noted earlier, the private medical profession appears to be just as insulated but a lot more avaricious than doctors working for government. The concentration of reformers upon *public* service providers shows considerable dogmatism.

The concept of 'empowering' the consumers of public service is too strong for the reality. There are gains from giving some genuine autonomy to individual schools and hospitals, encouraging some competition between them, and involving parents or consumers' representatives in their administration. These developments themselves demonstrate that public services need not be so hidebound as the critics claim. However there are also intrinsic limitations to the process set by the weak information available to consumers, the involvement of dependants (children and the mentally handicapped, for example) whose rights must be considered, and the relevance of professional judgements about need and treatment. For example, the quality of health care depends a lot upon relationships of trust and high standards of medical practice and ethics, which are often best implemented through durable associations and long-term contracts rather than open competition (Maynard, 1989).

Improving the quality of public services often requires not the stimulus of competition, but the flexible and imaginative use of public powers to regulate standards, provide advice and offer special services and financial assistance. This is just the sort of joint exercise of public powers which ought not, on the basis of 'transaction cost analysis', to be fragmented or dissipated. Moreover action of this sort is essential to overcome or modify the inegalitarian tendencies of a more competitive public system. For example, the danger that children from poor homes in poor areas will virtually be 'written off' educationally has to be tackled by a mix of special courses to encourage school attendance (here variety of provision is an asset), remedial teaching and counselling, and financial assistance for those who can profitably continue their studies. These results will not occur spontaneously from competition between schools umpired by a public authority.

Another example is the state's role over preventive health care as a means both of cutting medical bills and of promoting positive health. This role may be especially important in the future for assisting old people to live healthier lives and to be less dependent upon expensive medical treatment for acute illness. Public authorities have both a strong financial incentive and various opportunities to pursue this course vigorously, whereas market incentives often work in the opposite way. Any comparison between private and public goods should recognise how many of the former goods promote ill-health (for example, smoking, alcohol, fatty foods) which the public health system must struggle to cure or remedy. In a context such as this the association of the market sector with 'productive investment', and of the state with wasteful spending, becomes absurdly baroque.

Growth of political cleavage

Is the social basis of state welfare changing? Developments in the 1980s produced a new theory of social and political cleavage, based upon the dependence of individuals upon either the public or private sector (Dunleavy, 1986). Conflict of interest between these sectors was stimulated by the growth of redundancies and unemployment in industry compared with the relative security of the public sector. Animus was also directed against the more entrenched position of public service unions and the more generous pensions which public servants had often acquired. Some of the political conflicts of the period can be explained in these terms.

However consumption patterns still leave most people with a mixed dependence upon public and private provision. In the case of transport, the private car dominates but many middle-class suburbanites use subsidised rail services, families of car-owners make some use of public transport and many car-owners support the case for good public transport as a stand-by facility or on environmental grounds. Education, health and basic income protection remain heavily dominated by state provision in most Western countries, with the exception of subsidised church schools. Private insurance often operates as an addition to the state system although tax-supported private pension plans are growing rapidly. There is little correlation either between production and consumption cleavages. Many white-collar owner-occupiers work for government, many or most public housing tenants do not. The one more homogeneous field is personal social services, where both providers and consumers are heavily dependent upon public jobs and services.

However it does seem that state provision in Britain and the USA has become more biased towards the interests of the middle and indeed upper classes. Analysing the expenditure of the Conservative government of 1979–83 against co-efficients of needs, Le Grand and Winter (1987) found a definite increase in the middle-class bias of public services (they also found, although only tentatively, a small opposite change under the previous Labour government). The middle class draw support from tax subsidies for private housing and pensions, while also enjoying an increasingly favourable position over access to the state education and health services. The carefully cultivated myth that state welfare is a matter of helping the poor not the affluent dies hard, and is supported by the assumption of an insurance basis to social security and by the belief that free tertiary education is a justified form of 'equality of opportunity'. Thus the more affluent may manage to rationalise their dependence upon the state, while maintaining a philosophic identification with privatisation. Rein (1989, p. 69) concludes that the pattern of financial shifts has become so complex in the USA that 'it is an illusion to think that empirical evidence will substitute for normative theory'.

This situation has led some writers such as Goodin and Le Grand (1987, pp. 222–5) to conclude that it is impossible to prevent a middle-class bias in state welfare services, and that the only possible remedy would be 'to adopt the less back-handed strategy of intervening directly in the market to try to make sure that it produces the right income distribution in the first place'. This strategy seeks an effective enthronement of economic rights such as minimum wages and full employment, with the desirable addition of some redistribution of wealth so as to provide every individual at maturity with an initial capital sum. The authors' emphasis upon the importance of economic policies is fully justified. Unemployment or low wages are now much the largest causes of poverty in Britain and the USA. However it seems utopian to hope that a society which will not distribute state welfare equitably will nonetheless agree to a fundamental redistribution of market income.

Neither is political history at all helpful to this particular argument. After all the social security system is an established form of income redistribution which could be (but has not been) transformed into the more comprehensive and widely floated device of a negative income tax. President Nixon's proposal of a family income plan, which would guarantee each family a basic income, failed to pass Congress, as did President Carter's version of the same idea. The cost was reckoned too high, and in Britain the Treasury is firmly set against any such proposal.

Is the pessimistic assumption of Goodin and Le Grand a correct one? After all comprehensive schemes of state welfare have had widespread popular support, and still do so in most European countries. They have the advantage of supplementing income guarantees with basic rights to education, health and housing. Glaring inequities in their provision ought not to be incapable of any remedies. For example in Britain the prestigious Rowntree Foundation inquiry chaired by the Duke of Edinburgh came out firmly in favour of phasing out tax relief on mortgages and allocating the money saved to low-income housing (Joseph Rowntree Foundation, 1991). In Australia a graduate tax has been introduced for university education which quite equitably requires graduates to repay their grants from subsequent earnings above a certain level (Chapman and Chia, 1989). In the USA political pressure is increasing for an extension of Federal health insurance to cover the present glaring omission of low-income workers and their families. While the resistance of existing interests to such proposals may be considerable, it is no more absolute than the once-supposed invulnerability of coalitions of state providers and consumers.

The dependence of social rights upon economic rights

The experience of successful welfare states supports the proposition that social and economic rights are mutually reinforcing. The more comprehensive welfare states are also the most effective redistributors of income and services. Norway actually has a more redistributive welfare system than Sweden, but because the Swedish system is bigger and has rather more generous benefits it achieves greater overall redistribution than Norway (Ringen, 1987). In Sweden the welfare system is complemented by full employment policies, utilising an active labour market policy, and by the protection of minimum wages through a corporatist system of collective bargaining (Castles, 1978). Moreover the high levels of public expenditure on welfare in Scandinavian and some other European countries have been accompanied in the past by higher economic growth rates than in English-speaking countries, where state welfare services are both less generous and less redistributive (Castles and Dowrick, 1990). Also, while governments certainly on occasion fuel inflation, there seems to be no general correlation between government spending and levels of inflation (Cameron, 1985). While there may be many causes of these economic outcomes, and while Sweden has modified its policies in the face of fiercer international competition, there is at the least no statistical basis for the frequent assertion that high welfare expenditure is inimical to economic growth.

How can these outcomes be explained? Ringen suggests that, while some economic disincentives may result from the high tax levels of Sweden and other large welfare states, they are more than compensated by the feelings of security and well-being engendered in the whole population by strong welfare policies. The growth of the welfare state has led to increased personal opportunities and interests, and often to a more rewarding family life, not the deadening effects which are often claimed (Ringen, 1987).

Corporatist theories offer a supportive explanation of the connections between welfare and economic policies. Crouch (1985) traces the success of eight European 'neo-corporatist' countries to the co-ordination of organised interests over managing economic change, restraining income growth and sharing resources equitably through wage and welfare policies. By contrast situations of open and unstructured confrontation between interests create a zone of instability where unemployment and inflation may grow simultaneously (Klein, 1985). If this confrontation leads to the dominance of a market ideology, the welfare system may also be undermined in an effort to discipline the working force and to give more room for capitalist enterprises. The likely results are higher unemployment and lower wages for many as well as reduced state welfare, so that the failure is both economic and social. These corporatist theories appear more plausible than Olson's public choice thesis that the American and British economies have stagnated because of the power of entrenched interests.

Recent theories of the welfare state stress the interdependence between state welfare services and the functioning of the labour market (Esping-Andersen, 1990; Mishra, 1990). The economic decisions of individuals over entry to and exit from the labour market are much influenced by the patterns of state welfare. Moreover there are significant differences between 'welfare state regimes'. For example in Scandinavia full employment policies have been linked with the absorption of labour (especially women) into state social services. In 1985 total employment in health, education and welfare (HEW) accounted for 16 and 17 per cent respectively of the labour force in the UK and the USA but for 26 and 28 per cent respectively in Sweden and Denmark; while in Scandinavia, unlike the English-speaking countries, almost all of this employment was public (Esping-Andersen, 1990, p. 158). Also in Scandinavia women are enabled and encouraged to work by generous leave entitlements for pregnancy and day-care facilities for children.

In the English-speaking countries no such coherent policies have developed. The employment of women has been modestly helped by equal opportunity legislation and day-care facilities; but many women can only find jobs in poorly paid and dead-end occupations. Conversely the problem of unemployment has been tackled by state schemes of early retirement (especially in Britain) and by measures for keeping young people off the labour market, often through training for jobs which never materialise. The welfare system has been subservient to, rather than attempting to cure, the adverse economic environment. This is not to say that the Scandinavian policies have been or are easy to sustain. Under adverse economic conditions they enhance the tensions between the market and public sectors and threaten the unity of the labour movement. Yet they still represent a determination to fuse the two elements (social and economic) of a viable welfare state.

The viability of universalist social services is undeniably threatened by the growth of unemployment and poverty. An increasing number of poor people increases the pressure for means-tested welfare and reduces its generosity, while simultaneously social polarisation produces political opportunities for state assistance towards private insurance or provision. These results are not inevitable. It is possible to redesign universalist schemes so that they keep their coverage and increase their equity; but not unless failures in the market system can be overcome.

Conclusion

The 'crisis' of the welfare state was precipitated by the onset of economic stagnation and by the restrictive and divisive public policies then employed to restimulate the market system. A second, partly independent, factor was a degree of disillusionment with the performance of public services. The first problem can only be tackled by international policies to establish a stabler market system which also provides more room for the satisfaction of basic social needs. The second problem requires a more humanised or 'user-friendly' treatment of state social services, which is already to some extent occurring but whose accomplishment is threatened by narrow doctrines of privatisation and competition.

A viable welfare state requires a normative foundation. While the growth of state welfare represented a rational electoral choice, the choice is not self-sustaining upon a narrowly egoistic basis. It entails a form of 'enlightened self-interest' which takes account of the individual's own long-term needs and has some regard and sympathy for the equivalent needs of others. Ultimately this approach involves some concept of shared citizenship within a society. This concept can be undermined by using a much narrower concept of self-interest to induce individuals to opt for privatised welfare.

Concurrently ideology plays a crucial role in both the processes of constructing and of dismantling state welfare. Its theme in the former case was the benefits of positive political co-operation to achieve mutually beneficial results; in the latter case, the inefficiencies of government action and the superiority of self-help. The extraordinary achievement of the latter ideology, drawn from the dominant school of public choice theory, has lain in the credibility given to wholly irrational arguments. As this chapter has demonstrated, it is generally false to argue that private provision of welfare will be more efficient than public provision – to the contrary, universalist schemes of social security and health insurance (or public service) provide better and cheaper protection against the vicissitudes of the life cycle and inequalities of condition. It is equally false to claim that privatisation saves resources – on the contrary it means that the affluent spend considerably more upon their welfare require-ments and total outlays increase while the poor suffer from inadequate provision.

The erosion of state welfare is due to subtle shifts in its structure and distribution of benefits which may open the gate to further erosion. In a favourite phrase, 'policies change politics' by altering the distribution of interests and patterns of behaviour. This theme is familiar to public choice writers as the 'tragedy of the commons' (Hardin, 1968), whereby the use of common grazing rights is progressively undermined by the rational but egoistic decisions of individual owners to put more beasts out to pasture. In the same way erosion of the social norms which sustain the welfare state could become a cumulative process. To reverse this result requires not only the gradual rebuilding of political coalitions in favour of state welfare, but also the support of normative theories of the role of the state that differ fundamentally from the dominant strain of public choice theory.

Restructuring Government

Political goals and public choice theories

During the 1980s substantial efforts to change the structure of government occurred in the English-speaking countries of the UK, USA, Canada, Australia and New Zealand. The goals of the political leaders were to slim bureaucracy, to assert political control, to revamp the machinery of administration, to change patterns of service delivery, and to introduce a new managerial philosophy of resource efficiency and expenditure control. The results of these efforts were a mosaic of administrative change, varying between the states in question; because of the large number of new arrangements, only selected examples can be given in this chapter. It may be premature to talk of a new administrative system, given the persistence of traditions of government and bureaucracy, but it is possible to examine the new directions which have been imposed upon the often resistant structure of the state. Nor can it be said that these directions are entirely novel, since in some cases they represent an acceleration of trends which were already present in earlier decades.

The influence of public choice

Public choice theory has contributed in the first place, as suggested in Chapter 3, to a highly critical view of bureaucracy and to attempts to subordinate bureaucracy more closely to the will of political leaders. These attempts are linked also with the influence of the 'new institutional economics', which seeks to remodel the machinery of government according to the idealised concept of a competitive market system. Key ideas here are to achieve an accurate listing and costing of all government functions; to break up public service monopolies and introduce competition with private or other public providers; to impose user charges where practicable; to overcome the alleged tendency of departments to be 'captured' by their clientele and to make policy advice to ministers more 'contestable'; and to increase the transparency and cost-effectiveness of the whole system. Linked with these goals is the influence of 'contract theory', which reduces organisational relationships to those between a principal and his agent, both motivated by rational self-interest, and which therefore seeks ways for inducing the 'agent' (the bureaucrat) to act in accordance with the wishes of the 'principal' (the minister).

This raft of theories aims both to move the behaviour of bureaucracy closer to a market model and to increase the power and discretion of the political leadership, who will thereby achieve more control over policy advice, service delivery, the size and functions of government and the actions of their 'agents' (the senior bureaucracy). A different and perhaps more influential path to administrative reform is offered by the 'new managerialism', which stresses the importance of comprehensive resource planning and of a stronger delegation of discretionary authority to line managers. This managerial doctrine shares with public choice an emphasis upon economic incentives and market techniques; but it is as much (or more) concerned with strengthening the role of public service managers as with tightening political control. The new institutional economies favours a polycentric and competitive design of the government system, which diverges significantly from the managerial emphasis upon corporate planning and co-ordination. Thus, within the machinery of government, conflicts arise both between concepts of political control and managerial discretion, and between a competitive and co-ordinated system of public administration.

Implications for democracy

A critical question is how these various policies relate to concepts of democracy. Public choice theory aims to align the provision of public services with the preferences of consumers as far as is possible. However the goals of national political leaders do not necessarily accord with the wishes of consumers or with considerations of service efficiency (Moe, 1984, pp. 766–7). Moreover the interest of citizens in the functioning of bureaucracy is not the same as that of political leaders. The latter may pursue highly partisan and discriminatory political goals, whereas citizens have an interest in impartial and effective service delivery. While elected political leaders do possess a democratic legitimacy which hands them authority over bureaucracy, a developed concept of democracy requires other factors to be taken into account than the political will of the leaders.

As Chapter 1 noted, one logical implication from public choice theory is the maximisation of democratic choice over the range and quality of public services. This argument has highly radical implications for both bureaucracy and democracy. In *The Intellectual Crisis in American Public Administration* (1973) Vincent Ostrom argues that the answer to the dysfunctions of big bureaucracy lies in the devolution of public services to the control of local elected boards. As a result public choice would be maximised and bureaucratic input minimised. If the clients or consumers of a service (say education or health) elected the relevant board, and paid directly for the service, they could make a rational choice of the amount and quality of the service they required. Bureaucracy would become again the servant of public choice. Ostrom's radical proposal is one possible interpretation of public choice thinking which is in striking contrast to the theory of maximising top-down political control over a large centralised bureaucracy.

Ostrom's actual proposal for a series of client-elected boards could only be very partially applied (for example, it has a weak relevance to the state's many regulative, protective and corrective functions), it has inegalitarian implications and it raises stubbornly difficult issues about the co-ordination of public policies and the capacity of citizens to elect numerous bodies. However, as Ostrom also recognises, many of these gains in democratic choice can also be realised through an enhanced measure of local self-government. *Political* devolution is a possible public choice answer to the problems both of big bureaucracy and of excessive political power at the centre; but it is an answer which also raises complex issues about the desirable structure of a devolved system. Also political leaders may resist and even reverse political devolution for partisan reasons, or because they are more concerned with promoting privatisation than with the democratic management of public services.

In line with these concerns, the next two sections on bureaucracy and administration are followed by sections on political decentralisation and its opposite, the centralisation of power. The conclusion relates public choice theories to a verdict upon the desirable relationship between bureaucracy and democracy.

The assault on bureaucracy

Public choice theories, with their stress on rational egoism, have posited two major defects of bureaucracies. One is the tendency of bureaucrats to 'build empires', maximise budgets and generally increase the size of government. The other defect is the weak control of bureaucracy because of the private interests of bureaucrats in distorting information, evading orders or shirking work (however shirking is at the opposite pole from frenetic empire building). Hence efforts by politicians to slim bureaucracy and bring career officials under tighter political control.

Cutting bureaucracies

Bureaucracies *were* cut in the 1980s. In Britain the Comptroller-General found that in five years (1979–84) over 100 000 posts had been shed, reducing the civil service by 14 per cent and exceeding the Thatcher Government's target (Hennessy, 1989, p. 600). In the USA over the same period Federal civilian employment declined by roughly the same amount (from 3.33 per cent to 2.78 per cent of the labour force). These are gross figures. A more detailed British study, using somewhat different data (decline of just over 12 per cent over seven years) finds that, contrary to public choice assumptions, the cuts fell most heavily on the *top* bureaucrats, the falls being 19.04 per cent for top level, 7.23 per cent for middle and 10.39 per cent for lower levels. Moreover part-time staff increased, contrary to the prediction that bureaucracy would shed its weakest members first (Dunsire and Hood, 1989, p. 103). Blue-collar workers fell by still more (34 per cent), but here the decline from rationalisation of production was long-standing and further accelerated by privatisation.

How far were these staff cuts genuine? The same British study finds that the adoption of more efficient work methods accounted for only 13.5 per cent of the staff cuts. Other reductions due to changes in workloads (13.7 per cent) and 'general streamlining' including lower standards of service (24.5 per cent) suggested quality cuts. The other cuts (48.3 per cent) referred to shedding functions by terminating them, privatising them, or transferring the function to a public agency outside civil service rules. This last activity (15.1 per cent) was plainly a cosmetic change which did not affect the real level of public employment. Precisely the same cosmetic tactic was used in the USA. However these figures do suggest that the bureaucracy did achieve some efficiency gains as well as accepting political instructions to lower standards and shed functions (Dunsire and Hood, 1989, pp. 145–55).

Political leaders stressed the need to cut wasteful use of resources in the public service. Undoubtedly such waste existed in these huge bureaucratic organisations, but President Reagan had absurdly exaggerated expectations – at any rate for electoral consumption – of the likely results of his 'war on waste'. He relied upon a private sector survey on cost control in the familiar American form of a top-heavy Commission (the Grace Commission) using numerous working parties. This Commission recognised that the salaries of top civil servants were inadequate – they were in fact tied to those of members of Congress – but it concentrated upon the case for cutting the more generous pensions and fringe benefits of the public service and reducing the opportunities for grading salaries upwards ('classification creep') which was a device used for getting around inadequate salaries. Not surprisingly, in view of their ideology and perhaps their own private interests, the Grace Commission placed heavy emphasis upon privatisation and contracting out as means of reducing costs. Reagan took the same line, using the Office of Management and Budget to urge privatisation where costs could be reduced by 10 per cent. Guy Peters (1985, pp. 19–42) notes the inappropriateness of these proposals for a public service which was heavily professionalised but had different responsibilities and much lower salaries than the business world.

The British inquiry into civil service efficiency was more modest and better designed and managed. Lord Rayner, an executive of Marks and Spencer, worked with a small civil service staff (the 'efficiency unit') on a detailed scrutiny of particular administrative tasks. Not sharing Mrs Thatcher's hostility to the civil service as an institution, Rayner was able to enlist the interest and enthusiasm of many civil servants in improving their workloads. Rayner believed in cutting down paperwork, such as the 50 volumes of rules used by the Department of Health and Social Security, and in a close look at specific activities which seemed wasteful. 'Rayner's Raiders' conducted 155 such investigations and identified potential annual savings of £421 millions. The Rayner inquiry certainly demonstrated a lack of 'cost-efficiency' within the public service (there were some glaring examples of waste), but another of his conclusions was that the skills of public servants were underused through lack of appropriate education and experience (Hennessy, 1989, pp. 589–622).

Increasing political control

The second goal of political leaders was to control bureaucracy more effectively. In the USA this took the form of increasing the number of Presidential political appointments, which had already grown in the post-war period from a mere 200 under President F. D. Roosevelt to over 2 000. Now Reagan increased these 'political executives' to 3 000 and used departmental reorganisations to rationalise their hierarchical control over the career civil service. The partnership between the rather erratically appointed and very temporary 'political executives', drawn largely from the private sector, and the senior civil servants is a difficult one at best. It was made harder by the hostility towards and ignorance about the public service which many of Reagan's appointees shared with Reagan himself. The result could be mirrored in public choice terms as a game where the public servants lacked enough inducement to comply with the erratic directions of the political executives.

The Volcker Commission (1990), which comprised business and political leaders, delivered a damning report upon political methods of bureaucratic control. It criticised the effects of 'layers of temporary Presidential appointments between the President and the career officials who deliver services' (p. 18). It wanted the number of political executives cut back to 2 000, and urged that they be more systematically selected (a familiar idea) and give more support to the career service. It pointed to the growing disparity of incomes between government and business, the exodus of top public servants into the private sector and the great difficulty of recruiting able graduates. It attributed many administrative crises, such as scandals in defence procurement, near-misses in air control, the collapse of loans and savings banks and the poor supervision of hazardous waste and nuclear weapon plants, to inadequate staffing and poor morale in the Federal public service; and all this despite the fact that 'the need for a strong public service is growing, not lessening' (p. 1). Necessary improvements included more devolution to the discretion of line managers, better salaries and better training, as well as the need for political efforts to rehabilitate the public service and to foster civic understanding of its value (in contrast to the cynical view current in the media). This report, endorsed and funded by business leaders, represented a strong answer to the advocates of restricting and controlling bureaucracy more tightly.

In Westminster-style democracies there is much less scope than in America for political appointments but there was an increased use of political advisers and private consultants as alternative sources of policy advice. In Britain an investigation by the Royal Institute of Public Administration cleared the Thatcher Government – albeit a little doubtfully – of using political criteria in administrative promotions, but it did suggest that these appointments had become more 'personalised', in their regard for the Prime Minister's own opinions and aims (Hennessy, 1989, p. 634). Simultaneously the hostile attitude of Mrs Thatcher towards civil servants generally, whom she regarded as an inferior breed to business managers, and the strong stress on cutting staff, lowered morale and created resentment. Sue Richards concluded that the impact of new managerial initiatives was undermined by the hostile atmosphere in which they were launched (Harrison and Gretton, 1987, pp. 22–41).

Reducing public service rights

Simultaneously security of tenure and other rights of public service workers have been reduced. The flagships of bureaucratic self-regulation were independent boards who controlled the conditions of recruitment and promotion, protected rights of appeal and prescribed standards of personnel management. In Britain, Australia and New Zealand the personnel functions of these bodies have largely been transferred to individual departments and their supervisory role has been diminished or eliminated. In Britain the Civil Service Department, which regarded itself as the custodian of good management and morale within the civil service, was abolished and its chief, Lord Bancroft (who was also Head of the Civil Service), took early retirement, observing that the 'grovel count' was rising among Ministers and some officials (Hennessy, 1989, pp. 623–5). In Australia the Hawke Government abolished the Public Service Board in 1987, leaving the residue of its powers to prevent improper appointment with a Public Service Commissioner and small staff. In both Britain and Australia responsibility for senior appointments was shifted to the Prime Minister's portfolio, a much more political location. New powers were taken in Australia and New Zealand to authorise staff redundancies and to reduce the appeal rights of dissatisfied employees. Pay comparability with the private sector was effectively ended in Britain and Australia. While these changes might be defended by the need to shake up over-protected public services, they also reduced the safeguards of a politically impartial bureaucracy.

The use of limited-term contracts for senior bureaucratic appointments has become quite common. The systematic development of this practice in New Zealand represented a deliberate application of the contractarian theory of principal and agent. There the chief executives of all departments are appointed by the State Services Commission for a maximum of five years with flexible financial packages. The Commission is now required to take note of ministerial preferences (in the last resort the government collectively can make the appointment) in place of peer review by senior public servants. Ministers are also expected to make 'performance agreements' with their chief officials which specify their tasks and objectives and are used to review the performance and pay of the official. Similarly the members of New Zealand's new Senior Executive Service, which is intended (like the Australian SES) to be a countervailing force to the increasing autonomy of departments, are appointed on five-year renewable contracts with scope for pay variations by the departmental head (Boston, 1991, pp. 82–113). Similar arrangements apply in Australian states and in the New South Wales Government the contractual approach has been pushed to the limit of one-year appointments for chief executives with annual reviews by the premier's department using outside consultants.

These arrangements have increased the flexibility but reduced the security of administrative appointments. They give political leaders more scope to intervene in appointments, to specify their wishes, to review performance and to terminate unsatisfactory contracts. However New Zealand experience suggests that ministers are often not keen to act so systematically and find it difficult to set objectives and monitor performance in what is often a turbulent political environment. Moreover the combination of short-term tenures for both ministers and their chief officials deprives government of its institutional memory, and reduces the continuity of public administration (Boston, 1991, p. 98). The use of private consultants over making appointments and appraising performance may be a check upon the back-scratching of a closed administrative circle; but it also underrates such factors as good staff relations and quality of advice which only 'insiders' are likely to appreciate.

Theoretical implications

What do these many developments suggest about bureaucratic behaviour? There is little evidence of effective resistance by bureaucracies against the staff cuts, the reduction in security of tenure, the privatisation of public functions, and the imposition of stronger political controls. Bureaucratic opposition, to the extent that it occurred, did not prevent politicians from imposing policies which were quite contrary to traditional bureaucratic beliefs and supposed interests. Certainly there was dismay and disaffection and no doubt some practical resistance to the implementation of change; but the thesis of a bureaucracy strong enough to stand up to its political masters cannot be sustained for the English-speaking democracies.

It does not necessarily follow that a permanent and radical change is occurring in the political–bureaucratic relationship. In terms of Guy Peters' (1987) five 'ideal models' of that relationship, discussed in Chapter 2, there has been a small move towards his first 'formal–legal' model where politicians command a compliant bureaucracy by virtue of their formal authority; but in the English-speaking democracies a subtle balance exists between the strong formal powers of the political leaders supported by the bureaucratic tradition of compliance with political will, and the bureaucracy's large resources of numbers, expertise and zones of *de facto* administrative autonomy. This subtle balance is not easily upset, but the co-operative relationship became a more adversarial one. Two public choice theories deserve special attention in the light of the changing situation of bureaucracy.

The bureau-shaping bureaucrat
The theory of the budget-maximising bureaucrat, insofar as it was ever plausible, has been vitiated by the experience of a decade of cutback management. Under these conditions a much more plausible public choice theory is Dunleavy's (1991, pp. 74–209) concept of the 'bureau-shaping bureaucrat'. This rational egoist observes that his personal interests will be best served by joining the bandwagon of politically inspired change. He can

carve a career for himself out of cutting staff, privatising functions and reorganising agencies, if he can occupy a controlling position within the administrative hierarchy. This opportunistic behaviour, to the extent that it actually exists, supports the thesis of dominant political control. The bureaucrat is acting like a well-paid hatchet man. In this form the theory is only applicable to a particular period of change, and also (unlike the maximising bureau chief) it is unclear *which* bureaucrats will behave in the specified manner, unless indeed such behaviour becomes a test of survival.

However Dunleavy (1991, pp. 200–2) seeks to give his theory a wider relevance by arguing that senior bureaucrats usually put a high valuation upon non-pecuniary personal benefits, such as prestige, proximity to political power, interesting work and a pleasant collegial atmosphere. This preference reflects their difficulty in achieving higher salaries since they do not enjoy the flexible financial packages of businessmen (however the contract system may be removing that constraint); moreover these non-pecuniary attractions are also reasons for choosing a public service career. These bureaucratic ambitions can be best satisfied by joining such central agencies as the Treasury or the Prime Minister's Department, which have small budgets and staffs but do interesting, influential policy work; or by acting as policy advisers to a minister at the apex of a politically significant department. Stripped of its opportunistic implications, this theory repeats the well-worn theme of the bureaucratic attractions of top-level policy jobs. Thus Dunleavy's theory may throw some light upon recent administrative developments which separate top-level policy advice from the strengthened managerial functions of hived-off agencies.

The principal–agent theory
The second theory needing examination is that of contractual relations between a principal and an agent. This theory is based upon the economic concept of 'transaction costs' (Williamson, 1975, 1985). The minister, according to this theory, faces problems of 'adverse selection' and 'moral hazard'. Public service rules in traditional bureaucracies do restrict the minister's possible choice by introducing considerations of seniority, career planning and independent administrative advice on top appointments. Thus the minister can avoid being saddled with an official he mistrusts by widening the field of candidates (including the private sector)

and by imposing frequent reviews and possibility of termination. However the scope for greater political control over top appointments can be achieved, as it has been in the Australian Government, without the use of contracts. In practice there must always be administrative as well as political inputs into the selection process (the issue being the desirable balance) and it is misleading to view the minister as an independent principal (top appointments usually require collective government approval).

The problem of 'moral hazard', according to the theory, is that the bureaucrat will always tend to substitute his own personal interest for the minister's wishes wherever these conflict. However a short-term contractual relationship may well increase this danger. The traditional administrative system does at least ensure that officials are committed to a public service career and imbued with certain values, such as compliance with ministerial directions even when these are disliked (although officials may sometimes drag their feet). An official on limited contract will have less commitment to the public service and may be more disposed to use his position to establish useful contacts and opportunities in the private sector. The best way to avoid 'moral hazard' would seem to be to develop an administrative system which produces predictable qualifications and attitudes of the desired kind.

A basic aim of the contractual model is to use economic incentives to achieve efficient performance by agents. On the assumption that all workers are inclined to avoid effort (a version of the 'free rider' assumption), the task of the manager is to improve performance by an appropriate use of carrots and sticks. To perform this difficult task the manager or bureaucrat supposedly needs a large financial incentive related to his performance. This is a very leaky theory to apply to public administration where quantitative tests of performance are hard to apply and often misleading because of considerations of equity and due process. Also such tests, for example of number of appeals heard or cases processed, tell nothing of the quality of the decisions. The monitoring of efficiency has often to be based upon professional judgement rather than quantitative tests.

The only easy test that can be applied to public service is that of cutting expenditure. In a climate of retrenchment the contracted bureaucrat may be more efficient and ruthless over saving money than a more traditional official, but the axe wielder may not stay to observe the consequences of his decisions. At the same time the strong use of economic incentives cuts across bureaucratic norms of teamwork, and thereby increases adversarial relations within the system. Because of these problems, economic incentives have so far been given only a limited application within public services; but they do show up in the increased capacity of departmental heads to control promotions and vary pay, in the widespread use of 'merit' pay increments, and in the use of flexible financial packages for top appointments. In a 'public choice' world these innovations would doubtless be taken much further.

The most curious feature of principal–agent theory is that it is concerned exclusively with the behaviour of the agent; yet the principal (who is often though not always in a more powerful position) may have the greater opportunity to exploit his control of the agent for partisan or personal ends (Perrow, 1986a, pp. 14–16). So far the main problem which has shown up in administrative contracts has been the incapacity or unwillingness of ministers to meet their responsibilities for specific directives and effective monitoring. However, once the bureaucrat is treated as simply the agent of a politician, the opportunity is there for a return to political patronage, nepotism and other forms of corruption which were stopped by the introduction of civil service merit systems.

Copying market models

Along with these assertions of political control over bureaucracy have come other changes in the methods and machinery of public administration inspired by public choice theory and business management. The convergence and tensions between these modes of thinking, both rooted ultimately in a prescriptive market model, will emerge in this section. British administrative reform in the 1980s suggests the influence of a big business model, while New Zealand developments provide a much purer example of public choice thought about the machinery of central government.

The big business model

The influence of the 'scientific administration' school can still be seen in modern managerial theories. They stressed the importance of clear objectives, a rational division of functions, a hierarchical structure of control and co-ordination, the avoidance of duplication and waste, and efficient methods of reporting and policy appraisal. However scientific administration paid little attention to human relations, and its strongly authoritarian and hierarchical principles are less acceptable today. Moreover scientific administration did not develop a specific theory of resource management.

The growth of resource planning
That theory developed in the 1960s and 1970s with the emergence of budgetary techniques such as PPBS (planning, programming, budgeting systems) in the USA and of programme budgeting in other developed countries (Self, 1975, Ch. 8). These techniques shifted the structure of national budgets (at least partially) from the traditional 'input' basis of costs to an 'output' basis of the products of government action; and because these 'outputs' can often not be evaluated in monetary terms, attempts were also made to link them to 'outcomes' in the form of indicators of the effectiveness of public policies. (There actually remains an enormous gap between the description of 'outputs', which can be done, and of 'outcomes' which are nearly always elusive and contestable.) Government departments were expected to specify their objectives (quantitatively if possible) and translate them into action programmes and budgetary estimates. Rolling budgets and forward estimates became the conventional practice in many countries, although in the USA the independent role of Congress largely precluded this arrangement.

This new 'science' of resource management suggested the desirability of changes in the machinery of government. Sir Richard Clarke (1971), a distinguished British Treasury official, argued that effective resource planning required government functions to be grouped into a small number of giant departments. The Cabinet in conjunction with the Treasury would then be capable of reviewing each year the objectives and programme of each such department, and of determining priorities and agreeing budgetary forecasts. The minister and top officials of each giant department would repeat the same exercise in relation to its major divisions, and each division would delegate responsibility for the implementation of its programme to line managers.

There was small likelihood that so theoretical a format would be closely applied to the political task of government reorganisation, but the requirements of rational resource planning were one main reason for the British creation of giant departments in 1970, and influenced the same development in the USA and elsewhere. The Australian Government's creation of several but smaller 'super-departments' in 1987 showed that the idea still had salience under the changed conditions of cutback management. Its purpose was to establish a more hierarchical structure of resource and policy co-ordination, which would assist the implementation of basic policy objectives (Pusey, 1991, pp. 146–52). However Clarke's hope that the Cabinet would concern itself with regular strategic reviews of objectives has been disappointed in Britain and Australia (it was never feasible in the USA). Instead powerful Cabinet committees have been given the hatchet job of controlling public expenditure, backed by the growing influence of the Treasury over public policy.

The switch from administration to management

In the 1980s the model of the big business corporation became more influential as a result of the extensive use of business consultants, the supposed superior efficiency of the market sector and the increase in the numbers of senior officials with economic or business qualifications. In this new world 'government' becomes 'the public sector' and administrators become 'public sector managers'. 'Management' is treated as a portable technical skill, divorced from specialised experience and knowledge about particular subjects, equally applicable to the private and public sectors, and primarily concerned with the efficient use of resources. The special features of government, such as its coercive powers of taxation and regulation, its responsibility for defence and law and order, its presumed concern with social equity and welfare needs, and its unique legal responsibilities, come to be regarded as 'constraints' upon basic principles of managerial efficiency. They are not held to justify a separate or distinctive framework of study and application, save perhaps in some specific policy or legal contexts.

The usual model of a big business corporation is of a strategic brain centre where the profitability and prospects of operating divisions or subsidiary companies can be evaluated and compared with each other and with possible new ventures. Within this framework of strategic resource decisions and guidance, the controllers of the operating units have considerable freedom to manage their own resources of finance and personnel and to

egate considerable discretion to the managers of small 'budget
ntres' (though there are many significant variations in actual
business practice).

Governments work in a very different environment. They lack
profit tests for determining objectives and have less ability to
close down activities and switch resources. Politics throws up a
great variety of shifting demands and calculations which require
'strategic planning' (if possible at all) to consist primarily in an
agreed political programme. Objective-setting of this kind is most
feasible for a newly elected or strongly entrenched government
with a cohesive philosophy; but this unity is easily diffused into
the separate goals of individual ministers, influenced by their
departmental advisers. Further down the line the requirements of
parliamentary and financial accountability (as well as service-
wide principles of personnel management) greatly restrict the
line manager's freedom of action (Self, 1975).

Despite these large differences between business and public
administration there can be some common ground. Bureaucrats
can be trained in the skills of resource and personnel management, especially since their deficiencies in these respects had
become the target of much criticism (it was the main theme of the
British Fulton Report of 1968). Ways can also be sought to get
round traditional administrative controls and confer greater
freedom upon line managers. The machinery of government
can also be revamped, as Clarke earlier urged, so as to focus more
closely upon efficient resource management. All of these ideas
were given a new stimulus by the economising philosophy of the
1980s. The ruling ideas were that wherever possible governments
should cut costs and reduce or privatise services, and economy
was enforced by cash limits on current spending instead of the
expansive forward planning of the 1960s. Efficient resource
management had become a dominant goal of governments,
albeit largely a negative one.

The British example
Developments in Britain in the 1980s can be understood against
this background. Michael Heseltine, as the minister for the giant
Department of the Environment, took an early initiative in the
form of MINIS (Management Information System for ministers).
His aim was to inform himself of the precise functions performed
by his huge department, of the resources available for these tasks
and of progress towards specified goals. Heseltine saw himself as

a chief executive, but other ministers and still more their permanent secretaries disliked this innovation. MINIS got Cabinet backing for general application and was followed by the Financial Management Initiative (1982) which was overseen by a small administrative unit eventually (in 1987) absorbed into the Treasury.

The purpose of the FMI was to improve methods of financial management and control throughout government and to delegate more responsibility to line managers. The FMI produced much more sophisticated systems of financial information and control, and led to an increased cost-consciousness among line managers. In the Department of the Environment, for example, responsibility for financial management was transferred to policy divisions and, in direct emulation of private sector practice, 150 cost centres were established whose managers had to forecast, budget, control and manage their administrative expenditure (Whitbread, 1987).

Many middle-level officials welcomed the prospect of getting more direct responsibility for the use of resources, but were disappointed by the absolute priority given to cost-cutting (Richards, 1987). Moreover FMI was concerned only with administrative costs not programme expenditures. It was thus more useful for departments with a heavy paper load such as taxation and social security than for sponsoring and financing departments such as health, education and environment (Gray, Jenkins, *et al*, 1991). For example, only 3 per cent of Environment's budget was spent internally, the remainder being allocated to local authorities and public boards. The system also favoured tasks which could be quantified over considerations of quality of service. One verdict by an economic advisor is that the FMI did little 'to clarify programme objectives and quantify outputs', and it is unlikely it saved running costs, but there was success in 'improved performance and clarity of management operations' (Whitbread, 1987, p. 103). A harsher verdict was that the government was becoming 'a financial reporting machine in which managerial freedoms were subjected to systems of central control' (Gray and Jenkins, 1991, p. 58).

Reforms might have ended at this very modest point had not the government's Efficiency Unit (1988) produced a dramatic new initiative known as 'The Next Steps', which argued that 'radical change in the freedom to manage is needed urgently if substantially better results are to be achieved'. The proposed change was to transfer the 95 per cent of the civil services said to be concerned with service delivery to hived-off agencies, each of which would have a chief executive, a contractual relationship with its parent department, and a corporate plan detailing its powers and obligations adapted to its special task. This proposed dismantling of the traditional Whitehall machine survived much initial scepticism and Treasury hostility to become government policy after the 1987 election. The government also set a tight timetable for implementation and within three years 40 per cent of the civil service had been transferred to 51 new agencies, with plans laid to move a further 20 per cent to another twenty-six agencies by mid-1992 (Hede, 1991, p. 36).

How did this big initiative get so quickly off the ground? It seems that senior ministers were content to be relieved of direct responsibility for their more routine functions and saw a possible opportunity for privatising or abolishing some functions. (A government directive required these options to be investigated before a new agency was set up.) Senior civil servants saw the advantage of reverting to their traditional role of policy advice, leaving managerial tasks to the hived-off agencies. Public service unions welcomed the prospect of greater managerial autonomy, but were worried by the pace of implementation. These motivations were sufficient to overcome the resistance and scepticism of the Treasury.

However the actual workings of the reform remain uncertain. Whitehall is being miniaturised into a vast number of agencies, some large (the Social Security Benefits Agency has 68 000 staff) and many tiny. The status of all these agencies will vary in a typically pragmatic British manner, but except for services financed by user charges central financial controls will not be lightly relinquished. The new system does stress the identity of each service (instead of submerging it in a vast department), encourages a service orientation to particular clients (who are quite often inside government) and facilitates to some extent a business-like treatment of costs and benefits. If the agencies get real freedom the effects are unpredictable – sometimes a more innovative approach, sometimes a neglect of traditional public service obligations.

The weakest link is the low democratic profile of the new agencies. The 'Next Steps' report wanted to remove them from ministerial responsibility and to establish a new constitutional code governing the responsibility to parliament of their chief executives. The government has not accepted this proposal: the chief executives will be expected to answer parliamentary questions and to appear before parliamentary committees, but ministers will retain a shadowy responsibility for their activities. This unsatisfactory compromise contrasts with the well defined constitutional relationship between ministers and devolved agencies ('royal boards') in Sweden. As so often, managerial reform in Whitehall may be moving pragmatically towards a half-way house between the traditional system and the new theory of 'letting the managers manage'.

The public choice model

Public choice theory has found its most ardent disciples not in its American heartland but in the remote, small islands of New Zealand. There a Labour Government between 1984 and 1990 made substantial changes in the machinery of government, abolishing fifteen of the thirty-four existing departments and creating twenty new ones, as well as developing new contractual and financial arrangements within the administrative system. These innovations were clearly inspired by public choice beliefs as the Treasury reform manual (1987) and articles by Treasury officials (Scott and Gorringe, 1989) testify.

The New Zealand example

The model which inspired these changes was not drawn from big business but from a polycentric market system. The New Zealand Treasury and some ardent Labour ministers such as Roger Douglas acted on public choice beliefs about the perverse tendencies of bureaucracy and interest groups. One ruling principle was to separate different *types* of government activity, such as policy advice, implementation, regulation and public enterprise, into separate departments or agencies. The dangers of 'policy bias' or 'producer capture' were thought to be partly due to the combination of functions in a single department. A more polycentric system of government would also reduce concentrations of state power and create more competitive relationships within government. The analogue of an internal 'administrative market', purged of its monopolistic elements, was discernible in these beliefs.

Consequently the New Zealand reformers had no liking for the concept of 'giant departments'. New Zealand government was already fragmented, with a minister often controlling several departments and some departments being responsible to several ministers. The effect of these very rapid, wholesale reorganisations was to fragment the system still further. Several new policy ministries, such as Education, Environment and Health, had been created by hiving off their operational functions. Four of the new policy departments were small units dealing with disadvantaged groups (Youth Affairs, Women's Affairs, Maori Affairs, Pacific Island Affairs) and there was also a Consumer Affairs Unit in another department. These arrangements, which have parallels in other reconstructed governments, followed the public choice idea that consumers rather than producers needed top-level administrative representation. They were also a reflection of the special ethnic problems of New Zealand.

Other changes represented the 'corporatisation' of such economic and conservation functions as the Forestry Service and the Land Corporation. Stronger arrangements for the review and audit of public services were introduced, such as an expanded Audit Office, the new Education Review Office and a Parliamentary Commissioner for the Environment. However the logic of the new system was not fully applied. Some departments retained mixed functions and the distinction between operational departments and hived-off agencies was grounded mainly in the exclusion of the latter from the provisions of the 1988 State Sector Act.

Some of these arrangements, especially the new corporatised agencies, had the same managerial objectives as the 'Next Steps' initiative in Britain, and posed similar problems of parliamentary accountability. However the claim that the new system would produce more 'contestable advice' to ministers has not been demonstrated. As Boston points out (1991, p. 255) there is no source of alternative economic advice to the powerful Treasury and there is no department with a general brief for social policy. 'Ideological capture' of government policy by the Treasury seems more of a present reality than 'producer capture' of departments. Its presumed justification was the need for policies which could overcome resistance to trade liberalisation and cuts in public and social services.

An ideological treasury
The influence of a polycentric market model can be seen in the favoured principles of the Treasury (Scott and Gorringe, 1989).

Ministers are viewed as consumer representatives buying services at the cheapest price. The performance agreements reached by ministers with chief executives should specify the required output of services. All activities should be fully costed and costs recovered from users wherever practicable. Departments should also pay tax and earn a rate of return on their capital. 'Profitability would be the key measure of efficiency' (ibid., p. 86). The goal is a 'level playing field' of competition between public and private suppliers or between different government agencies. All subsidies to particular interests, such as the costs of trade protection, should be transparent and monitored by a central agency.

Another performance agreement, which reflects a minister's other role as trustee for public assets, should specify conditions about departmental efficiency, such as an appropriate financial management system. Chief executives should be given wide discretion in their choice of inputs and they should have control over appointments, promotions and pay, subject to some guidance from the State Services Commission. Industrial relations should approximate to those in the private sector. The possibility of chief executives abusing their wide discretion is conceded, and an answer sought in offering stronger economic incentives for efficient management. Also the old spectre of the empire-building bureaucrat is enlisted to support legislative or contractual restrictions upon the extent of departmental operations (ibid., p. 87).

These principles express clearly the strong ideological direction of the New Zealand 'reforms'. They have not been fully implemented. Bureaucratic resistance has been surprisingly weak, but the theory runs up against those public service values which cannot be expressed in terms of costs and profits. The political side of the equation has been hardest to achieve. Ministers have in fact made little progress in developing coherent objectives across departmental boundaries, or in relating their output targets to desired policy outcomes (Boston *et al.*, 1991, pp. 396–7).

The cost of these New Zealand reforms has been high, both financially and politically, but they have produced a sparser and leaner administration with narrower policy goals. The unpopularity of the public policies with which these changes were linked led to the exit of the Labour Government and in turn (in 1992) to the still lower esteem of its successor National Government; but bureaucratic change has continued in accordance with the Treasury objectives.

An unfinished agenda

The administrative changes in Britain and New Zealand show in different ways the prevalence of market models of the way governments should operate. The difference is between the more co-ordinative or 'big business' framework of the British reforms and the purer competitive or 'public choice' model of the New Zealand ones. A critical distrust of bureaucracy is present in both cases, but is more marked in New Zealand. There are also common elements in the adoption of many private sector concepts of efficient management, such as comprehensive accounting systems, performance contracts, economic incentives (such as 'merit pay') and decentralised management. Similar developments can be observed in other public services such as those of the USA, Canada and Australia.

However it would be facile to suppose that governments are actually coming to resemble closely either big business corporations or competitive market systems. The political and legal environment of public administration precludes this result. Nor, a few zealots apart, do politicians or bureaucrats really want this outcome. What is occurring is a subtle shift in the structure and performance of public administration which, if continued, will have cumulative effects.

Both the significance and the limitations of the new theories can be seen in the development in Britain and New Zealand of a revived distinction between 'policy' and 'management' and its articulation in new, more differentiated structures. This development appears to combine recognition of the distinctive nature of policy work in government with the claims of the 'new managerialism'. It seeks both to empower managers in new hived-off agencies and to reinstate the traditional role of top bureaucrats as policy advisors. However a system of this kind is not easy to work and could undercut the managerial model through rejecting its application to top levels of government.

Decentralisation, American style

Public choice theory can suggest the desirability of a decentralised political system. Just as competitive markets work ideally through satisfying a diverse range of consumer preferences, so (it can be argued) should the political system meet a diverse set of preferences for public services. The more heterogeneous are individual preferences over public services, the stronger becomes this argument; and critics of the homogeneous institutions of the 'welfare state' do often claim that the requirements of individuals are becoming more diverse.

Public choice and American local government

The new institutional economics favours a strongly decentralised and differentiated system of service delivery. The best examples of the way such a system might work are to be found in American local government. While American local government may not fully realise the public choice ideal, its multiplicity and variety of institutions, and its numerous specialised authorities do seem pragmatically to reflect these principles and to offer an experimental laboratory for testing them (for example, the Association of Bay Area Governments centred on San Francisco contains nine counties, about 100 municipalities and over 500 special purpose districts). Moreover city governments are also highly differentiated internally, with varying roles for the mayor, the city council, board of estimate, the chief administrator (where separate from the mayor) and various partly independent bodies such as the planning commission, redevelopment authority, and so on.

Some public choice principles for a decentralised system of government can be listed and briefly illustrated (see Ostrom and Ostrom, 1976, 1977):

1. Small local government units more accurately reflect the preferences of their electors than large ones, and can control bureaucracy more effectively. Thus fragmentation of local government within metropolitan areas, very marked in the USA, can be a democratic advantage (Ostrom, Tiebout and Warren, 1991).
2. Equally competition between a large number of such units is advantageous. The individual citizen can choose to live in the local district which best satisfies (subject to other constraints) his or her preferred mixture of local services and taxes (Tiebout, 1956).
3. Specialised functional agencies have the advantage of matching supply and demand for a service more closely than where a city performs multiple functions; and they facilitate the 'user pay' principle. Co-ordination between authorities can be achieved by bargaining and contractual agreements.

4. The 'demand' function (whereby a local government purchases a service on behalf of its citizens) can be separated from the 'production' function (the question of who produces the service). This separation, as noted earlier for central government, facilitates a flexible approach to service delivery, which can be contracted out to a private firm, a non-profit body or a different public agency. For example, Lakewood, a small, rich suburban municipality is Los Angeles County, purchases most of its services from the county administration or other sources. The Lakewood plan enables small elected authorities to buy their services in the cheapest market and to utilise technological or economic efficiencies of production (Ostrom, Tiebout and Warren, 1991, p. 153).

These claimed advantages of a highly pluralistic system of service delivery, geared as closely as possible to the wishes and interests of the final consumers, also have important limitations. The new institutional economics admits the desirability of correspondence between the unit of supply and the area of benefit. For example, residents of suburban municipalities benefit from the parks, roads, public transport and cultural facilities provided by a central city. Either they should pay for these facilities or, if that is impossible, some metropolitan-wide system of government seems indicated. Again many measures for the control of pollution are effective only over wide (sometimes very wide) areas, and need to be tackled by appropriate levels of government in terms both of effectiveness and of the incidence of costs and benefits. While false claims are often made about the 'economies of scale' obtainable by large units of government (see next section) such economies can be considerable for many technical services, such as electricity generation, water supply, sewage and waste disposal, and underground railways.

The practical issue for the new institutional economics is how far the general case for decentralisation and pluralism can or should be extended in the face of countervailing considerations. One possible compromise is to argue that something like the American Federal system, with its multiple levels of government, is capable of getting the best of both worlds. This theory argues that whenever possible functions should be transferred downwards from Federal to state and from state to local governments. This argument does not answer the question of how far a fragmented system of government is intrinsically desirable. Its advantages in terms of market tests of service efficiency have to be scrutinised against democratic tests of political purpose.

1. The fragmentation of constituencies places a heavy load upon the individual voter. The complexity of the system is hospitable to the influence of specialised interests and local oligarchies. The public choice virtue of 'transparency' may provide opportunities for comparisons of service delivery costs, but is lost in the complexity of institutional relationships.

2. Integrated political action, which aims at general goals across a range of issues, is difficult to achieve through fractured institutions (such as many city governments) and jurisdictions. The concentration upon service efficiency overlooks such significant political goals as equity between groups or the improvement and transformation of the local environment. Co-ordination of public functions is hard to achieve through market-like relations between different authorities, especially given the rigidity of institutional interests which public choice theorists themselves emphasise. Of course, since public choice theorists are suspicious of broad public purposes, it may be rational for them to advocate a system which promotes a minimalist view of government. An exclusive stress upon 'efficient service delivery' has just this effect.

3. A fragmented system of local government is highly inegalitarian. Tiebout's thesis is vitiated by the fact that other considerations (such as familial roots and access to work) are usually more significant influences over the decision where to live than are local government considerations; and in any case choice of location is limited by the individual's wealth. A fragmented system polarises rich and poor into separate local governments, especially given the capacity of rich suburban municipalities to 'zone poverty out of existence' by the use of planning codes. These effects can be partly offset (and sometimes are) by state schemes of fiscal equalisation, but only at all adequately in special cases. (In California the courts have mandated a substantial equalisation of education costs as representing an essential public purpose.) It is true that a metropolitan-wide authority may not equalise effectively either but at least the opportunity is there if the political will exists; for example, Metro Toronto successively equalised education and welfare costs throughout its territory (Self, 1982, p. 76).

The impact of financial constraints

President Reagan came to power dedicated to unscrambling big government and devolving Federal responsibilities to the states. His actual achievements were much more modest than his rhetoric. He secured the consolidation of 54 Federal grant-in-aid programmes into nine block grants, totalling just over $7 billion, but the cuts in Federal grants were not matched by equivalent reductions of Federal controls. In important programmes such as AFDC (Aid for families with dependent children), Federal conditions about eligibility for aid were tightened. Congress was also reluctant to relinquish its considerable influence over the way Federal money was spent.

State governments reacted very variously to this situation of reduced funding. There was some tendency to see the adequacy of specific Federal programmes as not a state responsibility, especially where strong conditions applied. Thus California simply passed on Federal welfare cuts to their recipients but maintained its own programme of support for human services. New York State on the other hand replaced lost Federal aid with its own welfare grants and tightened administrative control over the counties who delivered welfare. Nathan and Doolittle (1987, p. 356) conclude that many states adopted 'coping strategies to modify the impact of Federal cuts, but that they gave more help for politically popular programmes having a broad incidence than towards welfare schemes for disadvantaged minorities'.

Simultaneously state and local governments had to cope with 'public choice'- type referenda aimed at restricting tax and expenditure levels. The most famous of these occurred in California where Proposition 13 (1978) drastically cut the property tax revenues available to local government to almost half their previous level. Other successful Californian referenda limited state expenditure (1979), indexed income tax against inflation (1982) and abolished inheritance tax (1982). However the analysis of tax revolts by Dye (1990, pp. 87–98) shows that over half the various state referenda on tax limits were defeated, and claims that those passed had a rather modest effect upon state and local finances with the important exception of California's Proposition 13.

At the same time the Federal–city partnership that had been established in the Kennedy and Johnson years was being eroded. It ran wholly contrary to the Reaganite philosophy of 'states' rights'. Long-standing Federal policies of aid to declining cities and regions were abandoned on the grounds that they conflicted with the market-based concept of a 'level playing-field' for inter-urban competition (Judd and Parkinson, 1990, p. 16). As in Britain, economic aid to cities became concentrated on triggering off private investment through urban development grants. The cities' dependence on the states increased.

Crisis of the big cities

Meanwhile the social polarisation of local government has accelerated. The white middle class and blue-collar workers have continued to leave the cities for suburban municipalities, and have been replaced by increasing numbers of blacks, Hispanics and Asians. By 1990 Detroit, Atlanta and New Orleans had black majorities and other big cities (Chicago, Houston, Los Angeles, Miami) had a majority of blacks and Hispanics. Several black and one Hispanic mayor had been elected in the main cities. The fact of a poorer (and sometimes smaller) population has had a severe effect upon city finances and services. Crime, arson and the deterioration of old neighbourhoods have become still more widespread. New York City, despite its slow recovery from bankruptcy, is overwhelmed by social problems which require major public initiatives over housing, transport, education, crime and drugs (Salins, 1988). The traumatic Los Angeles race riots of April 1992 reflected not only black anger at police brutality and legal injustice, but the startling inequality of social conditions which had developed between the big cities and the richer suburban jurisdictions.

Because of the narrowness of their tax base in real estate, all American cities have a strong interest in economic growth and a corresponding inhibition against financing redistributive welfare schemes through local taxation (Peterson, 1981). This incentive is enhanced by civic 'boosterism' – the tendency to judge success by the splendour of downtown skyscrapers and civic facilities. This growth imperative became still stronger in a period of economic restructuring caused by the decline of industrial employment and intense competition to attract corporate headquarters, convention facilities and tourists. However success in the competition depended a lot upon global financial trends and other factors outside the city's control (Fainstein, 1990). Boston, at the centre of a region specialising in advanced research and technology, successfully revitalised its downtown and attracted middle-class workers back to the city. Detroit, at the centre of a declining motor car industry, faced an almost helpless task in trying to check its slide into deprivation and squalor through subsidising new offices and a convention centre.

Despite these formidable difficulties in the 1980s, some big cities did see the emergence of broad-based coalitions committed to social welfare which contradicted to some small extent

Peterson's assumption about the impossibility of redistribution at the local level. Under a black mayor, Harold Washington, with support from its black majority, Chicago switched from its previous politics of machine patronage and business-led downtown investments to policies for neighbourhood rehabilitation, affirmative action and support for small ethnic businesses; but the precariousness of this switch against the economic tide was shown in the modified policies of the next mayor, the second Richard Daley. San Francisco, an economically more favoured city, produced an anti-growth coalition which restricted the spread and height of new office buildings, strengthened environmental protection, and supported the rights of ethnic groups and of its colony of gays and lesbians – a move in this case to 'post-materialist values' (for individual cities see Savitch and Thomas, 1991).

The very fragmentation of local government produces a certain political vitality. In some cities, citizens' groups form to oppose the fragmentation of jurisdictions to achieve much needed environmental improvements and controls, and try to fight fiscal restraints to help rundown neighbourhoods. The battle is a hard one, however, and in some places it never gets off the ground. Thus Yates (1977) pictured local government as the scene of 'hyper-pluralism', of endless, inconclusive 'street fighting' between different interests and authorities, and of a basic 'ungovernability'. Although it may have been too extreme, the tougher economic conditions and reduced Federal aid of the 1980s have strengthened this gloomy verdict.

The tensions of federalism

How does this brief review of 'decentralisation, American style' match up to the earlier public choice theories? In a structural sense, the USA is clearly a highly decentralised and pluralistic society. However the patterns of decentralisation are subject to continuous tension. Traditional Federal theory saw the system in 'layer-cake' terms as a neat division of independent powers between two levels of government, but a 'marble-cake' description captures much better the flexible and shifting distribution of overlapping functions between the Federal, state and local levels (Grodzins, 1960). Despite Reagan's own adherence to the traditional concept of Federalism, his period of office did not change the basic situation.

However the marble-cake model produces two difficulties over effective decentralisation. First, each government builds up its own specific political constituency and interests. Theoretically this may be hailed as a desirable balancing act which enables disaffected citizens to take their case to another forum and protects the autonomy of local communities; but it also gives an extra purchase to the more powerful interests and produces a highly unequal distribution of resources in relation to needs. Second, the system easily fragments (as public choice theorists would prefer) into discrete but complex systems of service delivery in which all levels of government often participate. The horizontal integration of public powers into coherent political strategies thus becomes very difficult, especially at the local level.

It seems agreed that Federal policy changes in the 1980s have had the effect of reinvigorating state governments – indeed this is the usual effect of conservative national policies. To some limited extent this produced a 'paradox of devolution' – Reagan's policies of retrenchment were undercut by his devolution of powers (Nathan and Doolittle, 1987, pp. 355–8). More basically it showed up the extreme variety of state policies, some being socially progressive and others extremely reactionary, a few such as Oregon leading the way with far-sighted environmental measures, others sticking to the aim of attempting economic growth at any cost. This situation may be allowed, in public choice terms, to represent fruitful emulation or competition among states (although few people are likely to move to another state for this reason). In any case a serious restriction on state initiatives is their limited tax base compared with the Federal Government. Dye's analysis shows that overall the combined incidence of state and local taxation is roughly proportionate to income, but the incidence is highly regressive in some states and progressive in the case of New York State income tax (Dye, 1990).

The impact of changed Federal policies upon local government has been much more negative, bringing reduced financial resources and increased state supervision. The partnership between the Federal Government and the cities has been severed, at least for the time being. The condition of American local government reflects not only public choice concepts of service delivery but the dominance of allied economic theories of 'free competition' and 'a level playing field'. The idea is that all local jurisdictions should struggle for their own growth or survival within a Darwinian world. The world in question is indeed Darwinian, because it is largely governed by environmental conditions beyond the influence of the individual local government, and by strong and accelerating differences in size and wealth.

Centralisation, British style

A striking contrast to the theory and practice of decentralisation in the USA is provided by its treatment in Britain. Britain is always thought of as having a strong tradition of local self-government. This is true in the sense that elected local councils were for a long time the main and almost the exclusive agencies of service delivery. Local government was democratised in the late nineteenth century and its functions steadily expanded until the 1930s to include most of the tasks of a modern welfare state. The big cities (known as county boroughs) and especially the London County Council were pioneers in service developments and municipal enterprise, and wielded an appreciable political clout.

Beginning in the 1930s this pattern of decentralisation was thrown into reverse. By stages such local functions as poor relief, health and trunk roads were transferred to national departments and appointed boards. Despite this loss of many traditional functions, local government expanded rapidly in the post-1945 period through the growth of its education, housing, planning, environmental and personal welfare service. It increased its total current expenditure in real terms by more than five times between 1930 and 1975, and by 1981 accounted for more than half of all government employment. Simultaneously central administrative controls became stronger, as a result of the actual or assumed responsibilities of ministers for expanding welfare services and the heavy dependence of local government upon government financial support as a consequence of its narrow and inelastic tax base in real property (rates).

In the 1980s Conservative governments mounted successive assaults upon the traditional role of local self-government. These assaults were driven by a desire to reduce local expenditure and to prevent local policies which conflicted with nationally set goals. The new institutional economics was interpreted in strongly partisan ways which reflected a drive for political hegemony and the reduction, not enhancement, of political choice. Dominating ideas were a search for managerial effi-ciency, privatisation when possible and the removal of political opposition. Policy changes came on three fronts – the system of local government, its powers and functions, and its fiscal base which will be considered in turn.

The structure of local government

In the USA the existence of the numerous local governments is protected, some would say too well protected, by state constitu-tional provisions and charters. In France the numerous small communes receive a *de facto* protection from the political influence of their mayors and the weight of local sentiment. In Britain (and to a lesser extent in other European countries) the local government system has been subject to periodic restructur-ings to meet considerations of service efficiency and movements of population.

Since 1945 British local government has been under almost continuous scrutiny from ministerially appointed commissions of inquiry. The biggest change came with the Local Government Act of 1972, passed by a Conservative Government and influenced by the report of a Royal Commission on Local Government (1969) which stressed the economies of scale in service delivery that a large local government could achieve, although there was little evidence to support this argument, which proved largely illusory (Benjamin, 1977). It was also influenced by the theoretical belief that a large local government could be more 'independent' (of central control) than a small one. In fact it was government departments who pressed most strongly the case for large unitary authorities and the Royal Commission noted that 'Government departments left us with the impression that, were it not for democratic considerations, they would really like a system of 30 to 40 all-purpose authorities' (Benjamin, 1977, p. 153). The Conservative Government, under pressure from its back-bench-ers, gave some heed to these 'democratic considerations' and rejected the Commission's proposal for establishing a system of large 'unitary authorities' outside the big conurbations. None-theless the 1972 Act left England and Wales with a two-tier system of only 400 elected councils compared with the previous 1000 (Scotland had a separate, parallel reform). Britain was handed, in the name of efficiency, the most streamlined system of local government in the Western world.

However the metropolitan system introduced for London and the provincial conurbations did represent a real recognition of the facts of modern social geography and their functional and political implications. Similar recognitions of the reality of the 'regional city' were occurring elsewhere with the creation of metropolitan authorities for Toronto, Stockholm, Paris and other great cities. The 1972 Act created a two-tier system of elected metro and district councils in the six largest provincial conurbations, which followed (in modified form) a similar reorganisation that had already been introduced for Greater London in 1964 (also by a Conservative Government). Problems soon arose over the division of functions between the metro and local councils, but some overlap and competition over such functions as planning, housing and urban redevelopment could be regarded (certainly by public choice theorists) as not necessarily undesirable or wasteful. The new metro councils filled a glaring gap in the general framework of government, but they had the initial problem of building a political constituency and carving out a strategic role. In trying to do so they got little support from central government (Self, 1982, Ch. 3).

Before they could show their full potential, the Greater London Council and the other metro county councils were summarily abolished in 1986 by the Thatcher Government. Their functions were variously transferred to the local councils, handed to independent trusts, made a ministerial responsibility or simply cancelled. Their abolition was justified on grounds of administrative simplification, but (unlike earlier reforms) it was done without any review or inquiry. It was in fact a partisan political act since all the seven metro councils were Labour-controlled and committed to such policies as cheap public transport, affirmative action, affordable housing and local economic initiatives which the government disliked. The consequent vacuum over strategic planning, transport, and housing and development policies in the big cities was soon apparent and led to renewed pressure in London for the re-creation of some co-ordinating metro body.

A similar managerial thrust was evident in yet another local government inquiry in 1991, charged with the task of recommending a simplified pattern of unitary authorities throughout the country. The minister's intention was to streamline the system of local government still further, and he made little secret of his preference for streamlining the elected councils also into small, more managerial and less political bodies. This latter concept has obvious affinity with the American council-manager system, but that system is locally chosen, not imposed, and has not been the choice of most big cities which continue to have strong mayors and active politics.

Diminished powers and political choice

The new institutional economics has been very selectively applied in Britain. The government has been keen to break the monopoly of elected local authorities as providers of such public services as education and housing. In other cases local functions have been simply transferred to central departments or appointed agencies, as in the case of the new city technology colleges and tertiary education.

Similarly local government responsibilities for urban regeneration have been largely transferred to appointed urban development corporations, containing strong business representation, starting with the London Docklands and extended by stages to most large cities. In the case of Sheffield the development corporation was centrally imposed even though several expert inquiries had reported that the city council had the experience and capacity to be entrusted with the extra resources being made available for urban regeneration. In 1992 the government proposed to establish yet another appointed corporation to develop what was claimed to be large areas of underused or vacant land in cities (a harsher description would be 'town cramming' to prevent the mainly Labour-controlled cities from spreading). Again the government has almost prohibited local councils from building public housing, even where they will pay the cost themselves. Thus in practice the doctrine of flexible service delivery has largely ended up as a policy of moving functions from local democratic bodies to managerial agencies of central government.

A second interpretation of 'flexible service delivery' is that local councils should purchase services from outside sources where that promises a better result. However the councils have not been left free to make this judgement and have been to some extent legally compelled to privatise the delivery of a growing list of functions. The government's ultimate aim is that local governments should become 'enabling' rather than 'providing' bodies. The co-ordinative role of local councils over such matters as welfare provision and environmental protection has grown, especially with the impacts of 'deinstitutionalisation' upon the provision of domiciliary care and of environmental legislation. However this local government 'enabling' role is also much limited by the independent status of centrally appointed boards, by its weakened financial resources, and by the considerable restrictions placed upon the use of local planning powers. On present trends, English local government is liable to end up as a sort of administrative dustbin for functions which no one else can perform or which represent awkward tasks (such as the implementation of European environmental directives) that embarrass the national government.

Other measures have further restricted the scope of local politics. The Thatcher Government rejected the previous flexible relationship of consultation and bargaining between central and local government, and sought to impose its will by law. Over forty major Acts concerning local government were passed between 1979 and 1987, some of which had retrospective application and negated successful court challenges (Stoker, 1988, pp. 142–3). Other Acts restricted the play of local politics by disallowing the right of local party leaders to establish an official co-ordinating committee (or 'cabinet'), by reducing the political rights of local officials, and by prohibiting local councils from expressing their views on politically controversial issues (Leach, 1989, pp. 101–22). The last injunction, coming at a time when the government's own publicity machine was being dogmatically used and expanded, showed especially clearly how local government was now regarded as an administrative appendage, not a separate if limited forum for political choice.

On the whole local councils have bowed to the constitutional powers of central ministers, have implemented laws they disliked and waited for better days. They were not wholly defenceless since ministers must rely for much policy implementation upon the large professional staffs within local government. Thus some councils used delaying tactics or 'creative accounting' to evade unpalatable edicts or resorted to legal actions which were usually defeated or overborne by subsequent legislation. More positively the onslaught from Whitehall caused many councils to cultivate their own constituencies more actively. New measures were introduced to improve service delivery such as decentralisation to area committees and more attention to client preferences. Local councils could still hope to re-emerge eventually as the champions of local choice against centralised controls; but the task was a hard one.

Mrs Thatcher's poll tax

Government attempts to control local expenditure in the 1980s culminated in the abolition of domestic rates and their replacement by a flat-rate 'community charge', universally known as a poll tax, payable with a few exceptions by all adults resident in a local area. This drastic innovation, unparalleled in the developed world, was the political solution to a long-standing Conservative promise to free house-owners of any direct tax on their property. It also represented, however, a very flawed example of public choice thinking.

The new system was claimed to increase fairness and accountability. It was argued that, as all adults and not just ratepayers benefited from local services, all should make some contribution to the local revenue pool. (The legislation also enabled, and could require, local councils to levy charges for specific services.) Accountability would be increased because virtually all electors would now be paying a local tax. Moreover, since the poll tax was paid by all and undeniably regressive, there would be strong local pressure to restrain expenditure. On the other hand it was envisaged that local councils, who throughout the 1980s had been subjected to various measures of rate-capping and penalties for overspending, would now be free to make their own expenditure decisions, thus increasing their responsiveness to the local electorate (Department of the Environment, 1986).

Closer examination and actual experience showed the fragility of all these arguments. As compared with rates, poll tax shifted the financial burden from occupiers of expensive to cheap housing, and from single residents to large families. There seemed nothing at all equitable in a bachelor Duke in his mansion paying one-third the charge of three adults living in a miserable tenement. Even on a benefit-received basis the system was inequitable, since the occupiers of large houses get more benefit from roads, lighting, police and fire services. Some rich owners were in fact sufficiently conscience-stricken to try to pay a higher tax. For the same reasons, rich areas generally benefited and poor areas suffered from the change (Travers, 1989).

The claims about enhanced local accountability and freedom of choice were equally flawed. Simultaneously with the introduction of poll tax, the levying of business rates was transferred to the government, put on a uniform basis and distributed among local governments according to population; and the rate support grant from government was split into another per capita distribution and a 'needs' element to compensate for differential service costs. These changes had the effect that roughly 75 per cent of local expenditure would be centrally financed. Local autonomy consisted of the need to finance any additional expenditure wholly from poll tax, which meant that on average an extra 5 per cent in total expenditure would entail a 20 per cent increase in poll tax. Given the inevitable degree of administrative arbitrariness, and the scope for political discrimination as well, in the 'needs' grant awarded to each local government, it was obvious that the necessary service expenditure to be financed from poll tax would vary appreciably between local councils. A transitional scheme was introduced to cushion the effects upon the needier local authorities with high service costs, but the rising burden upon poor localities (as well as poor families) was quickly apparent. Thus the theory that the essence of local choice lay in free decisions about marginal expenditure (as claimed by the government) was unreal. The truth was that poll tax would vary substantially, not simply from local decisions, but from circumstances and decisions outside local control.

Poll tax would certainly have checked local expenditure severely and undermined local preferences for better public services. In addition its administrative costs were extremely high and difficulties of collection horrendous. However the government's hope that these problems would be seen as issues of local accountability was quickly disappointed. Poll tax was seen, quite rightly, as primarily a centrally imposed levy. The government's reaction was to cap the poll tax which individual councils could levy, thus cancelling the claim that it would increase local freedom and accountability; and also to introduce more exemptions for hardship cases, thus reducing its universality. Nothing could save the poll tax and, after Mrs Thatcher's departure, the government moved to reduce its impact by supplementary grants and to phase it out by stages. The experiment, a pet project of the Adam Smith Institute, had decisively failed; but it left local finance in a shambles and local councils (for the time being at least) more dependent than ever on government grants.

The Conservative Government's treatment of local democracy in the 1980s was dominated by the wish to restrict local political choice almost to vanishing point. This aim was linked with a strong political animus against Labour-controlled local councils who were dominant in the large cities. The justification for many of the government's measures was the need to restrain local expenditure. Since the biggest spenders were urban Labour councils, they suffered the most. Their high expenditure was partly the product of deliberate local choice, but it was also the product of greater welfare needs (for personal social services and housing) and higher local costs (for example, for land and buildings). This political animus was blatantly expressed in the abolition of the Greater London and other metro councils. The other administrative reorganisations and interventions of this period reflected the wish to reduce the role of local democracy (under the guise of 'simplification' and 'rationalisation'), to minimise local politics and to subject local government to strong central controls.

The only possible 'public choice' justification for these measures was the general argument for rolling back the frontiers of the state to make more room for the market system; but the implication was that only national ministers had the right to determine the range and quality of public services. This assumption not only gave a very narrow and authoritarian interpretation to the concept of 'political choice', it was also, in terms of the new institutional economics, a very inefficient way of organising service delivery. It required national civil servants, who were anyhow ill-equipped for the task (having no local experience), to make detailed judgements about the supposed 'needs' of each local government, to allocate resources accordingly and to recommend penalties and prohibitions against those councils said to be 'overspending'. Simultaneously local councils, heavily dependent upon central finance and authorisations, had little incentive to order their affairs wisely; and the poll tax experiment, which was supposed to remedy this situation, actually made it worse. Finally the 'rationalisation' of local government eliminated features of competition and variety that are essential elements of the new institutional economics. Instead Britain moved closer to a centralised and hierarchical system of service delivery, governed by lean managerial norms, not local or clientele wishes.

Bureaucracy and democracy

This chapter has ranged widely and selectively over recent innovations in the machinery of government and the theories which underlie them. The connecting threads are the treatment of bureaucracy and democracy. Public choice theory is highly critical of bureaucracy. It seeks to slim bureaucracy, reduce its degree of autonomy and influence, and makes it more 'accountable' – but to whom? Here public choice theory is more ambivalent. In principle bureaucracy should be accountable to the consumers and funders of public services. Logically therefore the greater the degree of citizen choice over public services, the better will individual preferences (the ultimate criterion) be satisfied. However public choice's critical view of the political process can also be adduced to resist this conclusion. The dominant goal can then be presented as being the restraint of state activities and the privatisation of services into the superior efficiency of the market economy. That conclusion is hostile to democracy, which becomes only acceptable when politicians with the right goals are in power.

The agency theory discussed earlier can be adduced to support the authority of political leaders. However this theory applies logically to the whole chain of political and bureaucratic relationships down to the street-level bureaucrat who delivers services. Thus in a parliamentary system, the ministers are in a sense the agents of the parliament (in the USA the dual control over bureaucracy by the President and Congress introduces an added complication into the principal–agent model; see Cook and Wood, 1989). Equally elected representatives are in a sense the agents of the electorate.

Thus the theory can also justify efforts to strengthen the chain of political accountability, for example by increasing the control of parliament over the executive or of the electorate over political parties by devices such as the 'doctrine of the mandate'. Such efforts aim to correct imbalances of power and strengthen democracy. However no-one can seriously view them as realistic applications of principal–agent theories. Elected representatives are quite reasonably conceded a substantial degree of discretionary power, and so still more plainly are political leaders, even if the extent of their power is considered excessive. Again front-line counter staff cannot be treated as solely and exclusively accountable to their hierarchical superiors, since they are also there to serve their clients.

Bureaucracy under pressure

As with these other cases the relationship between politicians and bureaucrats needs to include some balance of their respective roles and responsibilities, not just a simple hierarchy (the formal authority of the politician is one element in the relationship, not the whole of it). In terms of American constitutional theory, a partly independent bureaucracy can be seen as one desirable element in a rational division of powers. For example, Millett (1966) defended bureaucracy as a partly autonomous system of administrative expertise working under the triple supervision of Congress, the President and the Judiciary – a view which denies the simple hierarchical assumption of Presidential control.

The accountability of bureaucracy cannot be understood in narrow terms of obedience to the current political leadership. The opportunism of political leaders has also to be considered, indeed it is actually a favourite theme of public choice theories (but one neglected in their actual applications). Political leaders can and do use their power over bureaucracy to pursue partisan and personal goals. As Eve Etzioni-Halevy (1983) argues, democracy *needs* bureaucracy and, one might add, vice versa. For all its faults, bureaucracy is a necessary instrument for the impartial and effective administration of laws. The laws themselves may not be impartial, but at least a bureaucracy protected by the merit system and imbued with appropriate values will apply them without fear and favour. Such a bureaucracy may also influence political decisions towards regard for equity. These results are not certain but the 'politicisation' of bureaucracy is liable to undercut those values which it is there to protect.

The urge to control bureaucracy has led to its discretionary powers being greatly restricted. James Fesler (1990) points out that the actions of Federal bureaux have become increasingly controlled by both Presidential directives (largely from the Office of Management and Budget) and tightly drawn Congressional laws which lay down detailed rules and timetables for enforcement. The idea that bureaucracy is out of control cannot be sustained. Rather there is the danger that it may be losing the capacity to promote public policies effectively and to respond quickly to crises or emergencies.

Because of its protected status and the complex nature of its work (entailing a balance of different values), bureaucracy has tendencies towards wasteful or inefficient use of resources. The 'free rider' hypothesis has some relevance here in the sense that job security and the difficulty of performance tests can shelter incompetence and laziness. However the public choice assumption that all individuals are self-interested and will shirk work or pursue personal gain where they can does not help to overcome this problem. It leads to an exclusive concentration upon individual performance, based upon unsuitable or artificial tests and the use of personal rewards and sanctions, which (anyhow beyond a certain point) undercut co-operative relationships and shared values. The many variations in actual bureaucratic performance suggest that individual motivation is not a constant factor but varies with organisational culture (and indeed social culture). Improved performance therefore depends upon achieving changes in that culture.

As Hood (1991) says, 'the new managerialism' emphasises one possible set of administrative values at the expense of their alternatives: 'sigma-type values' (a spare, frugal and tightly coupled system) are exalted as against 'theta-type values' (rectitude, fairness, due process) and 'lambda-type values' (resilience, risk-aversion, spare resources). Hood also argues (p. 16) that the quest for administrative frugality removes traditional protections and assumes a culture of public service honesty; actually such honesty is not assumed and bureaucratic compliance is sought through controls and incentives. While previously resource efficiency may have been seriously neglected, an acceptable administrative system requires space for all three of Hood's value clusters. Indeed the American public choice writers who celebrate the values of redundancy and competition subscribe to the third set of values.

Democracy and decentralisation

The issue of efficiency leads back again to the meanings of accountability and democratic control. 'Efficient' public services are those which the public prefer and are willing (collectively if not individually) to pay for. Efficiency in this sense cannot be guaranteed from decentralised managerial agencies loosely coupled to remote and restricted ministerial supervision. This is paradoxically a recipe for a complex bureaucratic system, displaying all the traditional tensions between staff and line, centre and periphery, and 'managers' and specialists upon an enlarged scale. Such a system could be a prelude to extensive privatisation, but hardly to an acceptably democratic pattern of administration. The outcome is both a big bureaucracy and centralised power – the very situation which Ostrom diagnosed as a negation of the expression of public choice.

In Britain the Conservative Government came to power dedicated to axing the numerous 'quangos' – representative appointed boards and agencies – which had grown up through previous corporatist arrangements. It did abolish or downgrade the tripartite bodies (representative of government, employers and unions) responsible for economic policy advice or administration. Economic and industrial policy became highly centralised. However, after an initial splurge of abolitions, the number of 'quangos' grew again. The chief difference was that their membership was now drawn increasingly from the business community, for example on the local councils of the new Training Agency, the urban development corporations, and the University and Polytechnic Funding Councils. Unions were excluded and other social groups weakly represented (Crouch and Dore, 1990, pp. 1–44). Thus corporatism continued to flourish at the level of detailed administration, and was increasingly linked with the interests and perspectives of the business sector. Simultaneously, notwithstanding the rhetoric of 'empowering consumers', the exclusion of local government from service provision went with increased managerial control over the main public services. The original opposition of the Conservatives to undemocratic bodies simply evaporated.

Thus the effective exercise of democratic choice is linked with the issues of political devolution discussed in the previous two sections. Interestingly there is common ground on the value of devolved institutions between public choice theory and traditional democratic and communitarian beliefs. Public choice theory seeks to maximise diverse individual preferences and to foster competition between service agencies. Alternatively, as de Tocqueville and J. S. Mill long ago stressed, municipal institutions can be seen as the basic institutions of any genuine, active democracy. As Ostrom (1991, p. 256) puts it, 'citizens cannot achieve self-organizing and self-governing capabilities without the experience of actively associating with their fellow citizens to accomplish tasks that require their joint efforts'.

Despite this confluence of opinion, embracing both the political Right and Left, significant differences also exist over the structure and purpose of democratic institutions. As discussed earlier in the case of the USA, public choice theory offers support not only for Federalism but for a fragmented structure of local government and an atomised pattern of service delivery. By contrast a democratic communitarian approach will lay stress upon the unified character of geographic communities and upon the integrated exercise of public powers. Elected local bodies should have some protection against frequent or arbitrary reorganisations and some respect is due to a locally identified sense of community; but the structure has also to be capable of handling functional tasks effectively and equitably, and of avoiding polarisation into a historically evolved pattern of very unequal governments (in terms of their size, wealth and capacity). There is a balance to be struck between homogeneity and variety and between too much and too little respect for 'local option'.

Conclusion

The influence of public choice thought upon the events discussed in this chapter has been ambivalent. If the market system is seen as intrinsically superior, privatisation of state services wherever possible will seem the most effective policy. Since the state shows no signs of withering away, determined attempts to reduce public expenditure and impose priorities from the centre can lead to restrictions upon democratic choice and an enlarged role for the national bureaucracy. While not perhaps a necessary outcome, this seems to be the direction in which British government has been moving.

Alternatively a more positive evaluation of political choice, combined with a wish to restrict and disperse the powers of government, will favour a strongly decentralised and pluralist system. Some public choice thinkers would like to move American government much further in this direction, especially by reducing the scope of the Federal bureaucracy. While that bureaucracy may be unnecessarily large, this theory is weak on understanding the distinctive contribution to a democratic society that can be provided only by a bureaucracy trained in strong and impartial values of public service. Equally, as

Chapter 8 will further explore, democracy cannot be adequately based upon the private wants of individuals but depends upon a distinctive ethic of citizenship which lies beyond the realm of most public choice thought.

7
Market Ideology and Public Policy

Politics and ethics of markets

Much public choice theory takes a free market model as its benchmark for evaluating political behaviour. It assumes that market systems are inhabited and operated by rational egoists and that under competitive conditions the results will be generally beneficial. This of course is a replay of Adam Smith's 'hidden hand', whereby the self-interest of butchers and bakers promotes the prosperity of the whole society. By contrast, according to these theorists, politics is a difficult and treacherous terrain for harmonising the self-interest of individuals.

It is now time to reverse the approach of the previous chapters and ask some questions about this market model. Does it actually work in the prescribed way? Is it dominated by calculations of rational self-interest? Is there a political theory of the market, just as there is an economic theory of politics? In the space available these issues can only be briefly considered. More fundamental for the subject of this book, we need to inquire into the impact of a dominant market system and an influential market ideology upon political behaviour and public policy. Is the vaunted 'market model' a constructive or a destructive basis on which to base public policies? And what is the relationship between the market system and the social foundations of politics and society?

Are markets efficient?

There is obviously a wide gap between the idealised market model of economic theory and the actual modern market system. In the ideal model, no firm commands a large enough share of the market to influence prices, and competition keeps down profits through equating marginal revenues with marginal cost. In the real world, large firms possess enough market power to set or influence prices, to buy out or swamp new competitors and to accumulate large surpluses that can be utilised not only for profits, but for extensive advertising and sponsorship, the acquisition of political influence and big fees and other benefits for their directors.

The large international firm or conglomerate bestrides the world like a colossus, disposing of the location of investment and employment in many countries, wooing public opinion with generous gifts for sports, arts, charities and even public services, and influencing governments and politicians through devices both legal and illegal. The giant multinational is light-years away from Smith's butchers and bakers and in a position to subordinate political power to economic power rather than vice versa. The market system contains a mixture of elephants and minnows. The minnows, such as small firms and family farmers, often operate in a highly competitive environment; but many of them are crucially dependent upon the elephants, in the form of contracts for supplies, franchises for distribution, or tenancies in large property developments.

Market theory tries to explain the growth of big firms in terms of a rational pursuit of economic efficiency. For example, 'transaction-cost analysis' argues that firms grow because it is often more efficient to internalise the costs of procuring supplies or organising distribution by a 'vertical integration' of related activities (Williamson, 1975, 1985); but there can be high costs of internal co-ordination and difficulties in getting as good performance from a subsidiary firm as from a competitive supplier. Often a more cogent reason for a firm's expansion is to aquire a stronger bargaining position vis-à-vis other firms. Collusive forms of market power include tacit or secret price-fixing cartels, hoarding of information such as patents, action to bar political competitors (as in the conspiracy to prevent Laker Airlines flying to America) and market co-ordination as in the many joint ventures of the 'seven sisters' oil cartel (Mokken, 1980). The significance of organisational power gets overlooked in these supposed demonstrations of market rationality (Perrow, 1986a, 18–31).

'Rational expectations theory' claims that the market will make the best possible use of all available information about the future profitability of firms and industries. Thus any new factor, such as a government intervention in industry, will be smoothly absorbed and equalised by the financial markets. However this fact only demonstrates the efficiency of the market in equalising expectations of profits on available information. It does not show that this test is a satisfactory guide to the efficiency of particular firms or industries, whose real rates of return vary because of sources of finance and other institutional factors, or that the market system is itself 'rational' by any wider test than its own closed circle of logic (Thurow, 1983). The allied argument that the threat of takeover is a sufficient incentive for firms to maximise their efficiency or face the consequences overlooks the fact that takeovers are often launched for short-term financial gain ('asset stripping') or to remove what may be an efficient but financially more cautious market competitor.

Self-interest and market outcomes

Public choice theory also has difficulty over demonstrating that the motive of rational self-interest leads necessarily to desirable market outcomes. Clearly this motivation has a basic and pervasive role in the functioning of the market. If, following Etzioni (1961), we classify motives as being either utilitarian, normative or coercive, it is clear (as he says) that economic organisations draw primarily upon the first of these motives. Politics by contrast draws also upon the direct coercive rights of the state as well as (despite what public choice theorists contend) upon normative motives of political idealism and loyalty. Economic life is largely motivated by material incentives, and the increasing 'commodification' of life through the widening ambit of monetary transactions has inevitably added to the significance of this motivation. Indeed the dominance of economic forms of calculation in modern life offers one explanation of the plausibility of economic interpretations of politics. The economic virus, so to speak, has infected the body politic.

The efficiency of a firm becomes dependent upon the often competing interests of its individual members (Jackson, 1982). Since the pioneering study by Berle and Means (1932, 1968), it has become evident that managers in big firms are often more concerned with maintaining the firm's stability or growth in the interest of their own jobs than with maximising its profits. Similarly shareholders are quite unable to control the enormous fees and 'perks' which directors vote themselves, while these rewards seem to bear little relationship to actual profits (Dahl, 1985, p. 103). Industrial sociology reveals the prevalence of conflicts between various groups of managers, specialists and line workers over methods of work and distribution of income (Crozier, 1964). Many of these conflicts are highly dysfunctional for the technical efficiency of the firm and its profitability. The benevolence of the 'hidden hand' seems absent in such cases.

However economic behaviour is by no means exclusively governed by material incentives. If good service and loyalty to a firm are repaid with security of employment, a satisfactory pension and social recognition, the loyalty thereby invoked may extend beyond material calculations and take on a life of its own, sometimes in the face of adverse financial effects. Japanese industry is a well-known example of the importance of long-term relations of paternalism and loyalty in individual firms (Dore, 1989). The effects upon economic productivity seem to be a lot more impressive than the results of the much more mobile pattern of employment in Western societies.

Loyalty and its converse, the irresponsible rivalries of financial entrepreneurs for power or prestige and not just profit, are significant elements in modern economic life which contradict public choice assumptions. Indeed the fall and bankruptcy of some high-flying entrepreneurs seems due to an insatiable appetite for power pursued in the teeth of economic rationality. While some firms in the West seek to build up durable relations of partnership and trust with their employees, the modern trend is towards a more individually competitive and mobile society. The loyalty of the Western 'organisation man' is often only skin-deep, since no-one is surprised when he transfers his declared dedication to the interests of his firm to one of its rivals. The public choice stress upon purely individual calculations of advantage endorses this behaviour.

Thus rational self-interest may be a useful spur to market efficiency but too strong a dose of this quality undermines effective performance. The paradox emerges that the most competitive firms are often those which achieve the greatest co-operation among their workers.

Market ethics

The market system cannot dispense with ethics. Honesty and fair dealing are crucial lubricants of efficient business transactions. Their absence much increases 'transaction costs' because more effort has to be spent upon legal checks and safeguards, and there is more uncertainty about the outcome of a business deal. The success of financial institutions in the City of London used to rest quite a lot upon their reputation for probity and prompt payment of debts and sometimes upon honouring even verbal commitments. Today these qualities are less evident in the City, as elsewhere. The quest for economic gain has always been liable to undermine business ethics, but increased financial complexity and scope for speculation have compounded this tendency.

There are certainly business leaders who are keen to maintain ethical standards, but their influence is liable to erosion in the modern market place. The celebration of individual acquisitiveness as an acceptable motivation ('greed is good for you') encourages a cynical view of ethical and legal constraints upon market behaviour. The eventual bankruptcy of a number of financial entrepreneurs in the late 1980s, and the disclosure of malpractices by some banks and other financial institutions, revealed the extent of irresponsibility and illegality within the financial system. A public choice writer such as Gordon Tullock can produce a cost–benefit analysis of burglary which concentrates upon whether the economic benefits to the burglar are likely to exceed his costs. No doubt Tullock does not write to encourage burglary, but his perspective abstracts individual behaviour from its encompassing framework of social norms and rules.

Despite the efforts of apologists such as Hayek (1960) to present an amoral market regime as being socially desirable, this viewpoint has never been acceptable to ordinary opinion. Concepts such as a 'fair wage' and a 'fair price' are not simply the property of muddle-headed egalitarians or socialists, but the common currency of debate about market dealing. The market in other words is expected to justify itself, in terms both of the equity of its internal operations and of its relationship to the wider social institutions and norms of society. Both the acceptability and the efficiency of the market system turn upon social norms which cannot be supplied by the internal logic of profit on its own. They have to be borrowed, so to speak, from the wider social system which encompasses and contains the operation of the market.

The need to prevent ethically unacceptable and damaging business practices has led to increasingly complex forms of public regulation. Quite often, as has happened in Britain and USA, this need is met through delegating powers of self-regulation to market interests themselves. The collective interest in business ethics is thereby given the boost of public endorsement and some ultimate possibility of recourse to direct government intervention, although the results of such self-regulation are often disappointing. The complex framework of diverse national laws makes effective regulation difficult; and the problem of recruiting impartial and effective regulators is made harder by the superior rewards which the market can offer them and the consequent scope for influence or bribery.

The market–political nexus

To summarise this section, the market system must be seen not simply or primarily as a spontaneous system of voluntary exchanges governed by objective economic laws, but as itself a political system. Despite the stress of public choice writers upon individual choice and calculation, this system shares some of the pluralist features of politics. Conflicts between and among trade unions and employers' organisations occupy the centre of this political stage. Strategic alliances arise between economic interests for such purposes as takeover bids, defeating competitors or the exploitation of latent opportunities for profit. The politics of the market system revolves around wide differentials in access to resources and to strategic locations in the production cycle; for example, Green Shield stamps was for a time a very profitable firm because it used the appeal of 'free gifts' to passing motorists to induce petrol stations to buy and give away the stamps.

Moreover the politics of the market is in continuous interaction with the political system. All market interests seek political support for their goals, whether these are aggressive or defensive. Large firms can augment their exceptional market power by achieving an equivalent superiority of political influence. Thus oligopolies or monopolist market leaders can fire two barrels to enhance their position (Etzioni, 1988, Ch. 13). The administrative advantages to government of dealing with big rather than small firms (or with trade associations led by big firms) also fit the common style and convenience of big bureaucracy, whether public or private. Politicians easily see or even exaggerate the importance of big firms to national prosperity, and the adverse political effects of losing this source of jobs and investment. For this reason, as well as through direct channels, business in America exerts a much stronger influence upon public policy than do labour interests – thus reinforcing market inequalities (Lindblom, 1977).

The exchange of favours between market and political actors is of course a principal target of the public choice critique of politics. Ideally this critique would insulate the two spheres from each other and leave the market to function autonomously according to its own 'objective' laws. Clearly such a result, if it were possible, would eliminate the numerous examples of special favours given and received through political channels. It would also remove many opportunities for bribery and corruption. Unfortunately this apparently simple solution would leave many problems unsolved. It would still be necessary for government to police the market system and to ensure acceptable levels of business ethics and trade practices. The market cannot police itself. Then, if political intervention is withdrawn, the intrinsic inequalities of market relationships will assert themselves with full vigour. If one result would be to deprive business interests of their political influence, another result would be to leave the weaker players in the market system more open to exploitation. A hundred years of market reforms would be cancelled or undermined. Finally, and more broadly, the question arises of how far the market system on its own can produce an acceptable type of society, and in what respects it needs to be steered, replaced or supplemented by decisions made within the political realm.

There seems in fact to be no alternative to substantial interactions between the political and market systems, the critical question being about the actual forms and terms of these interactions. What is the 'right balance' between state and market? There are obvious dangers in allowing excessive power to either system – in the state's case of too great a control over economic and social life, in the market's case of neglect of social welfare and justice. The special concern of this chapter is to explore whether the increasing range and grip of the market system, and the influence of its accompanying ideology, are undercutting the capacity of the political system to perform its distinctive role at all adequately.

Markets in theory and practice

Before considering the impact of market ideology upon politics, it is desirable to ask how far the performance of the market system lives up to the claims of market theory.

Values and institutions

Market theory postulates the existence of a spontaneous but continually changing equilibrium between the demand and supply for goods whereby the 'utilities' of consumers will be maximised. This model has two basic flaws. In the first place, the equilibrium position which will ensure that all available resources are deployed in their most profitable use (in terms of the ultimate wishes of consumers) is an elusive one. Market theory is weak on dynamic analysis. Theories of the trade cycle, or of long-term cycles of boom and slump, demonstrate the existence of severe market instabilities; but no solutions for these problems have been found outside of political intervention.

Secondly the concept of individual 'utility' is either circular or meaningless. In its pure form the theory holds that individuals maximise their preferences through the prices at which goods exchange or bargains are struck. However the concept of 'consumers' surplus' points out that individuals would often pay a higher than necessary price for some good which they badly require and economise elsewhere; but the extent of this 'surplus' cannot be known or measured save notionally. More fundamentally many 'utilities' (satisfactions) which individuals value cannot be achieved at all adequately through market transactions. Thus the concept becomes merely a way of describing or dignifying the outcomes of market choice (Robinson, 1962, pp. 48–70).

These criticisms do not destroy the value of a competitive market system as a social institution, but they do suggest its limitations. Price and profit mechanisms are very useful mechanisms for producing and allocating a wide range of goods, but how well any given set of market institutions perform this function – and at what cost to other values – is a different matter. Abstract market theory, with its closed internal logic, spreads an unwarranted patina of respectability and inevitability over the actual market system.

Market theory has a weak correspondence with the actual institutions of capitalist markets. Capitalism can be described as the 'dominant social formation' of Western societies (Heilbroner, 1985), in the sense that owners of capital have the power to provide or withhold investment and employment and thereby to determine the conditions of economic life. Owners of capital may wield considerable political influence but the basis of capitalism is the exercise of property rights which are protected by the state and can be freely deployed in the market. The ownership of property is extremely unevenly distributed and its control is still more concentrated. Thus capitalism is not so much an integrated power bloc as a subtle set of market relationships which dominate economic life.

Moreover capitalism is a dynamic system which changes its direction according to the opportunities for profit offered by advances in technology and by the deliberate creation of new wants and tastes. Its scope is also much affected by the system of laws, the activities (or non-activities) of government and by social beliefs and expectations. Capitalism is not a system anchored in perpetuity to some harmonious equilibrium, but is subject to structural changes which alter its effects in unforeseen ways. In the modern world the range of capitalist markets has expanded steadily into new arenas. This expansion has been accompanied by a growing dissonance between the benefits which the market system claims to deliver and its actual outcomes. Two important aspects of the performance of the market system which need to be briefly considered are its contributions to economic growth and to international trade.

The paradoxes of economic growth

Economic growth has come to be regarded as a political imperative and as almost the supreme value of Western societies. Today it is widely assumed, much more so than in the past, that the market system is the basic and essential engine of economic growth. Consequently the health of the market economy is the first preoccupation of politicians. Public services occupy a subsidiary and dependent position in this scheme of things since it is generally assumed that their improvement – for example in the form of a better welfare system – is contingent upon market-led growth.

Economic growth can be broadly defined as improvements to the material standard of life, although conventional economic statistics do not reflect this concept accurately (for example, increases in wages spent on longer journeys to work show up as economic growth, but may actually represent a fall in living standards). In the international wealth league Japan now has the highest income per head and Australia ranks only sixteenth; yet a comparison of Japanese and Australian cities shows that on almost every criterion – hours of work, goods that can be purchased per hour of work, cost of food, travel costs, recreational facilities – the Australians have a significantly higher standard of living than the Japanese (Castles, 1992). These results reflect partly the greater population pressure in Japan, partly the better endowment of public services in Australia. They also of course reflect the artificiality of comparisons based upon the international exchange market; Japan seems very rich because of its favourable balance of trade.

Despite the misleading character of wealth statistics, it is clear that the market system has been instrumental in achieving large increases in the living standards of the populations of Western nations. In the post-1945 period especially large numbers experienced the basic benefits of cheaper and better clothes, improved housing, household durables, paid holidays and so on. Further instalments of growth have had more mixed effects. There are certainly technical gains in changing from an old-fashioned gramophone to a long-playing record to a cassette to a compact disc to whatever comes next, but they involve rapid replacement costs for the benefits gained. A surfeit of plastic dolls and an explosion of mass tourism are gains of a kind, but they hardly match the solid satisfactions of good food and clothing, a washing machine and a telephone.

Simultaneously the indirect costs of economic growth have clearly grown. Mass tourism, often pursued over long distances, has brought problems of pollution and congestion to the tourists themselves and to local citizens. Economic growth has produced such dire effects as acid rain, the ozone hole in the atmosphere and the greenhouse effect, although sometimes governments have been as responsible for these results as the market system. The multiplication of cars, yachts, second homes and so on. among the affluent has produced the exclusionary effects associated by Fred Hirsch with 'positional goods', meaning goods which occupy scarce space and impede or restrict the enjoyment of others (Hirsch, 1976).

It can be argued that there need be no limits to economic growth since human wants are insatiable. Even if this dubious proposition were true, the satisfaction gained from more consumer goods seems to decline among the already affluent. Economic growth is not exempt from the law of diminishing returns. One example is the emergence of 'post-material' values.

Another is the findings of much psychological and sociological research that, once they have a reasonable standard of living, Americans are more dependent for their happiness upon the nature of their work than their level of consumption (Lane, 1991). Quality of life, including a clean and safe environment, becomes more important. So in particular do personal sources of happiness, such as family and friends and living in a stable community. Economic growth in its present form is having adverse effects upon these personal and community values (Mishan, 1969, 1977).

Conversely very many people are still shut out from great gains to be had from more elementary forms of economic growth. The proportion of the population living below the official poverty line in some Western countries is actually increasing, and many members of these societies still occupy bad housing in blighted surroundings, have few resources or amenities and (with deteriorating public transport) enjoy little mobility. They constitute large islands of deprivation in a sea of affluence. In the world generally, possibly as many as a third of the total population suffer from hunger and a higher proportion live in severe poverty. This situation seems to make the drive to produce ever more sophisticated consumer goods for the already affluent seem positively indecent.

The market system continues to show enormous gains in technical productivity, although a substantial part of these gains derives from publicly provided education and research. As primary and manufacturing industries shed labour on a massive scale, much of the slack was taken up by the growth of public bureaucracies and social services. This balance has been upset in many countries by the strong priority given to market-led growth and by restrictions on public expenditure and investment. Surplus labour cannot be shifted to socially necessary but neglected tasks where such tasks are insufficiently profitable, too long-term, dependent on public initiative or otherwise unattractive to market entrepreneurs. Economic growth continues to be an urgent requirement for many people over much of the world. The market system is not responding at all well to this task because of the way it concentrates purchasing power among the already affluent. On the other hand the economic viewpoint of treating work as a painful necessity for producing the pleasure of consumption is wearing thin. Other values are increasingly conflicting with the consumption values of the market.

Those thinkers such as Friedman and Hayek who laud the market system, and want it to operate largely free from control, seem to be living in a vanished world. Theirs is the world of individuals bettering themselves and their society through hard work, enterprise and savings in some useful trade or occupation. It is interesting, for example, that two strong critics of the American welfare system, Stockman and Peterson, both had fathers who worked and saved remorselessly to make a go of a small business. Such individual efforts are still highly valuable to society and still continue to be made. They are the continuing inspiration of the 'American dream', yet they seem rather far removed from modern economic realities. The virtues of hard work and savings lose much of their moral appeal in a society where economic growth is directed more towards titillating individuals into consuming luxuries than meeting more basic needs; and the virtues of private enterprise seem less obvious when it takes the forms of financial speculation, monopolistic profits or tendentious advertising.

Problems of international trade

Market theory stresses the economic gains of free and open international trade. The principle of comparative advantage stresses the gains from free trade through the process of international specialisation. Actually this argument is not correct even at an abstract level. According to the 'theory of the second best', if any of the conditions of perfect competition are lacking (as they certainly are in the modern world), the advantage to any given country of free trade can no longer be demonstrated.

It is the conventional economic wisdom and in a sense it is certainly true, that the big expansion of world trade since 1945 has been a major cause as well as result of economic growth. International trade is conventionally seen as essential to further growth, and the imbalances between creditor and debtor nations and the recourse to protective measures are seen as principal causes for the decline in economic growth in the 1970s and 1980s (Shonfield, 1982). However the gains which free trade offers to consumers are offset by its often destabilising effects upon local labour markets and economies. Large firms roam the world in search of the most efficient or cheapest locations for their new investments, and open markets produce quick changes in the demand for particular products. Orthodox theory sees these effects as 'transitional costs' that require appropriate adjustments in employment and wages to produce a new equilibrium; but the costs of rapid economic change are high, in both economic and human terms, the adjustments painful and the desired new 'equilibrium' may never emerge or be quickly superseded. Thus the general benefits of international trade depend upon effective mechanisms for keeping the system in balance and controlling or limiting its adverse side-effects.

The productivity gains from international trade are also often secured at the cost of creating large-scale unemployment in the metropolitan centres. Mobility of labour, while much more restricted than that of capital, has created large enclaves of immigrants in Western countries. The onset of unemployment in those countries has been a major cause of racial tensions, as well as of crime and vandalism, and has fuelled the re-emergence of extreme right-wing or neo-Nazi parties in France, Germany and other countries. 'Guest workers' have been sent home from Germany, and many immigrant groups elsewhere suffer from poverty and unemployment.

The export of manufacturing jobs to poor countries which has produced this result does boost employment and incomes in those countries, although sometimes the wages paid are very low and attention to environmental pollution minimal, while the profits largely flow back to the metropolitan investors. Some smaller Asian countries have achieved very rapid economic growth through trade, but many poor countries remain dependent upon exporting primary products under very adverse terms of trade. These adverse terms reflect the fact that primary production remains much closer to the concept of perfect competition between a myriad of small producers than does manufacturing production by large firms using brand products. The heavy burden of third world debt was much increased by unexpected rises in metropolitan interest rates and a substantial proportion of these loans have gone to raise the Westernised lifestyle of the local élites. The USA has been ready to intervene frequently, and sometimes through extra-legal and revolutionary means, to maintain regimes in these countries which will accept a dependent economic relationship. This lopsided relationship traps the masses in the poor countries within a cycle of debt obligations, external restraints upon local schemes of development and attempts to expand exports which further worsen the terms of trade (Brandt Report, 1980).

A severe disequilibrium has developed in the world between creditor and debtor nations. Theoretically this problem should be resolved by such institutions as the International Monetary Fund (IMF), the World Bank and the General Agreement on Tariffs and Trade (GATT). However these institutions are dominated by the richer nations, especially the USA, and reflect the ruling market orthodoxy. Paradoxically perhaps its economic power has not prevented the transformation of the USA itself from the largest creditor into the largest debtor nation. America's large resources and internal market and the international role of the American dollar have so far protected the USA from the severer effects experienced by smaller debtor nations, but its trade deficit adds to the instability of world financial markets. Growing trade conflicts and widespread depression and unemployment in national economies contradict the benefits which the world market system is supposed to produce (Strange, 1986).

Economic rationalism and public policy

The last two sections have given a critical account of the social effects of the evolution of the capitalist market system. Economic growth is bringing a mixture of diminishing returns and maldistributed resources. International trade is not bringing the large benefits claimed for it by upholders of the system. Thus the system is far from neutral or objective in the realm of human values and aspirations. It satisfies some and negates others.

A brief discussion of economic theory will illustrate this argument. Keynesian theory constituted in its time an intellectual revolution which showed the weakness of neo-classical equilibrium theory (Robinson, 1962, pp. 71–93). Keynes demonstrated that the rate of interest which was supposed to balance the supply of savings and the demand for investment did not function at all efficiently. As a consequence the market system could not utilise all available resources and was liable to produce high levels of 'involuntary' unemployment such that many people who wanted a job could not find one. Keynes therefore argued that governments should act to maintain an adequate level of effective demand in the economy through public investment or budgetary deficits (Keynes, 1936).

The adoption of Keynesian policies after 1945 maintained high levels of employment in most Western countries. However these policies contributed to inflationary trends which represented a converse form of economic 'distortion' to that analysed originally by Keynes. The argument then advanced by many market theorists, especially monetarists such as Friedman, was that government should deflate the economy by cutting public expenditure and restricting the money supply, thereby exercising a downward pressure upon wages and prices.

Although monetarist theories have already been somewhat discredited, the general thrust of this economic counter-revolution has been to try to rehabilitate the neo-classical thesis of the spontaneous balance of the market system; for example, wages are assumed to have some 'natural' level which will equate the supply and demand for labour. Unemployment will also have a 'natural level' which can be reduced by greater efficiency and productivity. Since trade unions are often strong enough to obstruct wage reductions and to resist technological change, the population must be persuaded to accept the existence of substantial unemployment at least until workers' attitudes change; and fear of losing one's job is one way of changing attitudes. This revival of Victorian laissez-faire thinking has persuaded governments to cut welfare services and public investment, to accept high levels of unemployment as a necessary evil, and to put downward pressure upon wages.

Economic rationalists at least take market theory seriously and try to base their presciptions upon it; but the problem with 'economic rationalism' is that it expects a great deal too much of a largely uncontrolled market system. The solutions which they offer for economic problems are grounded in micro-economic theory which cannot cope with structural problems. Thus policies for economic efficiency which are based upon shedding labour and increasing productivity have a zero-sum effect on trade deficits if most nations follow them, or lead to the export of unemployment from more efficient to less efficient nations. Unemployment and low wages compound the problem of deficient effective demand and the widening gap between rich and poor nations and people. These issues can only be tackled by stronger government 'macro' policies which the 'rationalists', wedded to abstract theory, are unwilling to accept.

Because market systems are strongly influenced by institutional and sociological factors, no economic theory can adequately capture their behaviour. All such theories have a value bias of some kind and seek to move the system in some preferred direction. From this standpoint the wrong lessons were drawn from the problems of Keynesian policies. Instead of developing more sophisticated models of the tensions and frictions of market systems, there has been a return to the unrealism of abstract theory. A revised version of Keynesianism would properly broaden, not narrow, the scope of government intervention in order to move the market system closer to acceptable human values.

Impacts upon public policy

Market theorists admit that there are many examples of market failures, such as monopoly or oligopoly (although writers such as Galbraith (1957) point out that oligopoly can produce greater savings and investment than is possible under full competition), coalitions in restraint of trade, adverse 'externalities' such as pollution, inadequate consumer knowledge and protection, and so on . Additionally there are the problems of unemployment and the trade cycle. Many economists looked to government to correct these failures and their influence was prominent during the post-war period of Keynesian stabilisation policies, attempts at economic planning and other political initiatives such as regional development policies and public ownership of monopolies.

However public choice theorists have reversed this approach towards market failures. Their contention is that governments have largely failed in their market interventions because of the perversions caused by special interests. Their general conclusion is that 'political failures' are in fact more serious and inevitable than 'market failures', so that government intervention in the market ought to be confined to an inescapable minimum of general rules.

The issue of political failure

This public choice argument raises some critical issues. It assumes that the fundamental test or yardstick of a good society is an efficient market system. The primary role of government therefore (apart from such classical functions as defence, foreign policy and law and order, plus perhaps a safety net for the poor) is to correct market failures in an impartial and objective manner – meaning in accordance with market theory. Since governments cannot or will not act in this limited way, but go on to expand the state's role and interventions for other reasons, they need to be sharply reined back so as to free market forces to function more widely and effectively.

It should indeed have been obvious to the earlier 'welfare economists' that the political process cannot be expected to function simply as a useful auxiliary to some theoretical concept of market efficiency. Politics activates a variety of interests and values and has its own internal logic and autonomy. The denial of any intrinsic worth to these elements in the political process amounts to questioning the value of democracy itself and to rejecting the idea that there are significant social values which the market cannot satisfy but which the state can or should promote and facilitate.

In English-speaking countries especially, the successive interventions of governments in the economy from the mid-nineteenth century onwards were justified piecemeal on the pragmatic grounds of recognising some special need or removing some special disability. They were not informed by any general theory of the state, although T. H. Green's definition that the state's role was to 'remove obstacles to the good life' was an attempt to provide one. The theoretical dominance of market theory went unchallenged, even though new policies were being introduced which could not be defined as simply remedies for market failure. Gradually the idea grew that government had a responsibility for such goals as protecting and improving the health of the population; widening opportunities for recreation and culture; developing a good education system for all; reducing inequalities of wealth; helping depressed areas; improving the housing and environment of the poor; guaranteeing a basic income; combating unemployment; and guiding the development and conservation of basic resources. Of course the extent to which and the ways in which governments should promote these goals have always been controversial, but the goals themselves attracted and still attract widespread support. One approach at least to the analysis of 'political failures' might be to judge governmental performance in terms of some such list of goals.

The dominant market ideology of the present day has little sympathy with this approach. The argument put forward is that all these policies involve concessions to particular interests and upset the 'level playing field' of the market. This argument rests partly upon a misconception. Inevitably many political acts will help particular groups or areas – that is their intention. They also may be intended to make the market work more efficiently or equitably. That also is deliberate. Political pathologies arise not because some interventions have specific effects (although all political goals are best pursued through general laws), but because some interests are unduly favoured or do not warrant political support. The dilemma of democratic politics is how to pursue desirable social goals without becoming exposed to the special pleading of what are often the more powerful interests. There is no easy answer to this dilemma but reliance upon the market system cannot solve it. Previous chapters have shown that attempts to slim the state and free the market do not abolish the influence of special interests upon political decisions. They simply change the interests which are favoured. Conversely governments have been persuaded to adopt market criteria for their activities in cases where such criteria are inappropriate on broader social grounds. It is difficult to make direct comparisons between the performance of government and market because their goals and methods are often very different. Some comparisons over the performance of social services were made earlier and need not be repeated. Here the aim is to look at some other activities where the use of market concepts has a baleful social effect.

Public enterprise and inappropriate criteria

According to market ideology, public enterprises (if allowed to exist at all) should operate on precisely the same commercial criteria as private enterprises. This doctrine has been preached and followed both by Conservative governments in Britain and by Labour Governments in Australia and New Zealand. There is, however, the significant difference that public enterprises are often starved of capital, even though it usually costs governments less than private firms to borrow money for investment. This irrational prohibition is then further used to justify privatisation, as has happened with Qantas and Australian Airlines. Whatever the intrinsic merits of this decision by the Australian Government, a main purpose was to add one billion (Australian) dollars quickly to the Government's resources shortly before an election. In such cases market ideology encourages political opportunism.

There are situations where a public enterprise can serve the purpose of promoting market competition which would not otherwise exist. Often, however, the point of creating a public enterprise resides in the intention that it should behave rather differently from a private firm, even though some of the same tests of efficiency are expected to apply. This point is lost when a public enterprise deliberately sets out to emulate the behaviour and methods of its private competitors, as happened for example with the state banks of New South Wales and Victoria in Australia. Originally these banks performed the useful task of collecting small savings and making loans for housing, small business and public works. Under the pressure of Federal-induced cuts in public expenditure, the state governments tried to turn them into money winners. The result was that the two banks engaged in the same furore of rash and speculative lending as the private banks, ending in their bankruptcy, yet one justification for a public bank should surely be to demonstrate financial integrity and act as a stabilising influence upon the banking system. Public enterprises at their best combine social goals with commercial enterprise (Stretton, 1987, Ch. 4). They can only pursue this difficult task if governments recognise its importance and appoint capable, public-spirited managers.

A clear example of the application of inappropriate market criteria concerns public transport. There is massive evidence of social and environmental havoc created by the explosive growth of private vehicles. The results are not only a necessity for heavy expenditure upon roads and their absorption of up to a third of the land area of cities, but massive traffic congestion, extensive air pollution, an annual toll of road casualties comparable to that of a major war, destructive effects upon buildings and upon the peace and quiet of the local environment. Transport economists have for a long time urged various forms of road pricing so as to internalise some at least of these indirect costs, while town planners have urged methods of traffic 'calming' and restraint, and bans on road traffic in city centres or other vulnerable areas. All experts are agreed upon the importance of public transport for reducing these traffic problems (Adams, 1981).

All this evidence was well-known in Britain by the time of the arrival of a Conservative Government in 1979. Nonetheless the government strongly opposed the 'cheap fares' policy of the Greater London Council and has insisted that transport under-takings should strive to become commercially viable. Some 'social subsidies' are reluctantly conceded for some transport routes, so as to protect those individuals without a car, but the government has shown no understanding of the case for substantial new investment and subsidies such as other

European countries provide (Britain also seems likely to maximise the environmental damage and minimise the possible benefits of the Channel Tunnel because of the government's insistence that all new rail links should be commercially viable). In Australia the same doctrine has produced the almost complete collapse of an already antiquated rail system. At the time of writing there is no longer any day train between Sydney and Melbourne, two cities of over three million people only 450 miles apart. More significant still on social and environmental grounds are the contributions which buses and light rail systems could make to the decent functioning of cities.

These examples of troglodyte thinking about transport suggest a double perversion of public policy by market ideology. There is indifference towards the clearest possible example of massive market failure, as demonstrated in the huge indirect costs of road traffic, and there is no recognition of social equity which requires a system that distributes the gains and costs of mobility widely and fairly, not one which places all its burdens upon the poor and those without access to a car. Of course it can be argued that massive evidence and the views of experts cannot compete with the political influence of the road lobby and the unpopularity of increasing the costs of motorists; but if these factors explain government behaviour, they also demonstrate the greater susceptibility of pro-market governments to the interest group pressures which they claim to reject.

A comparison of time horizons

Public choice writers such as Brennan and Buchanan (1985, p. 76) suggest that the political process is inevitably shortsighted, because individual voters and politicians have little personal stake in long-term outcomes; by contrast private owners are said to have a clear personal interest in the long-run management of their property. It is certainly true that modern democratic politics is disposed towards short time horizons. The electoral interest of politicians inclines them towards policies which produce quick popularity and postpone any consequent costs. Frequent elections increase this tendency even though they also provide more opportunities for the removal of an incompetent or unpopular government. In Australia, for example, the close interactions between Federal and the various state elections, each (until recently) at intervals of only three years and often much less, aggravate this tendency to political myopia.

However it would be wrong to assume that politicians necessarily follow this electoral pathology. In the past, certainly, democratic governments have often launched long-term development projects whose benefits or failures will not be felt until the politicians concerned are well out of office or dead. Cabinets are often divided between the merits of seeking some 'quick fix' for the sake of popularity or of staying with policies which they believe (rightly or wrongly) to be in the nation's long-term interest. They do not always take the former course. Politicians are not just self-interested calculators of electoral advantage, but also sometimes at least individuals with a social mission and vision. Professional bureaucrats often are or anyhow were strongly disposed towards long-term development plans which engage their particular specialism. Indeed public choice thinkers also argue that politicians and bureaucrats are prone to devising expensive long-term plans for which they will not personally have to pay, and there are plenty of examples of this alternative pathology, such as the development of the Concorde supersonic aircraft and other expensive public investments in high technology (Hall, 1980).

On the other hand, private ownership hardly seems to demonstrate the virtues which Brennan and Buchanan claim. Farmers working no doubt under competitive pressure have created extensive soil erosion which governments must then try to remedy through financial and technical assistance. A system of subsidised farm prices such as French farmers enjoy and market theorists continually deplore does help the maintenance of the French countryside as well as giving some protection to the economic stability and welfare of the rural population. The rape of the Amazonian rainforest and other natural resources is largely the work of private entrepreneurs keen on quick profits, not long-term conservation of assets. Aristocratic landlords in England certainly maintained and enhanced their beautiful properties, and some still try to do so, but these attitudes were shaped by centuries of tradition and continuous inheritance, and usually made possible by the application of profits from commerce. Perhaps all that these examples tell us is that neither market theory nor political theory are very helpful about the conditions under which property or land will be well maintained.

The influence of modern market ideology must therefore be analysed in a more restricted way. When, explicitly or implicitly, market returns are accepted as the basis for new investments, there is a bias towards those that yield a quick or safe profit. Market-led investment may produce fashionable tourist resorts and areas of high-rise offices which large firms will rent for reasons of prestige out of their surplus profits, but it does little to repair or to extend basic infrastructure unless subsidised or otherwise assisted. When market interest rates are high (at 10 per cent or more) or unstable, the discounting of future income makes gains which take over twelve or more years to materialise of little significance in the overall estimates. This point has often been borne out in the cost–benefit studies of proposed major projects.

However any civilised society needs to protect its environmental resources and to build an infrastructure which will serve its future needs and not add to existing problems of urban congestion or resource depletion. Such functions as environmental conservation and urban development need to be judged upon broader criteria than market standards. However market ideology exercises the baleful effect of inhibiting such calculations and diminishing the responsibilities of government for the future of society.

Private ownership and the public estate

The market system works through the private ownership of rights in land, minerals, property, machinery, materials and other assets. Market theorists profess to see no objection to the indefinite extension of this process of private appropriation, except for a few public goods and a ban on those transactions which should be treated as criminal (an issue on which there is much controversy, for example over the legalisation of drugs). It is claimed that public ownership creates problems about the maintenance of assets and the reconciliation of individual rights, whereas disputes between private owners can be settled on a common law basis of proven injury. Some extreme theorists, in defiance of all the evidence, suggest that private ownership of all natural resources, such as state forests or common land, would solve environmental problems and avoid such situations as the 'tragedy of the commons'.

This type of thinking has already had a baleful effect upon the quality and care of the 'public estate', meaning by that all resources which citizens are supposed to hold in common. The pollution of the common resources of air and water is an obvious example. Far from offering an answer, privatisation of natural resources facilitates their quick exploitation where that is in the financial interest of the owners. In America, for example, the vast areas of Federal land in the West, the product of an early conservation movement which reserved the land in perpetuity for national forests and national parks, are increasingly being handed over for commercial logging, mineral extraction and cattle grazing.

The public estate comprehends all the land, buildings and community facilities which are open and freely available to all citizens. Of course many recreational and cultural facilities can reasonably be provided by voluntary clubs and associations and paid for by their members. As public authorities have withdrawn from the direct provision of facilities, under the pressures of financial restraint and market ideology, voluntary clubs have filled some of the gaps, sometimes with the help of public subsidies. However these arrangements do not meet the needs of all citizens. One can contrast the availability of recreational facilities in the USA and Australia. America has lavish country clubs for the rich but few facilities for poorer citizens. In Australia even the smallest local government ensures, directly or indirectly, that many facilities, such as a cricket oval, a swimming pool, bowls and golf, perhaps a fairground, a library, sometimes an indoor recreation centre and a museum or arts centre, are available free or very cheap to all local citizens. The common culture of these little country towns and urban municipalities in Australia is a good advertisement for local government (although even the Australian system is now threatened by the application of the fashionable 'user pay' principle).

Once upon a time, municipalities were proud of their free museums, libraries and art galleries, of their dances in the town hall, of their well-kept parks and well-lit streets; today the streets are often dirty and unsafe, the parks ill-kept, the cultural facilities run down and subject to user charges and early closing. The combination of public squalor and private affluence is one obvious cause of crime, hooliganism and vandalism which, often directed blindly at common facilities, adds further to problems of maintenance. A converse trend is the restoration of historic buildings and zones for cultural and entertainment purposes, but the safest and most more attractive urban areas are often designed more for tourists than for local citizens.

If one seeks an example of the sorry impact of market ideology upon the life and condition of cities, the deterioration of London over the last decade provides one. London is the centre of the most prosperous part of Britain, yet a survey of citizens' satisfaction with quality of life placed it thirty-fourth out of thirty-six British cities. Obvious reasons are the increased air pollution, the severe traffic congestion and the dirtiness and lesser safety of the streets. London's once excellent public transport has become less efficient, less safe and more expensive under the impacts of market deregulation and cuts in subsidies. The museums, art galleries and libraries are less well maintained and sometimes charge entrance fees and close earlier. The Regent Park Zoo has closed. Boating on the Thames has become less safe. A walk along the embankment reveals large numbers of homeless, arrived there because of cuts in municipal housing or a vain search for jobs. The only factors which seem likely to stir the government to action are the effects upon tourists and the invidious comparisons now being made with such cities as Paris or Vienna.

Yet London shows one notable example of publicly sponsored and subsidised development, the plan for the regeneration of docklands. Here a public corporation has made land available for massive office developments such as Canary Wharf and upper-income riverside housing. Since planning permission was not required in an 'enterprise zone', which covers much of Docklands, this massive development could largely go ahead without any public inquiry or local consultation. The local residents have gained little benefit from the scheme, but had to endure so much disruption, dust and injury to their health from living on a gigantic building site that they finally sued the corporation for damages (the saying is that Mrs Thatcher accomplished what Hitler could not do). In Docklands public power and resources have been used to subsidise development for the rich at the expense of the poor, at the same time as the 'public estate' of Londoners has been left to deteriorate (Brindley *et al.*, 1989, Ch. 6).

Why does the maintenance of a good 'public estate' matter? In the first place it contributes to community cohesion and shared enjoyment. Even if 'rational egoism' is rampant, it is surely desirable to have some opportunities for an alternative lifestyle. Secondly the results are environmentally far preferable to the endless multiplication of privatised facilities. Public parks, beaches, sports grounds and the rest enable far more people to enjoy recreation than if each person must acquire and pay for her own facilities. As things stand the expansion of privatised 'positional goods' is shrinking the resources available to the general public. Finally it can be said that the existence of good common facilities is vital to the very notion of citizenship and a civilised society.

The most striking erosion of the common value of citizenship is the growth of private security forces (who in some countries greatly outnumber the police) and the privatisation of prisons. While recourse to paid security systems may be a natural response to increasing violence for those who can afford it, its use undercuts the principle that all citizens are entitled to the *equal* protection of the laws. The privatisation of prisons reduces public responsibility for the criminal justice system and the treatment of offenders. The civic as opposed to the market response to lawlessness must be to strengthen the public police force and to reform the system of criminal justice.

Assault on public goods

The previous examples bring out the importance of social values as a motive for political action. By contrast market ideology ties political intervention to the support of market forces. Sometimes the effort is made to stimulate the market into helping the poor – as for example in the efforts of Michael Heseltine as Secretary for the Environment to encourage private firms to invest in the blighted areas of northern English cities. The efforts have not been very successful but they were tried. This is because the easiest way to stimulate market forces is to favour profitable activities, such as the conversion of Liverpool Docks into a tourist attraction. Liverpool has gained an attractive facility, but not one of much help to its 80 000 unemployed citizens.

The supreme political task comes to be seen as one of satisfying the requirements and promoting the growth of the market system with all other goods treated as subordinate to this basic goal. Associated with this belief are the ideas that public goods are somehow less 'productive' than goods sold in the market and that only market growth will produce 'real' jobs, that is durable ones which contribute positively to economic growth. These are curious beliefs. In terms of human welfare, it is difficult to suppose that, for example, the profitable manufacture of plastic dolls is more 'productive' than the provision of education or health services by a public agency. There seem to be two reasons for making these assumptions. One reason is that the market sector is usually the main source of a nation's exports. This need not be so, however. Some government services and enterprises can and do make contributions to exports, and contributions by public agencies which utilise sophisticated scientific or social research are becoming more valuable internationally. Conversely the commercial export of primary products such as woodchips from forests, wheat from eroded soil and scarce minerals depletes a nation's natural wealth.

The second explanation is that public goods often depend, wholly or partly, upon taxpayer's contributions. Even in public choice terms, it is hard to fault this arrangement if individuals prefer, as a matter of principle or efficiency, to pay for some goods through a common pool of taxation rather than individual user charges. The decision is a matter of political preferences, but in a political climate which favours tax cutting, the provision of public goods will decline unless politicians demonstrate their necessity or equity and find fair ways of sharing their cost. Assertions about the 'unproductive' nature of public goods also drew upon a situation in which the government sector was absorbing an increasing proportion of available resources at the expense of the market sector (Bacon and Eltis, 1976). This argument loses its basis where there are substantial unused resources.

On the other hand, the unproductive aspects of market behaviour seem often to be accepted as a fact of nature or as being somehow (if obscurely) beneficial to 'the economy'. A good example is the explosion of jobs (often very lucrative ones) in the financial sector, which is treated by many commentators as a useful and continuing source of economic growth. In fact this financial explosion is largely due to the instability of the global money and commodity markets, which causes banks, transnationals and financial institutions to protect their funds by placing hedging bets on the forward exchanges. This system, far from being beneficial, is especially burdensome to farmers, small businesses and other groups who cannot forecast their earnings with any confidence (Strange, 1986). It may be hard to decide whether the frenetic activities of the speculators add to or reduce the underlying instability of the exchanges, but the most favourable interpretation can only see their activities as a necessary (and very substantial) cost of world trade.

The comparison of political failures and market failures is bound to end in the quicksands. Each sector has its distinctive potential and pathology, and a good society requires the right balance and mix of their contributions. An overdose of market ideology obscures and contradicts the protection of those social values which can only be underwritten by governments, even if they often fail in the task.

Dominance of the media

The modern market culture is so pervasive that its impact upon political culture may not be immediately apparent. Despite what public choice theorists say, the citizens of modern societies tend to locate politics in a different mental box from markets, and to treat politics cynically in practice but idealistically in theory as the vehicle of a sacred possession labelled democracy. Thus the ways in which the market relays and interprets politics to the public may escape close scrutiny simply because these ways have now become so familiar.

The influence of the media

The monopolistic elements of modern markets enable leading firms to spend very large sums on advertising their products and improving their 'image'. Market competition or simple emulation generalises this form of market behaviour. As a result newspapers and commercial television have become wholly financially dependent upon a flood of expensive advertising. A curious market structure has emerged, which hinges upon high production costs and the need for a large circulation or viewing audience in order to attract advertisers. Media ownership has become highly concentrated in some societies. For example a single individual, and he an American citizen, controls 60 per cent of the print media in Australia.

These market arrangements have a very large impact upon mass political attitudes and beliefs. A few large media proprietors wield substantial political influence which is often exercised in support of right-wing governments or parties. A proprietor's influence upon the editorial policy of his newspaper varies (some are content to be fairly neutral), but the influence can be appreciable, as some admit. The owners' influence upon news presentation is much more limited, although it seems to have some responsibility for a deliberate trivialisation of politics and concentration upon political scandals.

In the case of Australia, the power of media proprietors is shown by the deferential and cautious respect paid to them by politicians. In the 1980s the Labour Government achieved favourable treatment from a few big proprietors which it was anxious not to lose. Undoubtedly this was a reason for the high level of television monopoly permitted under Labour's Broadcasting Act of 1987, and for the strange failure of the Liberal Opposition – despite their theoretical belief in competition – to question this measure more than marginally. When Rupert Murdoch came to Canberra in 1991 he did not not call on the political leaders but was visited by them. In Australia at any rate politicians not only curry favour with media proprietors but are plainly afraid of their criticism.

Television advertising has a deep impact upon popular culture. Many people watch television for up to 40 hours a week, and the continuous injunctions to buy goods and services of all kinds bids up popular desires for consumer goods and helps to legitimate market growth as the essential objective. The irrelevant equations of advertisers, such as the identification of soft drinks with sun-tanned bodies or of beer with sporting prowess, may produce some sceptical reactions but probably do more (through sheer repetition) to glamorise consumer goods. Commercial sponsorship of sport and culture may be considered a more beneficent activity. After all, artists have always depended upon some kind of patronage, and that of an insurance company may be as good as any; while a sport such as cricket which has strong nostalgic and patriotic appeal but rather low attendances would probably not survive without sponsorship. Many people may reasonably think that money for sport and art can only be good since these activities are, in the economist's phrase, 'merit goods'. The arrangement is only questioned when tobacco companies use sponsorship of sport to create dangerously misleading connections between the product sponsored and the product sold. Sponsorship may transmit a much too benevolent view of a firm's actual practices. More mildly, when such a famous venue as London's cricket Oval becomes retitled the Foster's Oval, the impact of market image is all too plain.

Political subordination to the media

The impacts of the commercial media upon the treatment of politics are considerable. The spotlight has come to focus more upon the political leader of a party, and less upon his senior colleagues, because presentation is thereby simplified and personalised. The 'image' of the leader – his physical appearance and way of speaking – get as much attention as what he actually says. Political messages have to be simplified and packaged like commercial advertisements and slotted into the same brief time spans. Public policy is thereby treated as being no more complex or problematic – or indeed important – than the question of which detergent washes whiter.

Politicians have not resisted this commercial debasement of their profession. Market considerations are allowed to rule. Bob Hawke, the Prime Minister of four successive Labour Governments, ended his political career with a paid announcement of his resignation on television and eagerly embraced a new career as a TV star. Ronald Reagan's whole Presidency was a sort of glorified Western with the hero riding off into the sunset, leaving behind a vast museum of personal memorabilia and a carefully doctored public image. Even the right of political leaders to put their case at election time has commercial critics who contend that all time on the air should be paid for, thus fully reducing the sphere of citizenship to that of the market.

Politicians have also failed to promote the many opportunities of the media for the diffusion of political information and education. While some public broadcasting stations do make a genuine attempt to perform this role, the general availability of good quality material is limited not just by popular tastes but by the economics of mass advertising and by the presumed need to justify public funding by engaging in the battle of 'ratings'. Hence much of the electronic media offers little to its viewers of genuine political substance.

In terms of market theory itself this situation should not have arisen. If competition is a necessary feature of efficient markets, it is doubly desirable in a sector concerned with the provision of information and the formation of opinion. Competition and variety have been increased by the advent of cable television, although at the cost of confining intelligent information and comment to a specialised public willing to pay for the service. The potentialities of new technologies for multiplying television channels and media outlets are enormous. Enthusiasts see this situation as a guarantee of genuine competition and diversity, although this result is far from certain beyond some small, specialised channels. The possibilities of creating a 'teledemocracy', which facilitates instant popular participation in the political process, are intriguing, although the achievements of initial experiments have been modest (Arterton, 1987).

The wider effects of the free rein given to commercial advertising and sponsorship and to media monopolies are adverse for any responsible concept of politics and citizenship. They create a popular culture made in the market's image which is favourable to market interests and values but indifferent or condescending towards those values which need to be cultivated and expressed through politics.

Assessing market influence

Some broader issues arise over the impact of the market system upon modern societies and their politics. Has the critical analysis of this chapter been overdrawn? Are some of the adverse impacts of the market which we have listed properly attributable to other causes?

Environmental issues

In the first place it may be contended that the grave environmental problems of the present age are not mainly due to capitalist markets. In support it will be said that the communist states of Eastern Europe produced an even greater degree of environmental degradation than have Western capitalist societies. This statement seems to be true of localised impacts, although Western capitalism has had a much stronger impact upon the natural resources of the whole world. Environmental degradation in Eastern Europe can perhaps be likened to the early impact of industrialisation in Western Europe, with the difference that the scale of production, especially in relation to urgent military priorities, was much greater in the case of Eastern Europe. By contrast the technologies of Western societies have become sophisticated enough, and their populations sufficiently affluent and vocal, for some of the cruder environmental impacts of economic growth to be at least reduced.

More broadly it can be contended that environmental degradation is not so much the result of any particular economic system as of the restless drive of modern humans to conquer and exploit nature for their own use and advantage. It is a product of modernity, not capitalism, sanctioned to some extent (until recently) by the Christian religion, which has opened a Pandora's box of unforeseen evils (Grant, 1969).

There is force in this critique, yet it overlooks the extent to which the uncontrolled assertion of technology has all along been associated with the search for profit of market entrepreneurs. Admittedly governments have often shared and acted on the same development philosophy under the influence of international competition for markets or the pressures of an international arms race in which commercial interests are also deeply embedded. Protection of the environment is in principle quite consistent with an efficient market system, but there would need to be substantial changes in lifestyles and a redirection of resource use. Many firms are coming to realise the special advantages to be gained from acquiring a 'greener' image, but it may be doubted whether this conversion to environmentalism goes very deep among business as a whole. This conclusion is borne out by the strong resistance of business interests to environmental controls and by the attempts of these interests and their political supporters to discredit scientific warnings. (One such contention is that scientists have a personal interest in conveying bad news, a view which reduces even scientific inquiry to a crass form of materialism.) After all it was oil interests which bought up public transport in Los Angeles and condemned the city to its ferocious smog (and who have been instrumental in similar action elsewhere).

Almost certainly public opinion could be 'educated' to accept considerable changes in lifestyles (people don't like pollution) if political leaders took the initiative over proposing and facilitating positive changes. The fact that President Bush would not even sign a very modest international treaty on wildlife preservation at the 1992 Rio 'Earth Summit', because of possible effects upon 'the economy', shows how powerful is the ideology and influence of a 'free market'. Obeisance to the existing system blocks the major advances in welfare which are technically and socially practicable.

Social issues

Another possible contention is that the problems of modern Western lifestyles are primarily due, not to the economic system, but to social change. Kinship and local community bonds have increasingly dissolved into a strongly individualist society. The result is a search for personal mobility and freedom, and an acquisitive attitude to consumption goods as an expression of both individual personality and social emulation in a world largely stripped of traditional constraints and satisfactions. America is the pace-setter for this type of society and California the pace-setter within America. Nathaniel West's novel *The Day of the Locust* (1975), brilliantly describes the rootless and anomic individualism of Los Angeles, and the way in which a crowd of unrelated individuals is open to demagogic swings of taste and attitude. This kind of society can be seen as producing the 'bread and circuses' of mass entertainment and the trivialisation of politics.

An emancipated individualism is, initially at least, a liberating experience. The individual no longer perceives social boundaries to the pursuit of his or her interests, tastes and ambitions. There is a childlike fascination in the acquisition of goods and the turnover of fashions. These facts explain the quick appeal of a Western lifestyle to Asian or erstwhile communist societies, just as they explained the appeal of American lifestyles to the more traditional societies of Western Europe. The pain of this lifestyle comes later with experience of the loss of community and the isolation imposed upon the old, the sick and the disadvantaged. This sociological analysis may be true but these social changes are nourished and promoted by the capitalist market system. That system flourishes under the conditions of what MacPherson (1962) terms 'possessive individualism'. It would seem that the acquisitive impulses of the capitalist entrepreneurs have become disseminated among the general public and that the Puritan work ethic has been transmuted into a hedonistic impulse to consume.

Another feature of modern Western societies is the rapid growth of litigation, especially and most markedly in the USA. One cause of this development is the legal remedies now available to individuals who experience ethnic or sexual discrimination, or who are injured by commercial fraud or public maladministration. While this stronger protection of individual rights is itself desirable, the other side of the coin is the greater exposure of individuals to dangerous drugs, real estate swindles, financial trickery and other examples of commercial malpractice. The growing complexity of the financial system increases the opportunities for illegal or improper manipulation of small savings and investments.

As the last chapter suggested, a favourite theory for explaining and justifying these developments is that of the contractual society. Individual relationships of all kind come to be seen as a form of contract based upon mutual advantage. This contractual concept follows market theory in disregarding inequalities of resources or capacity. It favours large organisations and the legally sophisticated but puts a heavy strain upon the capacities of ordinary individuals. It means that trustee relationships, such as those between a client and his or her doctor, solicitor or bank manager, cannot be safely grounded in mutual trust but must be protected on both sides by legal requirements. Personal relationships such as marriage or cohabitation are also increasingly the subject of specific contracts. As the 'transaction costs' of doing business increase, the efficiency of the market is itself undercut in a society of growing litigation and diminishing trust.

It can be accepted that the social and environmental problems of modern society have a wider range of causes than the market system. Nonetheless these causes are entangled in the evolution of that system into a dominant constituent of social behaviour and its extension into a widening range of activities. These developments of 'market imperialism' block the visibility and feasibility of alternative ways of conducting human affairs, even as they gradually undermine the benefits to be had from competitive markets themselves.

Conclusion

This chapter has given a critical account of the influence of economic beliefs upon public policies, the conduct of politics and society generally. These effects derive from the mistaken assumption that economic theory can be 'value-free' and from the identification of the present market system with the merits (but not the limitations) of competitive markets. This strong dose of market ideology blocks possible reforms in the market system itself – an issue continued in the last chapter – and leads to the adoption of inappropriate market solutions for a variety of policy issues.

There is no suggestion here that politics can produce easy solutions for the defects of the market system. Both systems are pervaded by often interlinked accumulations of power. Market capitalism has the helpful prop of a coherent if abstract formal theory, whereas the role of government has not – and in fact cannot be given – the intellectual support of any overarching theory. Politics follows a pragmatic course inspired by diverse pressures and mixed motivations. Twenty years ago 'piecemeal social engineering' was admired for its democratic character, but the lustre has now gone. Economic rationalism offers a simplified alternative to the 'overload' problems which harried governments in the 1970s, but it is a destructive simplification.

Much public choice writing holds up a spontaneous market order as a much better way of reconciling individual interests than politics can provide. The idol thus worshipped has feet of clay. The merits of competitive markets are real enough in their place but cannot be generalised into the foundations of a social order, and how well or badly markets work depends crucially upon the nature of politically made laws. If, as public choice theorists often suggest, the political process is necessarily perverse and corrupt, there can be no salvation from politics either. To this question we must now turn.

8
Public Choice and the Public Interest

This chapter reverts to the general discussion of public choice theories begun in the first three chapters. Its subject is the nature of the 'public philosophy' offered by mainstream public choice thought, with investigation of alternative public philosophies which may provide a sounder basis for the maintenance of a tolerably equitable and harmonious civil society. The final chapter follows this more theoretical discussion with some reflections on the public policies needed to establish a better society.

The concept of 'public philosophy' refers to the beliefs which inform our understanding of the desirable role of politics and government in a democracy and of the relationships which should exist between the public and private realms. This is a large subject. It is necessary to consider in the first place what meaning (if any) can be attached to the concept of public interest, and then to explore the significance of this finding in terms of the classic democratic issues of individual liberty and social justice. These reviews lead to conclusions about the failure of the 'market model' of society to offer an adequate or acceptable basis for the conduct of politics, and the need to introduce a more positive view of the function of responsible, active citizenship. The questions throughout are whether the pessimistic public choice view of politics is necessarily correct and whether a good society can be based upon any other foundation than responsible political behaviour – hard as that may be to achieve.

Is there a public interest?

Does public choice have a public philosophy at all? The question must be asked because many writers deny meaning to such terms as 'public interest' or 'public good'. This conclusion is linked with their strong methodological individualism which holds that only individuals have wants or values. The idea of a 'public good' is seen as a sort of holy grail, external to individual preferences or values and waiting to be discovered by some co-operative inquiry (Brennan and Buchanan, 1985, pp. 37–9). When allied with the power of the state, this search for the public interest becomes an 'organismic monstrosity'. Mrs Thatcher put the same idea in a more homely way when she claimed that families exist but 'there is no such thing as society' (but while she rejected society, she certainly did not reject the state).

There seems no reason to dispute 'methodological individualism' if it means that the only subjects of consciousness, experience and thought are individual beings. An organisation can make choices and issue decisions through collective processes, but it does not feel or think as a single entity. Individual feelings of mutual sympathy and shared beliefs can produce so strong a sense of social cohesion that it may be likened to a 'collective consciousness' or a 'group mind', but they still rest upon individual choices, commitments and possibilities of withdrawal. To that extent methodological individualism is true. The key question then is how individuals make their evaluations and whether these leave space for a 'public interest'.

Public and private interests

The history of the term 'public interest' gives some support to Brennan and Buchanan's interpretation. Originally the term was similar to the French 'raison d'état', and was a way of saying that the interests and especially the survival of the state justified extreme measures which would otherwise be morally opprobrious. Governments continue to act on this maxim. 'Public interest' also came to be used pragmatically as a way of justifying almost any government policy and in this form it is indeed an authoritarian rationalisation. 'Public interest' or more often 'social good' is also appealed to by moral reformers keen to remedy some claimed social abuse. In this case, and where governments justify their policies on moral grounds, the idea of 'public good' can be seen not as a futile appeal to some utopian 'holy grail', but to some widely shared moral principle or belief.

However, given their assumption of rational egoism, public choice writers assume that such moral uses of political authority will be rare or non-existent. Buchanan and the Virginia School consequently pursue that old dream of the utilitarians of founding a political system upon a spontaneous harmony of purely private interests. They contend or assume, very much against the evidence quoted in the last chapter, that markets offer such a system in the economic sphere. They can see that the situation is still tougher in politics and pin their hope on the contractarian theory of a restrictive constitution. They hope that all rational individuals will see that it is in their personal interest to place permanent limitations upon the scope of government and the powers of its office holders. However, realising that their assumption of self-interest will often incline individuals to a contrary conclusion, they find it 'necessary to resort to some version of 'general interest' or 'public interest' as the embodiment of a shared moral norm' (Brennan and Buchanan, 1985, pp. 146–7). So the critics of public interest find this concept essential after all as the only hope for realising their preferred society.

It is impossible to confine Buchanan's concept of a shared political norm to a one-off settlement of a constitution, even if individuals could agree upon its nature. Constitutionalism has a legitimate part to play in a satisfactory political system, but constitutions like all political decisions will in practice favour some individuals and disadvantage others. Even rigid constitutions become gradually reinterpreted as circumstances and public opinion change. Indeed it is a curious feature of the Virginia School that time has stood still for them. They write as if they were still living in a fairly egalitarian society of farmers and small businessmen recently escaped from the tyrannical intervention of an English king. However, if 'general interest' and responsible citizenship make sense in a constitutional decision, why should these qualities be viewed as impossible in the more normal situation of political decisions?

Rational egoism in politics

If voters did in fact act simply as 'rational egoists', the political outlook would be extremely bleak. If I had no children there would be no reason for me to support public education; if I was too old to worry about the greenhouse effect and other such dangers, there would be no reason for me to support environmental controls; if I lived in a comfortable tree-lined suburb, why should I bother about the blighted and crime-ridden problems of inner cities? And so on. It would require an extraordinary act of faith to suppose that economic markets will solve these problems without political action; but where is the reason to support such action?

To answer this question, public choice theorists might take refuge in the old utilitarian concept of 'enlightened self-interest', or alternatively they might concede some beneficial role to the existence of 'altruistic preferences'. Neither answer is adequate on its own. It may indeed be in my long-term private interest to reduce the spread of poverty, squalor and crime which could threaten my way of life; but such judgements are contingent upon my age, circumstances and foresight and there must always be some reluctance to make immediate personal sacrifices for the sake of remote hazards on purely prudential grounds. Any such inclination is undercut by the 'free rider' theorem, in the absence of some moral or emotional commitment to the interests of others.

On the other hand the 'altruistic preference' concept treats social obligation as a sort of personal aesthetic taste and fails to give it any binding quality. Moral norms have an essentially different character from personal feelings and express obligations which often run counter to personal inclination. It is a misunderstanding of political norms to reduce them simply to the status of private preferences. In any case rational egoists presumably do not have many inclinations of this kind.

However political norms can be of little relevance unless they actually exist and are applied. Like all norms these political beliefs have to be socially learned and the mental political map which an individual inherits depends on her society and is subject to continuous change. In a society where independent thought is possible, these learned beliefs are subjected to the scrutiny of individual judgement and evaluation. This is the valid element in Buchanan's claim for the primacy of 'individual evaluations', but it operates against a background of political indoctrination, requires an independent capacity for reflection, and cannot be compared with a personal choice between tea and coffee.

Arrow (1967) contends that a voter necessarily chooses not a preferred personal outcome but a preferred social state. The sociological conditions of politics support this contention. Thus, as public choice theorists themselves have demonstrated, it is most difficult for an individual to vote rationally for his or her own private interest. Democratic politics revolves around the articulation and reconciliation of group interests, including the interest of the nation itself as an overarching collectivity of individuals – not necessarily as an 'organismic monstrosity'. It is natural therefore and necessary too for the individual to identify his or her interest with one or often several communities of interest, whether a party, a cause, a profession, a city, an ethnic group or the nation as a whole. To some extent these different kinds of interest can be expressed in different political forums, but for the aware citizen there are always issues of priority and balance. Moreover in each case the meaning of 'interest' is not objectively given but is always contestable, and involves adjudication of competing claims.

In this situation it is rational for individuals to be guided by normative beliefs and identifications rather than by direct personal self-interest. Of course they may hope or even expect that the outcome will benefit them personally, but this is not a sufficient basis for political choice. Given the normative character of political argument and the uncertainty of outcomes, it is natural too for ideology – in the sense of an often simplified view of the way society does or should function – to play a substantial part in political debate. These seem to be intrinsic features of politics.

Much evidence supports these interpretations of political behaviour. Chapter 3 quoted cases of American voters taking positions on such issues as unemployment and defence which are ideologically based and run contrary to apparent personal interest. In post-war Britain, farmers obstinately voted Conservative in the belief that the result was 'best for the country' even though a Labour Government had wooed them with guaranteed prices and other material benefits (Self and Storing, 1962, Ch. IX). Much 'single-issue' voting is based upon adherence to non-material ends such as the protection of wildlife or wilderness. Voting is often driven by economic calculations, but voters seem to be concerned more with the overall state of the economy (a social state) than with personal calculations, although no doubt the voter assumes that a more prosperous economy will benefit her.

It is true that many public choice writers would like to change this state of affairs by establishing more direct linkages between personal interest and public policy. Schemes of 'consumer democracy' can enable individuals directly to choose and also to pay for the public services which they want. This idea has the merit of creating a direct democratic community of interest. However, as Chapter 6 pointed out, it cannot cope realistically with a wide range of public services and it has strong inegalitarian implications – for example, poor parents would be gravely disadvantaged by a school system run on this basis unless a centralised equalisation fund was also introduced; but recourse to such a fund brings back some idea of public interest.

'Rational egoism' in political life occurs much more among active participants than among the general population; but here too one must recognise the relevance and sometimes the dominance of other motivations. Thus, as public choice theory stresses, selfish groups and factions have many political opportunities to pursue their own material interests. However the extent to which they can and choose to do so is not the product of some invariable law but depends upon the rules, structure and norms of political life: on whether or how, for example, their claims have to be arbitrated within some broader and less biased forum of public opinion. Moreover these factors will affect the articulation of sectional claims. An interest group's strategy does involve the issue of how far its claims should be modified (either from principle or expediency) so as to respect other interests or social values.

Political loyalties and passions

Public choice theory fails also to recognise the complexity of political motivations. There is ample evidence that individuals are influenced both by personality factors and social identifications. The distinction between authoritarian and liberal, or 'tough' and 'tender', types of personality is now well-known. While the distinction is too absolute, it does show up in individual evaluations of social issues, such as the extent of reliance upon government assistance or self-help for relieving poverty and other hardships. Views on this matter seem to have a weak relationship to personal material circumstances, although they are certainly influenced by the political culture of the society in question. Social identifications lead individuals to align their interests with a particular class, party or regime in ways which may not correspond at all well with their material interests. Rational egoism is in limited supply in politics at the mass or popular level. Equally these examples do not show that individuals are driven by moral concern for the good of society, although they do suggest the importance of ideological beliefs.

Group loyalties play a large part in politics. Political allegiances often represent 'collective identifications in the face of uncertainty' (Pizzorno, 1985, p. 275). Individuals in other words seek protection, comfort or a sense of purpose through their attachment to some group or cause. Group loyalty will often reflect an individual's understanding of his or her own interest, but it can also draw on feelings of sympathy or empathy for the needs of other group members. Public choice writers generally view these other-regarding sentiments as individual properties ('altruistic preferences') which play rather little part in politics. However, as Adam Smith clearly recognised in *The Theory of Moral Sentiments*, emotional sympathy for the needs of others is a universal human quality, as indeed is its converse, hostility towards others when the safety or welfare of the group is threatened. These emotions operate politically in limited contexts. Mutual sympathy is most marked among groups sharing strong common characteristics and experiences, such as ethnic communities or isolated groups of workers such as miners. It also is related to propinquity, for example in supporting the life of local communities. Richard Jeffries somewhere gives a wonderful picture of how, when one member of a small English village cut his leg chopping wood, all the other villagers felt a sympathetic bleeding. Local sentiment is much weaker in the modern mobile society but still exists. Despite the existence of the 'global village', feelings of mutual sympathy and concern are much easier to arouse within a nation than across frontiers.

As already suggested, group loyalties are a necessary response to the political limitations of individual action. They also produce feelings of hostility and aggression as well as of mutual sympathy and support. In terms of any concept of public interest, 'communitarian politics' is two-faced. It can produce beneficial involvement in shared interests and purposes, for example in local community life or the pursuit of some common cause. Conversely it can take the form of highly aggressive attitudes towards other social groups. The modern world reveals all too many (and seemingly growing) examples of ethnic conflict or domination fed by aggressive passions. This pathological version of group loyalty is clearly inconsistent with democratic principles or a viable concept of 'public interest'.

The growth of political apathy

In Western democracies there is increasing political apathy and alienation, which is expressed in the decline of membership and of active participation in political parties and in falling turn-outs at elections. The causes of this situation seem to include a perceived narrowness of choice between the policies of the major parties and disillusionment with the ability of governments to deliver their promises. The appearance of a Texan billionaire with no political experience (but plenty of money for propaganda) as a serious candidate for the 1992 American Presidential election is a vivid illustration of this point. Behind these attitudes (although not clearly recognised) lies also the sense of powerlessness engendered by the often harsh and destabilising impacts of a world economic and political order that seems beyond the reach of control by national governments.

Many conservatives view this growth of political apathy with indifference or even approval. There have been articles on the merits of not voting. For some romantics politics is a dull matter of national housekeeping and individuals can better spend their time on 'higher things'. For others in the Oakeshottian tradition politics is a specialised profession best left to those fitted by birth or education to understand its requirements. For defenders of the existing economic order, the existence of a passive population is a considerable asset.

The traditional teaching of 'civics' in schools has been largely replaced by introductions to the more critical standpoints of political science. That is a gain for realism, but the limitation is that political science becomes another specialism, of interest mainly to a small intellectual minority. 'Civics' was no doubt too often presented in an idealistic and uncritical way and needs to be replaced with a more positive introduction to the duties and problems of responsible citizenship. In any case political norms gain little concrete meaning unless they are actively practised. Harry Eckstein (1973) has shown how Norway has developed its democratic culture through the practices of homes, schools and workplaces as well as in the polling booths and political committees. Such practices are much less widespread in English-speaking countries.

In the longer run political apathy undermines and will eventually destroy democracy. It deprives democratic politics of the essential lubricant of individual concern and participation; it starves the political process of inputs of belief and opinion; and it runs down the maintenance, let alone the improvement, of political norms which lose their moral force if few are interested or believe in them. The growth of apathy is sometimes defended on the grounds that it is at least preferable to the arousal of partisan passions or utopian expectations that the state cannot satisfy. However it seems rather to be the case that apathy paves the way for demagogic partisan movements. The rise of extremist and authoritarian right-wing parties in France, Germany and elsewhere, preaching ethnic hostility and discrimination, is helped by the political indifference of ordinary citizens as well as the economic failures and social tensions which governments have failed to ameliorate.

Back to the public interest

There is no room for complacency about the nature of politics as described in this section. On the contrary, the dangers of political tyranny arising from the dark side of 'communitarian politics' are real enough and abundantly demonstrated in the history of societies. Thus it is not being claimed that politics is necessarily a more moral forum of human action than the market system. It may be a better realm or a worse one. Conversely the beneficial uses of politics can also be undermined by political apathy and alienation, and by the increasing scope for opportunistic behaviour caused by a breakdown of acceptable norms and practices. As Aristotle said long ago, democracy can turn into demagoguery, to end as tyranny.

However elusive the concept, it does seem that all reflective thought about politics must lead to some idea of a 'public interest'. This concept cannot be reduced to Buchanan's narrow basis of a constitutional agreement, nor can it be constructed upon a basis of rational egoism. Equally it cannot be identified with what governments declare to be the common good, or treated as a 'holy grail' about which all citizens will agree. Connolly (1981, p. 91) suggests that the common good is not a set of interests but 'a set of shared purposes and standards which are fundamental to the way of life prized together by the participants'. This is a good description of the beneficial ways in which the citizens of a locality or the members of a political party can work for a common cause. Such activities are usually not free of material interests, but they can also pursue ends which are not selfishly motivated or perceived. More broadly 'public interest' in a modern democracy must refer to the normative standards and practices which guide the political life of the society. Behind these standards there will always exist some version of a 'public philosophy', which seeks to define the acceptable role of the state and its relationship to other constituent elements of society.

Public philosophies are inevitably contestable, and in a society which values individual freedom of thought there can be no hope of achieving general agreement. The ultimate moral judge, as Brennan and Buchanan say, can only be the reflective individual. Here, however, public philosophy has to turn back upon itself and ask about the conditions under which individuals can make wise and responsible judgements and choices. This project in turn requires further confrontation between the negative theory of politics held by public choice and allied thinkers, and its positive alternatives.

The liberty card replayed

Liberty is the trump card played by the upholders of limited government and 'free' markets. They argue, quite rightly, that political liberty is a precious and precarious value, and that when it has been established it is too easily taken for granted. They further contend, and can again appeal to much historical and comparative evidence, that the chief threat to individual liberty comes from a too powerful state. They claim, once again correctly, that the protection of individual liberty requires a distribution, not a concentration, of power within society. Finally they say that a strong and autonomous market system is a vital condition and support of liberty, because it is based upon a system of voluntary exchange and disperses power among a large number of actors. It thus balances and holds in check the threat to liberty which would otherwise be posed by the state, and complements constitutional constraints upon the exercise of government powers.

These arguments are appealing but their force depends very much upon the structures of both the state and the market, the relationships between them, and the social values and norms which influence the workings of each system. It can certainly be agreed that the concentration of both political and economic powers in a single centralised authority is an invitation to tyranny. Stalin decisively demonstrated this point. It is also clear enough that economic markets form one important element within a free society and that some separation of political and economic power is desirable. These points do not resolve the issue, however. It needs further exploration, both at a theoretical level and by reference to modern Western democracies.

Concepts of liberty

Libertarians often appeal to Isaiah Berlin's (1969) well-known distinction between 'negative' and 'positive' liberty. Negative liberty consists in the absence of external constraints upon the individual's freedom to act as she pleases. Positive liberty consists in the capacity of an individual to choose for herself under whatever constraints exist. Under the Berlin formula, negative liberty becomes the crucial form of liberty for political life if the state dominates the extent to which the free choices of individuals are externally blocked. 'Positive liberty' is a form of moral autonomy, which is possible even for a slave who can decide whether to obey his master or take the consequences, just as a senior official can decide whether to obey orders or resign on a point of conscience. However Berlin also points out that the scope for the exercise of positive liberty can be facilitated (though of course not guaranteed) by improving the opportunities open to deprived individuals for pursuing their personal goals instead of just struggling to keep alive.

Libertarians equate liberty wholly with its negative version and then argue that the principal source of external coercion is the state. By contrast they claim that market relationships are non-coercive and voluntary. Berlin himself does not make this mistake. In the second edition of his essay (1969, pp. xlv–xlvi), he recognises that 'the bloodstained story of economic individualism' has led to 'brutal violations of negative liberty' and that 'the case for intervention, by the state or other effective agencies, to secure conditions for positive, and at least a minimum degree of negative, liberty for individuals, is overwhelmingly strong'.

Coercion is not a simple concept and its uses and moral acceptability vary with circumstances. The state is expected to protect individuals from physical assault and robbery and increasingly from domestic violence as well. The state's use of its coercive powers to order arbitrary imprisonment is a very different matter from its use of those powers to levy taxation or to regulate trade. The levying of taxation on the rich in order to provide basic welfare for the poor is hardly a negation of liberty, but rather a redistribution of the opportunities available to individuals to exercise free choice. If faithfully carried out, it probably results in net gains for both negative and positive liberty. Of course if the taxes are used to improve the stipends of politicians or bureaucrats, the situation is once again different. There must be a *prima facie* case against any coercive use of power unless defensible gains in individual opportunities are thereby achieved.

Upon examination the distinction between negative and positive liberty tends to dissolve (Ryan, 1984). The possible uses of liberty depend upon the range of constraints and opportunities that are actually open to any individual. The responsible exercise of individual choice is best described as moral autonomy and not, despite the urgings of Rousseau, as a form of 'positive' liberty. The circumstances which limit and channel an individual's range of possible choice include unalterable factors such as genetic inheritance and family background, as well as the specific constraints and opportunities offered by the social system. Libertarians urge the right of the individual to maximise his economic opportunities, including the unconstrained inheritance and acquisition of personal wealth. Meritocrats desire state intervention to achieve (so far as that is possible) more equal opportunities for personal achievement, but accept the conse-quential inequalities of outcome. Egalitarians look to state action to bring about not only more equality of opportunities but more equality of outcomes.

These different philosophies, which are the stuff of modern political argument, entail varying uses of state power. The libertarian needs the state's coercive power as strongly as the other groups, but in order to protect his assumed right to inheritance and property and to ward off the claims of less fortunate individuals. So far as liberty is concerned, the other philosophies (if they can be fairly and consistently applied) favour a more balanced distribution of individual opportu-nities. This qualification is once again the libertarian's trump card. Can the state be trusted with such a difficult task? Alternatively though, how will the liberty of individuals fare if left to the play of 'market forces'?

Capitalism and democracies

It is time to consider the issue of liberty empirically. When Berlin wrote his essay in the post-war period of the mixed economy, he assumed that capitalism had been effectively 'tamed' and brought under control, and that future dangers to liberty were more likely to arise from a too powerful state. That diagnosis now looks very out of date. As the last chapter showed, the market system has led not to more diffusion but to increasing concentrations of economic power. The international reach of capitalism has outdistanced the capacity of national governments to control its activities or to pursue independent policies. Some governments, especially in English-speaking countries, have chosen deliberately to move with the tide and to favour and encourage market forces while cutting back the responsibilities of government. If the liberal thesis about state and markets is right, the effect should have been a strengthening of political liberty.

The example of Britain suggests otherwise. A decade of Conservative government witnessed a steady growth of authoritarianism, summarised by the *Political Quarterly* (January 1989, p. 1) as 'a disturbing story of gradual, incremental encroachment on much of what has hitherto been taken for granted as a secure pluralist democracy'. Some of these authoritarian developments have been described in previous chapters. They include the imposition of central controls upon what were largely autonomous institutions such as the universities; the rejection of consultation with interest groups such as the trade unions; the haughty and dismissive treatment of cause groups and professional bodies; the transfer of many local government functions to centrally appointed 'quangos'; severe controls and restrictions upon elected local bodies themselves; more partisan appointments to official positions; a strong use of the Official Secrets Act to prevent discussion of the behaviour of the state's security forces; the 'doctoring' of official statistics; and an unprecedented extension of the government's public relations machinery to promote its policies and hobble its critics. All this was accompanied by an angry and intolerant attitude towards both opponents and independent critics such as the Church of England and the British Broadcasting Corporation.

These acts were possible partly because of the absence of constitutional contraints upon the powers of a British Government holding a parliamentary majority. They were exacerbated by the personality of the Prime Minister and modified after her departure. These facts lend support to the advocates of constitutional constraints upon the powers of government. Pluralist democracy in Britain had the support of unwritten conventions and norms which have been eroded but not finally destroyed by the government's behaviour. Some of these conventions, such as the possession of some reasonable degree of autonomy by locally elected bodies, now require the support of constitutional protection such as they receive in many other democratic countries. Federal systems of government suffer from rigidities in the distribution of functions, but they are a strong barrier to autocratic behaviour by the centre. In fact the advantages of some division of political power can be obtained constitutionally without running into the rigidities of federation. Such arrangements are a protection both for political liberty and for the exercise of democratic choice. Both these values would also be improved by a constitutional change to the British electoral system, which at present enables a party to achieve a large electoral majority on a minority vote.

Thus recent British history does support the old liberal thesis of the need to restrain political power, even if it remains uncertain as to how far this goal can be achieved through the instrument of a written constitution. However the government saw its authoritarian behaviour as necessary in order to pursue its strongly pro-market agenda, which would be justified by the results. In this case the market was not being called to the aid of political liberty. Political liberty and democracy were being endangered in the interest of freeing market forces.

The British case may be exceptional, but it is possible to see similar trends at work in the other English-speaking democracies. The usual answer of libertarians is to argue that, while some capitalist countries are certainly not democracies, the only extant examples of political democracies also have capitalist market systems. The collapse of communist systems has given a strong but misleading impetus to this argument. Some necessary association between democracy and market systems can be allowed without difficulty. The real issue concerns the relationship between capitalism and democracy.

The support of capitalism by Western governments, especially the USA, has been pushed to the point of actively assisting a growing list of undemocratic and sometimes highly exploitative national regimes, on the grounds that a likely alternative government – even if popularly chosen – might upset the workings of the market system. Despite the rhetoric capitalism is increasingly preferred over democracy, or at the least the often precarious institutions of democracy are manipulated to favour or protect capitalist institutions.

On the other hand some countries have managed to combine strong democracy with effective reforms of the market system. In Scandinavia political liberties are well protected and democratic participation is fairly widespread, not only in politics but, as Eckstein (1973) noted for Norway, in other forums as well. However these are also countries which restrict the impact of the market system with strong social and environmental legislation. It is true that their governments have made some concessions to the international impact of capitalism in terms of public expenditure cuts and reduced taxation of higher incomes. However these adjustments are still modest compared with the concessions to 'market forces' made in Britain, the USA or New Zealand. The Scandinavian democracies would not enjoy more political liberty or democracy by adopting the prescriptions of Thatcherism or Reaganism.

To conclude this section, individual liberty is threatened by excessive concentrations of power, whether political or economic. If decentralisation and democratic participation are desirable features of the political system, they are equally desirable for the market system; but they will not come about spontaneously and they depend upon a politically determined framework. The liberty trump card can be reversed and played against forces within the market as well as forces within the state.

Economic rights and social justice

Any discussion of public philosophy must include the issue of individual rights. This subject can be seen, for our purposes, as a battlefield between the claims of competing economic and social concepts of the rights of the individual. The economic approach derives these rights from principles of private property and voluntary market exchanges, whereas the social approach derives them from principles of equal basic entitlements. (Of course it is not being suggested that all economists would subscribe to the former position, but it represents one important strand in economic theories of politics.)

Claims about individual rights have a long history, going back to medieval concepts of 'natural law' and earlier, and including the contractarian theories of Hobbes, Locke, Rousseau and others that are continued today by the Virginia School of political economy. The idea of 'natural rights' which every individual once possessed before he joined a civil society has no historical basis. Claims about individual rights are essentially moral arguments which appeal to principles of social justice. As such they can have no absolute status, but depend upon the strength and appeal of their supporting arguments and upon the physical and social capacity of any actual society to realise them. Nonetheless they occupy a pivotal place in any conception of social justice or the 'public good', and they are a source of impassioned political debate in the modern world.

The rights of property

Modern theories of the rights of property go back to the contractarian ideas of John Locke in the seventeenth century. Locke (1946) believed that an individual was entitled, as a condition of belonging to a civil society, to receive the protection of the state for his person and property. Property was seen by Locke as an essential element in the rights of the individual, so much so that, while a rebel against the King might have to forfeit his life, his heirs ought not for that reason to be deprived of their inheritance. However Locke's concept of property rights was also restricted. He contended that a property owner was entitled to as much of the fruits of his labour as he could reasonably enjoy, and no more, and he lamented that the invention of money enabled individuals to acquire much more wealth than they could reasonably require. Thus Locke's theory is actually cold comfort for the property entitlements of modern millionaires, despite its hallowed position in the defence of property rights.

Locke's grounding of the right to property upon the direct labour of its proprietor seemed a plausible argument in an age of small farmers and businesses. Its modern relevance is a radical one, since it would support the break-up of large agricultural estates into family farms, the diffusion of industrial ownership and priority for small businesses. Similar ideas figure in the modern teaching of the Catholic Church about property rights and their limitations, and these ideas have at least some influence upon the policies of those European parties and governments with religious affiliations. These beliefs run quite contrary to the assumed logic of the capitalist system, which sets no limits upon the process of acquisition and allows uncontrolled market forces to determine the distribution of capital assets.

Locke is also known as the originator of the labour theory of value. This theory was appropriated and reversed by Marx, who used it to explain the 'surplus value' which capitalists could appropriate from the labour of their workers. Modern theories of the market completely drop the moral assumptions of either Locke or Marx about economic rewards or rights. They are left with the need to justify the market system on utilitarian grounds, instead of pretending that it conforms with any principle of individual desert. Popularised versions of market theory explain that investors get rewards for 'deferred gratification' or for taking risks, and that workers get rewarded for their skills or their efforts. There is just enough plausibility in these descriptions to spread a weak patina of morality over market operations, but not enough to prevent continuous social pressures directed towards making markets more moral.

The Pareto principle

Probably the most influential defence of the exchange basis of modern markets, in terms of a redefinition of individual rights, is provided by the Pareto principle. This principle, derived from the Italian sociologist Vilfredo Pareto (1848–1923), actually has two legs. The first leg argues that the 'utility' (satisfaction) derived by an individual from any goods, property or other source is a subjective affair which other individuals cannot experience or know. Consequently interpersonal comparisons or additions of the utilities of different individuals are unscientific. The second leg argues that in consequence a change in total welfare can be justified if and only if at least one individual gains and no-one loses.

The extraordinary appeal of this Pareto principle to many economists, which might amaze Pareto himself, seems to rest upon two circumstances. One, the technical factor, is that the theory seems to provide at least a bottom line position for economists to make authoritative pronouncements about human welfare. Who can object to changes where no-one loses? (Actually even this argument is uncertain since an initial welfare gain can occur in ways which produce a longer-term loss.) The second, political reason is that the Pareto principle is actually highly conservative and defensive of existing property rights.

Once again these results come about in two ways. By denying interpersonal comparisons (and thus seemingly recognising the autonomy and unique experience of each individual), the Pareto principle also rules out any comparison of the marginal utility of a rich and a poor person. It is therefore not possible to claim that a poor man will get more satisfaction from a square meal than will a rich man from an extra helping of caviare (each costing the same). Thus the old utilitarian conclusion that transfers from rich to poor will increase the total sum of welfare is undermined. Secondly the principle will justify a welfare change which makes the rich better off and leaves the poor in their existing state, but it will not justify any redistribution from rich to poor. Thus the application of the principle is as likely to increase as to diminish the extent of 'relative deprivation' within any society.

In practice the Pareto principle can hardly ever be applied. If the 'utility' of an individual depends upon his or her own private valuation, he or she can block almost any project if his or her valuation is high enough. The Roskill Commission into the third London airport found its cost–benefit analysis hobbled when some householders put an infinity value upon the loss of their home and familiar surroundings. (It refused to allow more than three times market price: Self, 1975, p. 83). This problem results not only from the likelihood of strategic misinformation by the individual affected, but from the fact that sometimes no monetary compensation will meet a person's perceived loss.

However power stations, dams, roads, airports, and so on, are unlikely to be held up on these grounds. The Hicks–Kaldor amendment to Pareto suggested that a cost–benefit analysis of such projects can be justified if the estimate of total benefits exceeds that of total losses, even if compensation to the losers was not actually paid. This concession to practicality negates the Pareto definition of individual welfare. Pareto himself made it clear that, where his principle of welfare does not apply, it is necessary to make decisions on extra-economic (ethical) grounds (Schumpeter, 1952, p. 131). Very quickly, then, must the economist yield to the social thinker and moralist.

The Pareto principle has an obvious affinity with Buchanan's belief that constitutional laws should be passed unanimously. Unanimity in politics can be conceived as the equivalent of voluntary exchange in the market. However the comparison breaks down not only because market exchanges are actually highly unequal, but because the collective processes of politics cannot produce anything approaching unanimity, save perhaps in exceptional circumstances of war or siege. Therefore the principle becomes primarily a way of defending the allocation of resources through the market against political interventions.

In any case the exclusion of interpersonal comparisons is absurdly unrealistic and actually immoral. This notion, fashionable only among economists, is a piece of intellectual baggage inherited from the subjectivist school of philosophy which shuts up the individual in the private world of his or her own sensations. In practice comparisons of the wants and needs of different individuals (or classes of individuals) have continually to be made in homes, schools, firms, bureaucracies and politics too. The critical question concerns the principles on which such comparisons are made, not the fact of the comparison which in the real world is inescapable. Nonetheless many economists use the Pareto principle to justify an agnostic stand on issues of distribution, which they leave to politicians, while boldly claiming to prescribe policies for economic 'efficiency' (meaning the maximisation of total wealth). Actually wealth cannot be maximised even in a formal economic sense without reference to its distribution (Self, 1975, pp. 139–45).

The case for more economic equality

The alternative and more ethically appealing approach to the issue of economic rights derives from the principle of moral equality. The idea that all individuals are equally entitled to the respect and concern of others has deep roots in Christian and humanist thought. This principle is notably expressed in Kant's 'kingdom of ends', which holds that every individual is an end in him or herself and must not be used for another person's gratification. It was expressed more graphically in the Levellers' dictum that the poorest he in England has a life to lead as much as the richest he. This idea of a moral equality commands widespread consent in theory, but is frequently violated and negated in practice.

The cutting edge of this concept of individual rights lies in its application to politics. The idea that all individuals should share the same basic constitutional and political rights is the foundation stone of modern democracies. But what of economic rights? Here

Rawls (1971) provides a more persuasive contractarian alternative to the assumed rights of property. If one accepts that equal individuals existing in a state of ignorance about their actual position in the world would will a society geared to the interests of its least fortunate members, it follows that such a society should be tolerably egalitarian. Economic differences of wealth could be justified only if they worked to the advantage of the poorest individuals. While such a society would still require some economic incentives, it could hardly require a highly inegalitarian distribution of property and income.

A more pragmatic approach is to stress the bias against marked economic inequalities which the principle of moral equality suggests. It is true enough, as the critics of egalitarianism continually stress, that any pursuit of absolute equality – whether of individual opportunities or, still more, of outcomes – is likely to prove chimerical and self-defeating. It would indeed lead to unacceptable and inconsistent results in terms of individual deserts, and to burdensome restrictions upon the exercise of individual initiative and enterprise. A society of full equality might be acceptable among saints, but not (as the fate of many communitarian experiments suggests) among even idealistically inclined individuals. However this problem is averted by accepting some distinction between 'wants' and 'needs' (Braybrooke, 1987) and by giving priority to meeting those basic needs which can be reasonably clearly identified before adding to the want-satisfactions of the already affluent.

There is plenty of historical and comparative evidence about different societies to show that moves towards greater economic equality are certainly possible without destroying the incentives to individual effort. As this book has shown, offering bigger economic incentives to the already affluent has not helped the poor but has widened inequalities of wealth; and the argument that a poor person may gain no more from an extra dollar's consumption than a rich one is insulting to poverty and contrary to common sense. Thus one cannot find a plausible utilitarian defence of an untrammelled market system to compensate for its lack of ethical appeal. Moreover, as the last section showed, greater economic equality is in principle fully consistent with a wider spread of individual liberty, viewed as a given set of opportunities and constraints. Given the strong market bias towards inequality, a political bias towards equality is morally desirable.

Just as absolute equality is an impracticable myth, so is the idea that a citizen of one country should give equal consideration to the claims of every other individual in the world. The practices of equality and liberty have to radiate outwards in diminishing circles of practical consideration. This constraint need not imply indifference to broader international concerns or causes, but simply a recognition that any practical application of individual rights has to be grounded in the circumstances and resources of a particular society, and requires the support of communitarian feeling to become effectively operative. Where these values are combined – when a belief in individual equality and liberty is linked with some positive sense of what Tawney (1935) called 'fellowship' – one seems likely also to find the most harmonious societies.

The good and the bad liberals

These contrasting conceptions of economic rights can be further illustrated by a brief excursion into the history of modern liberalism. In the nineteenth century liberalism stood for a belief in the virtues of the market system, of laissez-faire and free trade. Herbert Spencer's *The Man Versus the State* (1884) represented the apogee of nineteenth century liberalism, but around that time a split occurred between what may be called the 'negative' and the 'positive' liberals. The negative liberals stayed with Spencer's thesis and his suspicion of any state intervention, the positive liberals shifted to the view that state action was needed to expand the opportunities available to individuals, especially but not exclusively among the poor and deprived. T. H. Green (1890), a professed liberal, saw the role of the state as one of 'removing obstacles to the good life' through educational provision and improvements in housing and the physical environment. L.T. Hobhouse saw the state as harmonising the conditions under which individuals lived. Green and Hobhouse may have inclined rather far towards an idealistic theory of the state under the influence of Hegel, but they started the tradition of welfare liberalism carried on later by such thinkers as J. M. Keynes and T. H. Marshall.

This split in the liberal camp has had a considerable impact upon the political history of Britain. The 'positive' or welfare liberals were prominent in the reformist Liberal Government of 1906–14, but with the later split in the Liberal Party many among them gravitated to Labour. In the USA the same intellectual movement ushered in the New Deal, which explains why in that country the term 'liberal' refers to the welfare or positive version of liberalism. The negative liberals in Britain gravitated into the Conservative Party where their doctrines were for long diluted by older traditions and beliefs until their triumphant re-emergence in the ideology of the Thatcherites.

T. H. Marshall (1963), successor of the positive liberals, contended that the twentieth century was witnessing a large move forward in the definition of the rights of individual citizens. Instead of being confined to the constitutional and political sphere, these rights were being effectively extended into the economic and social sphere. Marshall believed that capitalism was being tamed by the will of political majorities and would yield the space needed for the achievement of new economic and social rights. Marshall was much too sanguine. The negative liberals, retitled libertarians, are struggling to put the clock back, but their theories of economic rights have little ethical or utilitarian justification to set against the strong if currently clouded tradition of the 'positive' liberals.

Failures of the market model

The last three sections suggest that the market model appealed to by public choice ideology cannot offer an acceptable basis for a normative theory of politics and government. It is flawed in at least three basic ways.

No understanding of the public interest

While the concept of public interest is elusive, the term does at least imply the need for a non-egoistic and non-private concern with the common affairs and shared concerns of society. This concern operates in a number of particular contexts such as the 'public duty' of the bureaucrat, the 'social responsibility' of the politician, and the goals or ideals of a cause group or political party (some of these concerns can be more precisely defined than others). It must show up above all in the social concern of the responsible citizen (see later). While all such 'concerns' are doubtless precarious and partial, and often offset by personal or (more often in politics) by collective opportunities of gain, this other-regarding sentiment is an essential ingredient of political life. This public interest aspect of politics requires an acceptance of norms and principles which often run counter to individual inclination, as well as some identification or sympathy with the needs of others. Such attitudes may always be present in some degree but are aided or hindered by the norms, beliefs and practices of a given society. By excluding these norms and beliefs from its political explanations, public choice theory minimises (mistakenly) their actual significance, and normatively has the effect of making egoistic behaviour appear as rational and universal, hence acceptable. Its alternative design of a political harmony of rational egoisms simply cannot be made plausible or possible.

Confusion of political liberty with market freedom

Giovanni Sartori's (1987) impressive study of democracy shows the error of equating political liberalism with economic liberalism (or 'liberism' as he calls it). Political liberty occupies a different and socially prior terrain to market freedom. Although Sartori believes strongly in the need to constrain and diffuse political power, and is opposed to populism, he does not see any particular relationship between political liberty and the size or functions of the state. Rather it may be a reasonable political objective to increase democracy and diffuse power within the market system (Sartori, Vol. 2, Ch. 14).

Political liberty cannot be treated as the dependent variable of a strong, autonomous market system. Such a belief ends by gobbling up political liberty in order to suppress or by-pass opposition to the rigours of the market order. The most that can be claimed is that liberty requires some balancing of the roles of the state and the market. The state's role, however, is structurally and morally prior to that of the market. The market system is a cultural artifact, dependent upon political rules and capable of being changed by those rules. Without wise and acceptable rules, market 'freedom' would soon degenerate into an atomistic chaos. As Berlin, Sartori and indeed most political philosophers would agree, individual liberty is not a one-dimensional concept but a bundle of opportunities and constraints which regulate social relationships. Whilst political liberty basically requires only 'non-rival' rights (my freedom of speech does not injure yours), a broader concept of liberty – including therein the effective exercise of political liberty also – turns upon access to resources which are institutionally controlled. Whatever the state does or does not do will have a considerable effect upon the distribution of those resources and of consequent individual opportunities to exercise liberty.

Confusion between wants and needs

The market concept of utility makes no distinction between 'wants', viewed as the particular personal desires of individuals, and 'needs', viewed as the basic requirements for a tolerable life which all human beings have in common. The fact that any definition of 'need' must take account of the circumstances and resources of a particular society does not vitiate this distinction. The concept of need is certainly open to abuse and special pleading but remains basic to any developed concept of social justice (Braybrooke, 1987).

Because of this error public choice ideology treats political wants as having the same logical status as market wants expressed through a different and inferior forum. The individual knows his own 'utility' best – indeed no-one else can know it. Consequently individuals' claims to moral consideration through the political process became illegitimate or at best somewhat peripheral, depending upon the personal altruistic tastes which some citizens happen to possess. Equally irrelevant is the idea that some forms of human welfare derive from the quality of relationships between individuals, not from their private wants. Such relationships may be sought through private associations or clubs, but they are assumed to have little place in politics.

It is not fanciful to suppose that many of the gross inequalities to be found in Western societies become legitimised (so far as that is possible) by this style of thought which treats the needs of the poor and the deprived as the claims of just another interest group. Conversely, if the market system produces large and increasing inequalities, the result can be ascribed to the necessary logic of a superior system to politics which must be given its head. The market treatment of individual rights is rooted in the protection of property, inheritance and contract. Consequent appeals to individual rights have a strongly defensive character, as in the Pareto principle or Buchanan's search for a constitutional agreement to restrict the powers and expenditure of government. This negative view of rights held always *against* and never *through* the state undercuts any positive expectations about the role of politics, and is deeply damaging to any belief in the possibilities of collective endeavour.

The return to citizenship

Every normative political theory embraces some kind of 'public philosophy' about the nature of politics, the role of government and the relations between government and society. Public choice theory offers a very negative philosophy, except for those thinkers who want to maximise the sum of individual preferences, but find this (as formulated in purely individualistic terms) an impossible goal. Thus the question arises: what alternative public philosophy can be suggested which will avoid or anyhow reduce the many failures and 'perversions' to which politics is said to be liable?

Some basic elements of an alternative public philosophy have already emerged in previous sections. Central to these findings is a concept of citizenship. However old-fashioned it may sound, responsible citizenship is the essential foundation of any society which values both liberty and justice. The responsible citizen will be a participant in those groups with which she shares a common interest, but she will also subject group claims where necessary to her own independent judgement. She will also be mindful of the basic rights and needs of those members of society who are external to her own interests and activities. In this way, and only in this way, can the vital 'communitarian' element in politics be combined with checks upon excessive partisanship and intolerance. Responsible citizenship protects liberty by checking sources of tyranny and the abuse of power, and it protects justice with a developed sense of social equity.

Public choice theory, with its egoistic assumptions and treatment of politics in terms of personal utilities or want satisfactions, offers a thin concept of citizenship. This is not true of James Buchanan who recognises the difference between responsible judgement and want satisfaction, but who confines judgement to a very restricted constitutional forum. Nor it is true of such a convinced market zealot as Hayek who shared with J.S. Mill (whom he greatly admired and whose letters he edited) an earlier liberal conception of responsible citizenship (a rereading of *The Road to Serfdom* (1944) would show that, compared with his modern disciples, Hayek actually had a surprisingly broad view of the role of the state); but citizenship as a positive and active function has little place in the writings of modern political economy.

Recognition of the political significance of individual judgement agrees in one sense with the 'methodological individualism' of public choice thinkers; but it is a very narrow correspondence because those thinkers take individual tastes and opinions to be free expressions of individual choice, whose social origins need not be known or considered. Any realistic view of the role of the citizen has to recognise that he or she forms opinions within a very weighty structure of social influences. There is a chicken-and-egg situation; responsible citizenship both creates and is created by a favourable political environment. It cannot flourish unless the right enabling conditions of a democratic society are present.

Political participation

Modern democracies are complex systems which are often pictured as processing the 'inputs' coming from voters, interest groups and political parties into the 'outputs' produced by legislatures, elected officials, bureaucrats and law courts. This familiar 'systems theory' is actually misleading, since legislatures are often more concerned with voicing demands than with passing legislation; political parties are concerned with legitimising or criticising governments as well as with developing policies; bureaucrats are often involved in the articulation of public demands, and interest groups engaged in the delivery of policies; while political leaders occupy the apex of the system where 'inputs' are turned into 'outputs' or alternatively 'outputs' are legitimised against hostile opinion. Political systems theory (Easton, 1953) suggests a smooth progression of political demands being processed through the system into laws and administrative decisions, and overlooks the capacities of modern executive governments to make independent decisions (independent, that is, of political preferences, not of the state of the economy), to legitimise their policies by propaganda and appeals to party loyalty, and to implement them by the co-option of interest groups or intended beneficiaries. Government from the top down is often a more accurate description of the modern democratic process than policy-making from the bottom up.

The case for a fuller form of active democracy gains cogency from these anti-democratic tendencies in the policy process.

While one need not accept the arguments of Riker and others about the 'meaninglessness' of mass voting, it should be clear that voting itself is only one important element within an active democracy. Despite the admitted problems of agenda setting and aggregating votes, it would still seem democratically desirable to make more use of referenda on issues of clear constitutional and political importance. The results will provide one important and where necessary decisive guide to the balance of public opinion, provided the political environment is supportive of responsible political choice.

The principal feature of an active democracy is not voting but active political participation. The declining appeal and legitimacy of political parties is closely related to the decline in their active membership. Remedies for this situation include fairer electoral rules which will give more weight to the representation of minority parties, as well as democratic reforms within parties themselves. Perhaps still more important is the democratic potential of elected local governments which possess genuine powers and vitality. John Stuart Mill pointed out long ago how essential was local government to genuine democracy, inasmuch as several hundred times more individuals could participate directly in local elected bodies than in a national parliament. It is true that narrow jurisdictions and fiscal inequalities often reduce the effectiveness of local democracy, but these are not necessary features of a society which genuinely values public participation.

Once pluralist democracy was applauded for its multiplication of organised interests. The influence of public choice thought is apparent in a more critical political stance towards interest groups and in the belief that they undermine the 'efficiency' and 'logic' of the market system. In practice, as this book has shown, political hostility towards interest groups has usually been partisan and selective, not principled. An acceptable democratic theory must recognise the legitimacy of interest groups within pluralist societies, but seek ways of judging their claims by standards of equity and practicability. Once again the exercise of responsible citizenship, among the members of the interest group itself as well as among the parties and officials to whom their claims are addressed, is a necessary solvent of this process, as is the existence of a bureaucracy committed to principles of equity and impartiality.

A special political ambivalence occurs towards those 'cause groups' which pursue a social or ethical goal rather than a material interest. To some market zealots, the very lack of a material stake in the economy disqualifies a cause group from political participation; others treat such causes as 'woolly idealism' or at best as worth only as much attention as they can command votes. Some cause groups invoke arguments which clash with such democratic principles as religious toleration, but short of this point religious principles can contain relevant social arguments. For example, the religious case against Sunday trading is one way of declaring that there are values (whether recreational or religious or both) which warrant protection against the restless omnipresence of market activity.

Many cause groups in fact stand for contrary values to those of the dominant market order. Their appeal to many thoughtful and idealistic individuals shows the extent of disquiet about the effects of that dominant order, and the search for alternative ways of life and systems of economy. That cause groups have varied aims, some of which are narrow or dogmatic, does not alter their value as pointers to a new civilization. They must walk a hard road in their opposition to dominant interests and ideology, and for this reason alone deserve the respect and attention of every genuine democrat.

One of the gravest democratic problems is the frequent opportunism of political leaders. This opportunism figures in the theories of public choice, but is forgotten in its political applications. The ultimate counter to such opportunism is a democratic system which produces leaders of social vision and personal integrity. Protection against this danger also requires some diffusion of power among different organs and levels of government, and a clearer demarcation of the roles of politicians and bureaucrats. As Chapter 6 argued, democracy needs rules and traditions which protect the impartiality of bureaucracy from its political controllers as well as from interest groups. There can be no effective regulation or impartial administration if bureaucracy is allowed to become a junior branch of business administration, modelled along market lines and allied with business interests. Bureaucracy needs two faces: a partnership with politicians and a sensitivity to clients over the design of public policies but an impartial autonomy over their implementation.

The democratic climate

This brief review of democratic principles has invoked a number of familiar maxims. It may be none the worse for that and at least it suggests that the political pathologies painted by public choice writers are not inevitable features of democracy. The workings of a complex political process will always give rise to some misuse of public powers and resources at the expense of a broader public; but these effects only become pathological when the democratic channels silt over and standards of political life decline into opportunism.

For some time the intellectual as well as the political environment has been unhelpful to the goal of responsible citizenship. Liberal thought has been dominated by an agnostic treatment of individual lifestyles and values as matters of personal opinion; but no such inhibitions apply to the strong influences of commercial advertising and mass entertainment upon individual tastes and perceptions. Chapter 7 showed how the political order has become trivialised and subordinated to the pressures for market growth and consumption in a variety of ways. The intellectual climate may be changing towards more recognition of the place of moral values in politics, administration and the market system as well. Liberal education is an essential springboard for developing independent thought and a democratic government should promote and develop such education on a wide basis in the interest of responsible citizenship. Given the competing influences on the individual, education also needs rehabilitating as a means of personal development and interest, not just (as is now mainly the case) for utilitarian economic purpose. Equally important for a genuine democracy is the break-up of media monopolies, and the promotion of multiple sources of news and opinion.

These concepts of democracy are pitted against the strong constraints of the existing economic and political order. As Connolly (1981) says, individuals view their range of opportunities and expectations within a given social structure, and their wish to be 'at home' in their society inhibits them from a critical view of the system as a whole (blame is instead shifted to some sub-group such as immigrants); but if the discordance between the society's legitimating ideology and their own actual experience becomes too wide, they may rebel. Connolly's account fits surprisingly well the sudden, spontaneous overthrow of the communist systems of Eastern Europe. It is possible, if the political order becomes too dominated by market imperatives, that a similar spontaneous revolt may occur against the capitalist system of the West. On the other hand, it may be the case that the dynamic of democracy is still sufficient to establish the dominance of a political order which expresses balanced social values, and thereby to avert the possibilities of social breakdown or collapse. The issue is still open.

9
Towards Better Government

Can faith be restored in the capacity of democratic societies to solve their economic and social problems? Is better and more constructive government possible? This final chapter cannot adequately answer these big questions, but it can suggest some possible ways of transcending the present limitations upon effective collective action. To do this, the chapter will first revert to the public choice analysis of the growth and attempted curtailment of the role of government, then consider the new political agenda which is beginning to unfold and the required conditions for developing a new paradigm of the goals of public policy, and move finally to international and national problems of achieving political change.

Explaining government growth

Very many explanations can be given of the growth of government (see Hood, 1991). However, one important distinction is between the view that government growth is due to the self-exciting nature of the 'political market', and the more traditional argument that this growth is a rational response to electoral wishes or (more broadly) social requirements. Both main causes are recognised in the public choice literature (for a summary see Mueller, 1989, pp. 320–47), but the more politically influential viewpoint stresses the first cause. Writers such as Brennan and Buchanan (1980) and Buchanan (1986) go so far as to hypothesise that *all* government growth may be explained by the self-interest of politicians and bureaucrats.

This viewpoint is associated with a distinction often made by public choice writers between the 'allocative' and 'redistributive' functions of government. The former function consists in the provision of public goods and the removal of 'externalities' on efficiency grounds, subject to the Pareto principle. The latter function refers to the redistribution of wealth (through income transfers or services) from one section of society to another. The allocative function is conceded to be legitimate, but the redistributive function is viewed critically and often assumed to be the dominant cause of government growth. It is the dream of public choice 'constitutionalists' somehow to get redistributive issues separately solved (or shelved), and to confine government to its legitimate (but supposedly small) allocative role. However, the conceptual distinction between these two functions simply will not stand up. All government activities, even local streets or drains, redistribute costs and benefits between individuals to some extent; and the suggested use of the Pareto principle as a limiting principle is vitiated by the objections in the last chapter. More fundamentally the concept of *redistribution* implies that there is some prior system of wealth distribution – namely that produced by the market system – which has some prior right or claim over the distributive decisions reached by democratic governments, a belief that was strongly rejected in the last two chapters.

These considerations do not deny that some part (on occasion perhaps, a large part) of government growth derives from the special opportunities available to powerful interest groups, politicians and bureaucrats for pursuing their private advantage. However, the extent of this distortion can only be guessed at, since it varies with the institutions, rules and ethical standards of particular societies and also involves normative evaluations of the claims made by particular groups (unless all such claims are viewed as illegitimate, some have more reason and justice than others). Moreover, it has to be recognised that, since the size of government will always be limited ultimately by fiscal considerations, the success of some claims upon the public purse will inevitably mean the rejection or diminution of other claims which may be more equitably and rationally based. Redistribution by government does not necessarily run from rich to poor; on the contrary, and especially in recent decades of right-wing governments, it runs also in the reverse direction. The 'right' size of government depends upon the extent of well-grounded claims for public action and upon the desirable mix of public and private activities. It is much sounder to conclude that government resources are inequitably and irrationally distributed than that the total size of government is necessarily excessive.

Public choice theory, with its exclusive focus upon the 'political market', fails to consider the extent to which government growth is related to basic changes in social and economic conditions. For example, the growth of government expenditure has correlated quite strongly with indices of economic growth, per capita incomes and urbanisation (Dye, 1972). Some elements in these relationships are fairly obvious. A more populous, urbanised and mobile population increases the number of collective action problems. Rapid technological change dumps into the lap of government many problems, such as the management of a large volume of traffic, environmental pollution of various kinds and questions about the safety of new drugs and other products. Industry requires a better educated workforce. Income security becomes more necessary and affordable under conditions of increasing wealth but rapid economic change. Economic change also produces declining industries and failed firms. Social change produces many vulnerable individuals who can no longer depend upon traditional family or community support. This list of environmental pressures upon government could be expanded a lot further (for a review see Self, 1985, pp. 23–47).

An alternative, neo-Marxist explanation is that the growth of government is due to the requirements of capitalism. Government helps capitalism by providing necessary but unremunerative infrastructure, by subsidising industries, by assisting the search for new markets, by taking responsibility for workers' education and health, and by buying off discontent through welfare payments. O'Connor (1973) traced the 'fiscal crisis' of the state in the 1970s to these capitalist pressures upon government. This thesis now looks less plausible, given the growing trend for the market sector to take over or supply numerous public services on a profitable basis, and the apparent capacity of some governments to cut welfare and other 'social expenses'. However these developments are consistent with government support for capitalism in other ways. Economic growth still depends upon substantial government inputs into education and training, financial support and rescue operations, basic infrastructure and other activities. A free market system which cuts wages and produces unemployment may also undercut the purchasing power of the mass market on which capitalism depends.

However these economic and social pressures upon modern governments are assessed (and other versions are possible), public choice theory fails to consider *why* so many and various demands have been addressed to the state. Of course there is no automatic transmission belt from a 'social problem' to a 'government response'. All such problems have to be translated into effective political demands before action can result. Sometimes the connection is fairly straightforward; no government can ignore environmental health or traffic problems, although the nature of its response will vary within limits. Often, though, the extent of the political response will be more open-ended, and many perceived social problems or needs may become blocked by the political process. These facts do not alter the point that the nature of modern society (and not just that of the political process) produces a large and indeed increasing agenda of collective action problems.

The question therefore is how the political process deals with the various claims or demands thrown up by the nature of modern society. Many demands for government action represent more than a narrow assertion of self-interest, and have at least some rationale of improving social welfare or relieving particular causes of distress or injustice. It was argued in Chapter 5 that the growth of the welfare state represented a rational response of the electorate to the economic and social circumstances of modern societies, based upon a mixture of enlightened self-interest and some recognition of the needs of fellow citizens. Far from government being politically impelled into endless new ventures, it often seems to take some disaster – such as a severe industrial accident and loss of life, a startling example of child abuse or some glaring case of commercial corruption – to prod the political process into corrective action.

A problem for political theory is that there is no simple way of differentiating between reasonable and excessive or unjustified claims for government intervention or support. All claims dress themselves in arguments about the 'public interest' even if the argument is sometimes hypocritical. Public choice ideology itself makes this appeal in its frequent claim that a slimmer state will also be a more impartial one, purged of the excessive weight of special interests. That claim too must be evaluated.

Size and impartiality

Previous chapters have analysed efforts to curtail the role of government in a variety of ways. They have been far from successful in terms of overall public expenditure and, despite some shedding of functions, Leviathan remains alive and kicking.

These facts confirm that the growth of government has deeper causes than public choice theory suggests.

As earlier chapters showed, governments have had some success in changing the direction of the 'political market'. Bureaucracy was slimmed and redirected, public service unions were overruled, interest groups embedded in state functions were cold-shouldered. However this reversal was balanced by favours to other groups who would gain from a market regime and the reduction of state commitments, such as the managers and shareholders of privatised industries, contractors and developers, financial institutions, housing owner-occupiers and wealthier taxpayers.

The political entrepreneurs who launched these initiatives clearly did not believe that public choice theory applied to themselves. They believed that they were acting in the 'public interest'. The New Zealand politicians and Treasury who sought to bind bureaucrats contractually and to divide their offices, in order to guard against 'bureaucratic opportunism' and 'producer capture', had no worries about imposing their own beliefs upon bureaucracy and the state. Thatcher and Reagan never saw themselves, as a public choice analyst would logically have done, as opportunistic entrepreneurs mobilising latent anti-state and pro-market interests to their political advantage. Admittedly these policies do not always bring political advantage because of their frequent unpopularity. Here ideological goals take over and the idea of impartiality is associated with the necessary conditions of the international market system and hence free of political bias. The hollowness of this imputation of equity to the market order and the disingenuousness of denying the existence of political influence from market interests should be obvious.

The political influences of 'corporate power' have clearly grown. In the USA the large companies, both individually and collectively, have allocated much-increased funds and efforts to the Washington lobby as well as to financing right-wing think tanks. Rising electoral expenses have increased the pliability of members of Congress towards these sources of financial support, while friendly Presidents like Reagan and Bush have appointed business councils able to protect corporate interests in the execution of the laws. The weight of these corporate interests, when contrasted with the much smaller resources of consumer, worker or environmental groups, has led to administrative emasculation of the reformist legislation passed by Congress at an earlier period (around 1966–72). The corporate lobby has assertive as well as defensive goals, as witnessed in the expensive government bail-outs of the failed savings and loans banks and of commercial banks as well. American government has been returned to its historic role not of a 'nightwatchman state', but of a lavish spender on behalf of business and a stingy paymaster for the relief of poverty or unemployment.

In Britain, Australia and New Zealand, business interests have been treated with respect and deference as the goose which lays the golden eggs, while labour interests have received much critical scrutiny, even from the Labour governments ruling in the Antipodes. In Britain, as Chapter 6 showed, 'corporatism' has not (despite much rhetoric) been dismantled but has been turned into a narrower partnership between government and business on appointed boards, with other interests largely excluded. The attack on labour interests by Conservative governments culminated in 1992 in a draconian proposal to reduce the once vast coal industry to a mere rump of the most profitable mines so as to speed privatisation. Coming in the midst of a depression, this proposal was so unpopular (even among many Conservatives) that it had to be largely postponed, although not necessarily abandoned, under parliamentary pressure.

The idea of impartial treatment of all interests by government is unrealistic, but governments can and should be judged by their openness to the full range of social interests and their concern for public opinion. These criteria suggest that the measures taken over the last fifteen years in the name of 'slimming the state' have produced not more but less equity and democracy in the conduct of government. Historical evidence suggests that small government and bias towards the strongest economic interests tend to go together. Democracy requires a return to a more balanced pattern of pluralist representation, while renewing its capacity to judge claims fairly and to control the more powerful interests.

A new political agenda

It may be useful to speculate on the public policies which may eventually be found preferable to those of the current orthodoxy.

First, *resource goals*. Automation and productivity gains are rapidly reducing the labour required in the market sectors of agriculture, manufacturing and distribution. Some surplus labour is being shifted into finance, tourism, entertainment and personal services, but these market sectors have rather little connection with unfilled human needs and are an inadequate way to tackle unemployment. Conversely there are too few resources invested in education and the care of children, the old, the sick and the handicapped; in urban infrastructure and redevelopment; and in environmental maintenance and improvements. While market firms and techniques can contribute towards these goals, the desirable redeployment of resources requires action by governments and depends upon government initiatives and financing. The costs will partly be recovered from taxation of new earnings and savings on welfare expenditure. Some new forms of public investment can reasonably be financed from borrowing where they contribute substantially to a sustainable society (after all large debts are incurred by the private sector for much more ephemeral purposes). A new mixed sector of employment may develop that is financed partly from taxation and partly from user fees. The extra taxation which these policies would still require would need to be justified by reflection on their overall benefits to society compared with alternative outcomes.

Second, *full employment*. This goal has to be not abandoned but redefined so as to meet conditions of equal opportunity for women, more time spent on education or training, more flexible retirement dates and the existence of redundant, unskilled labour. Generally it seems desirable to make lifetime career patterns more flexible, so that (for example) either the mother or the father can get time off to care for young children and so that individuals in reasonable health can pick their own retirement date subject to differential pension rights. A shift of resources into neglected social needs would largely resolve the unemployment problem, although at some point working hours might be able to be reduced all round. Shorter working hours could then go with fuller opportunities for community service and political participation. The most serious problem – that of a superfluous underclass – could be tackled through training in basic skills for new community and environmental tasks. There is also a case for at least slowing technological change where its main effect is to destroy the livelihood and self-respect of workers with little opportunity for alternative employment. Governments would have the task of co-ordinating the labour market and implementing equitable employment laws.

Third, *social welfare*. It has been sufficiently argued that basic social services are best provided within a comprehensive public framework as civic entitlements. There remains much scope for argument as to the role of the private sector over providing additional facilities, delivering public services and acting as a forum for innovation, experiment and checking upon the quality of public provision. Private provision in such matters as health insurance and pensions is undercutting the quality of public provision and efforts to contain costs, and in the case of education adds to class stratification. However some opportunity for private provision may still be a necessary safeguard for the exercise of individual choice, especially if not confined exclusively to the rich. Service delivery is a different matter, since voluntary bodies in particular have a distinctive contribution to make in the care of the sick, old and handicapped, provided too much is not expected from their efforts.

Fourth, *environmental goals*. The full extent of the 'environmental revolution' has still to be appreciated or assimilated into public policy. It will require, and is gradually receiving, a new form of economics or social accounting, which will analyse and try to measure (however roughly) the necessary requirements of a sustainable society. Immediate requirements include effective conservation and control of energy resources, measures to reduce pollution and substantial efforts to reverse the degradation of soils and forests. Market incentives can and should be harnessed to these objectives, but they need the backing of basic standards of performance. The necessary initiatives and standards, together with a substantial programme of public works, again depend upon government initiatives. Additionally the protection of wildlife and of the few remaining areas of wilderness has become the most popular – although hardly the most fundamental – of environmental causes. The case for effective action here rests primarily not upon some static notion of ecological equilibrium but upon the speed and ruthlessness with which these natural resources are being irreversibly destroyed.

Fifth, *the equity principle*. The hardest task of all is to pursue these various objectives in an equitable manner. For example, short time horizons mean that environmental arguments and warnings are likely to be undervalued in both politics and the market; yet it is also true that some environmental fundamentalists and single-issue advocates bother too little about the extent and particularly the distribution of the immediate costs. The problem of equity is that a great variety of policy decisions, taken separately and in different forums, produce a total distribution of costs and benefits which may be far from equitable. It would be utopian to suppose that an adequate accounting of these effects is possible, since many of them are qualitative rather than quantitative and incapable of adequate expression even in notional monetary terms (Self, 1975); but a further use of social accounting (including the use of social indicators) would still be helpful. In the end, however, the best guarantees of equity are that taxation should be clearly progressive, social security should be clearly redistributive, social services should be generally allocated according to criteria of need, and the costs of environmental measures (for example, higher petrol prices) should be modified to protect the poor and those most adversely affected, such as the inhabitants of remote rural areas.

This brief account of a desirable political agenda stops short of any theoretical or programmatic synthesis of its various elements. That large task cannot be attempted here. However these pragmatic considerations may at least have the merit of widening political discourse beyond the narrow paradigm of economic rationalism. The appeal of 'economic rationalism' has lain partly in the apparent simplicity of its ruling criteria in contrast to the greater complexity of 'piecemeal social engineering', but the simplification excludes too much that is important in the life of the community. The return to a more complex view of the purposes of government action may be intrinsically incapable of finding any fully adequate theoretical base, but at least the conditions for the construction of a new paradigm can be explored.

The construction of a new paradigm

How does a new paradigm of the role of public policy get established? Here we can draw some lessons from the earlier dissemination of Keynesian ideas which also help to explain the success of the current ideology. Of course Keynesianism represented only one part of the post-1945 political consensus, being supported by the parallel concept of the welfare state. Moreover Keynesian policies were actually quite limited, concentrating upon the manipulation of effective demand to sustain full employment by mainly fiscal means. Still the widespread (but far from complete) influence of Keynesianism in the post-war world offers valuable clues as to the way in which a new paradigm might be designed and diffused.

In *The Political Power of Economic Ideas*, Peter Hall offers four explanations of why Keynesianism was adopted in many countries, but not in others such as Germany and Japan (Hall, 1989, pp. 361–92). The most important factor from this analysis was the appeal of Keynesianism to the ruling party. Left-wing parties representing rank-and-file workers eagerly seized upon a recipe which offered full employment. Right-wing parties were more cautious, although in the post-war conditions of rising prosperity some saw Keynesianism (as did Keynes himself) as a necessary device for 'saving capitalism' with the support of a contented labour force. In a similar way the now dominant ideology appeals to parties which represent capitalist interests. The ability of the current doctrines to win a wider degree of grudging acceptance rests upon their supposed demonstration that, under the conditions of an integrated world economy, there is no feasible alternative to the liberation and encouragement of market forces.

The second factor concerned the ability of Keynesianism to permeate the public service and the central institutions of economic management. Where economic management was already highly centralised as in Britain, Keynesianism had an easy ride once the top officials in the Treasury were converted. Where a key role in economic management was performed by an independent and powerful central bank as in Germany, Keynesianism was effectively resisted. The current ideology has won success by the same route of converting top financial officials, most remarkably in Australia and New Zealand. Its exponents also stress the value to a nation of an independent national bank dedicated to 'sound money', such as the German Bundesbank. The dedication of the Bundesbank to a close control of inflation, regardless of the existence of widespread unemployment and economic depression in European countries, produced financial dislocation and conflict in Europe in 1992 and seriously threatened the implementation of the Maastricht Treaty. This is a contradiction that the current ideology could only circumvent through compelling all countries to pursue the same monetary policy, regardless of other considerations.

Thirdly Keynesianism was successful where it could be fitted into the current political discourse of a society, often in different ways. For example, in Britain Keynesianism was politically acceptable as an alternative to the theoretical belief of socialists in comprehensive state planning, whereas in the USA it endorsed the Democrats' stronger disposition than the Republicans towards welfare spending. Similarly the current ideology, in Britain and Australia for example, has been able to build strongly upon the perception that the main obstacle to economic growth is the restrictive practices of trade unions. This thesis has the political asset of building on the frustrations of skilled workers whose earnings were held back by the 'social contracts' agreed between government and unions in Britain in the 1970s and Australia in the 1980s; and by the fact that the most obvious source of disruption to the public comes from union or 'wildcat' strikes.

The fourth factor which aided the spread of Keynesianism was World War Two which among the victorious nations (especially Britain) gave a new respectability and plausibility to the ability of government to manage the economy efficiently and equitably. The same conclusions were not drawn in Germany and Japan. Because another disaster would threaten the elaborate card house of the international capitalist economy, its defenders are keen to play down the significance of environmental 'threats' or social tensions such as the American race riots, and to use a 'bush fire' approach for stamping out localised conflicts which might threaten the existing order.

Clearly a successful new paradigm will need to draw upon the same sources of support as these previous examples. It will have to provide the intellectual basis for a governing political coalition, which can bring together interests concerned about unemployment, social welfare, environmentalism, ethnic and sexual discrimination and the life of local communities. The fact that these interests are diverse points to the need for a new paradigm of resource management and social equity. The rising proportion of low-paid jobs in all developed societies offers a strong economic basis for a new coalition. The future paradigm will need to restore the role of macro-economic management upon a broader basis than the present narrow concentration upon monetary stability by forging institutions better capable of integrating economic, welfare and environmental goals. Central banking institutions will have to be harnessed to this task. The elements of a new political discourse have already been suggested.

Finally, on a realistic view, an environmental or other major disaster seems all too probable sooner of later in the modern world. Its shock effects might compel attention to environmental constraints and reintroduce more priority for basic human needs, but the methods would more likely be authoritarian than democratic. The tensions of unemployment, poverty and personal insecurity consequent upon any further breakdown of the world economic order will increase the risk of the re-emergence of authoritarian and racist governments. The best chance of democratic solutions to these problems lies in the hope that deteriorating conditions will alert the public sooner to the need for new policy initiatives.

Reforming the market system

The biggest obstacle to change is the entrenched nature of the international economic system. Capitalism has become truly global in its reach and character. In place of the earlier balance in most countries between international and domestic fractions of capital, the former element has become dominant in the shape of multinational conglomerates and of interlinked banking and money markets. As a consequence free trade has become the ark of the covenant of modern market ideology and has been spread so successfully that the many departures from it are almost universally condemned as irrational. Thus any balanced treatment of free trade which, as Chapter 7 suggested, recognises its potential benefits to consumers but also its often damaging side-effects, becomes submerged under a dogma which reinforces a particular economic order.

The limits to national action

This international system creates, in terms of public choice methodology, a series of 'Prisoner's Dilemmas' over the adoption of socially beneficial policies. For example, the adoption of more effective anti-pollution laws is hobbled by the considerations that nations (and cities within nations) are competing for a limited supply of industrial investment and jobs, and any extra costs to local industries may discourage their growth or cause their departure.

More broadly the ability of a national government to improve social welfare or to harness its idle resources to long-term forms of investment is checked by the likely repercussions on the international money market. If a nation will not comply with financial orthodoxy or give complete priority to restoring 'market confidence', its foreign exchange rate will soon deteriorate. The one instrument still available to national governments for preventing this outcome – namely an increase in interest rates – also has adverse effects upon employment and investment. Thus national governments become more influenced by the fear of an adverse credit rating from Moody's than by the spectacle of unemployment and wasted resources.

It may be suggested that the economic success of Germany and Japan, two countries who never followed Keynesian prescriptions, shows the effectiveness of supply-side economics and close monetary discipline. However the success of these countries came through a substantial surplus of exports and it is obvious enough that this policy recipe cannot be universally applied. Exporting is a zero-sum game unless backed by an international system of macro-economic management which maintains trade equilibrium and a rising distribution of effective demand across countries. The case of the central bank which maintains monetary discipline in one country at the expense of depressed economies elsewhere is in the same category of Prisoner's Dilemmas. The idea that financial discipline by national governments will restore a satisfactory equilibrium to world markets suffers from the basic flaw of all market equilibrium theories: they do not tell us when or how the desired equilibrium will come about or what will be the costs along the way. In the long run we are all dead.

International co-operation

Since it is almost impossible for any national government (even a big one) to act independently, a natural reaction is the formation of regional economic *blocs*. The initial motivation is usually the promotion of free trade within the region, as in the European Community's objective of a single market and the free trade agreements between the USA, Canada and Mexico. This policy represents not only an extension of free trade, which will work more smoothly when the nations in question have a similar common culture and level of development, but also enables the new bloc to control and regulate its economic relationships with the rest of the world to an extent impossible for a single nation.

However the possible advantages of a strong regional organisation or confederation (as the EC might already be described) extend beyond trade. A super-government has a much stronger capacity to pursue social and environmental objectives, if its members agree, and to control the operations of transnationals and money markets. Political power is raised closer to the level of economic power. The intention of the Maastricht Treaty was to strengthen European environmental and social legislation, although the British Government in particular wants to restrict European union as closely as possible to the free market goal. Despite such conflicts the opportunity to pursue collective interests exists for any like-minded group of nations.

The economic power of a super-government such as the EC can weaken the position of small nations, especially poor ones. They may have the option of running for cover into their own economic bloc, but this alliance may still be weak, unstable and poor. The gross inequalities between nations can only be tackled by measures to stabilise the prices of primary commodities and otherwise improve the terms of trade for poor countries, to write off third world debt, and to provide technical and financial assistance suited to the actual needs and aspirations of the masses in those countries. However an enlightened European Community or similar body could do all these things more efficiently and humanely than the present set of international economic institutions, and need not be an obstacle to the eventual reform of those institutions.

The creation of a super-government such as the EC is bound to produce some drawbacks of democratic remoteness. One suggested solution has been the creation of a 'Europe of the regions' whereby national governments will gradually fade away and be replaced by smaller regional ones based upon historical territories such as Wales, Brittany, Tuscany or Catalonia. This vision, however appealing, is remote politically. A more feasible approach is to rehabilitate the importance of elected regional and local governments which can bring democratic choice and the control of service delivery closer to the people. This goal would be helped by a super-government strong enough to increase the stability of the economic base of local communities. The EC has offered increasing aid for regional development, although within a framework of accepting the centripetal pull of market forces; and it is also trying to promote democracy at the regional level.

Reforming market institutions

No civilised society can dispense with a market system. Nothing in this book is meant to deny that competitive markets can offer the benefits of allocative efficiency and consumers' choice. These are the virtues celebrated by market theory. However that theory takes little or no account of inequalities of bargaining power or the actual institutions and structures through which markets operate.

Yet there is nothing immutable about the market system which renders it incapable of reform. Some modest possible reforms should appeal to market theorists themselves. For example, changes in the taxation system could make directors more responsible to their shareholders and curb the purely speculative aspects of takeover bids. A switch from corporate to personal taxation would prevent companies from hoarding resources at the disposal of their management; and a denial of tax relief on borrowing to finance takeovers would tend to confine such activities to cases of genuine gains in efficiency (Kent, 1989, pp. 95–112). Stronger measures could be taken to control the growth of monopoly power, especially in such sectors as the media. Other measures to protect the weaker players in the market game and to strengthen the rights of both shareholders and consumers would be practicable.

More fundamental reforms would seek to democratise the market system. A favourite candidate here is the legislative promotion of share partnership schemes or more basically of workers' co-operatives. Such arrangements would distribute the fruits of economic growth more equitably, although they would not of themselves overcome market tendencies to instability or inequality. Dahl (1985) stresses that the economic success of big corporations is based upon social contributions of education and research, not just entrepreneurship. Hence their boards should include politically appointed representatives of the general public.

Other reforms would require the renewal of a positive role for government. A fundamental switch would be to replace the dominant goal of market growth with the broader aims of enhancing the quality of life and sharing the fruits and sacrifices of this policy equitably. Governments would need to engage strong constraints and incentives to steer the market in this direction, while supplementing the market's role with such measures as research and demonstration projects in energy conservation and public investment in low-income housing, environmental improvements and regional development. The vital goal of full employment would be addressed by these means as well as through labour market policies of retraining and financial support for some long-term projects. A likely consequence is that society would have to accept a flexible statutory system of income restraint. Competitive markets would have a more limited but still substantial role in such a society.

Some of these ideas form the basis of new theories of 'market socialism' (Miller, 1989). In the present economic climate they may look somewhat utopian, but they at least suggest alternatives to the policy of simply acquiescing in the directions of the market system as it currently operates.

Empowering democratic government

There are signs that the political tide of the last two decades is beginning to turn. The election of President Clinton, backed by Democratic majorities in Congress, heralds some change of direction in American policies. In Britain the Conservative Government of John Major has been heavily discredited and nearly lost parliamentary support as a consequence of its mishandling of the coal industry and European monetary union. In New Zealand the electorate has voted strongly for proportional representation out of disgust with the harsh economic and social policies imposed against popular opinion by successive Labour and National governments. In Australia the belated drift towards Thatcherite policies is being strongly contested. In Canada there is much disquiet that the policies of the Mulroney Conservative Government, especially the free trade agreement with America, will undermine Canada's distinctive social policies and institutions.

A book such as this cannot rely upon current political events which change swiftly. All the same it does seem likely that the political concerns of the next decade will be appreciably different from both the pro-market, anti-state emphasis of recent history and the Keynesian and welfare policies of the previous period. In history there can be no more than a partial turning back of the clock. Equally some part of the recent political initiatives will remain and be preserved.

Democratic government has suffered a loss of both legitimacy and effectiveness, because of its failures to meet social aspirations at all adequately and the spread of critical opinions about its capacity to do so. However the public has not been fully persuaded to accept a public choice verdict of 'diminished responsibility'. Government still seems to be much needed to tackle the urgent 'collective action' problems of modern societies, and is expected to do so in acceptable democratic ways.

One declared goal of recent government policies has been to make public services more flexible and responsible to the wants of their clients. Future policies will need to accept this goal but to implement it in a more effective and balanced manner. Decentralisation of authority to micro-institutions such as schools and hospitals brings benefits of local management and greater variety of provision, but can also degenerate (as earlier chapters showed) into state endorsement of what prove in practice to be oligarchic institutions with some resemblance to private clubs. The concept of 'empowering consumers' is taken from a market model which has some, but very limited, relevance to the administration of public services based upon criteria of equality and need. The decentralisation of public services, while a desirable goal, needs to be pursued within a local democratic framework and subject to safeguards over access to services.

The cold climate and financial stringency which has affected government in recent decades has also stimulated more innovatory and economical ways of tackling social problems. Many examples can be given from the USA of public 'entrepreneurship', based upon specific initiatives and a flexible use of available powers and finance (Osborne and Gaebler, 1992). City governments, faced with lack of funds for public development projects, now often enlist the support of the private sector, voluntary bodies and public opinion for achieving civic improvements or improving zones of urban blight. Such policies often tread an uneasy path between service to business interests and broader social goals, but community partnership and involvement is a welcome change from previous, more authoritarian methods. However local initiative on its own cannot be adequate (and is also less likely) in the many places with big problems and small resources.

Thus a much larger question is whether large public initiatives, such as characterised the Roosevelt or Kennedy years in the USA, are likely to be revived in America and elsewhere. Looking at the appalling physical and social state of many American cities, or at the pressing case for energy conservation and other environmental measures, the case for such initiatives would seem plain. They are held back, not just by financial stringency, but by the now conventional wisdom that it is no good 'throwing money' at social problems. This seems a strange conclusion for a nation which 'threw money' vigorously and effectively at putting a man on the moon and building a vast nuclear arsenal, and whose government is also ready to throw money at bailing out banks and bankrupt firms. However the argument goes that social problems reflect intractable features of character and ethnicity, and that anyhow the Federal government lacks the political muscle and means to implement its policies effectively; for example Pressman and Wildavsky's study of implementation (1973) was a typical product of disillusionment about government.

The ending of the cold war has presented the USA with a unique opportunity to redeploy substantial resources for a different kind of assault on the blight, poverty and crime that afflict so many of its cities. The large pools of urban unemployed could be offered training and support to help improve their own living conditions. The new repertoire of methods and techniques which governments are starting to engage suggests that the implementation of such a policy ought not to be dismissed as impracticable. This is only one major example of the public policy initiatives which may again come to be seen as necessary. If such ideas are to be practicable, public administration has to be rehabilitated as a profession after the ideological hammering of the last two decades. While lessons may be learned from the best business practice, administrative issues of equity, accountability, the reconciliation of diverse objectives, and the uses of coercion, discretion and inducement have no close parallels in the private sector. Government does need to attract the services of the 'best and brightest' if it is to cope well with its formidable tasks, as the Volcker Report (1990) recognised. Unfortunately, especially when compared with business administration, few resources have been put into creating professional schools of public administration in English-speaking countries, apart from some outstanding institutions in the USA, such as Harvard's Kennedy School. This fact alone suggests a lack of creative thought about public policy.

It is equally true that the best administrative institutions could achieve little without effective democratic support and supervision. There seems to be a widening gap between the range and number of the laws and their observance and implementation. Whatever the dictums of public choice, the 'regulatory state' continues to grow with steady accretions in environmental and health legislation, civil rights and equal opportunities, the control of monopoly and restraints of trade, administrative justice itself and other arenas. The growth of legislative and administrative regulation parallels that of collective action problems, as well as new pressures to protect individual rights, in increasingly complex societies. However legislators often imagine that their work is done when they have passed another law and neglect the question of how far it is being obeyed or implemented.

The need for simplifying and clarifying laws is plain enough but there are daunting problems of achieving compliance with them. The public administration 'problem' has been redefined as one of inducing or influencing desired patterns of social behaviour. This goal calls for skill and ingenuity over methods of implementation, and for a sensitivity to public opinion which does not degenerate into numerous concessions to powerful interests. The distinctive nature of public administration has to be recognised and the support of public opinion re-engaged. This is a task for politicians who are not so obsessed with the needs for control and accountability (important as these are) as to forget the requirements of effective and impartial administration.

Conclusion

Any measures to improve the performance of government will be fruitless without the reinvigoration of democracy itself. The points made in the last chapter need not be repeated. The basic need is to affirm the importance of and increase the opportunities for responsible citizenship, not just through voting but through active participation in parties, local governments and interest groups. Election rules need revision to achieve greater equity of representation, tighter control of election expenses (so as to reduce the advantages to wealth and the financial temptations to politicians) and increased opportunities to present political viewpoints, including minority ones, through the media. The political process should be as open and transparent as possible. Civics should be rediscovered in a more realistic but positive way.

These reforms are quite practicable, but it is a tough task to rescue politics from its opposite tendencies towards apathy or extremism. The capacity of democratic societies to take charge of their affairs and to find more effective and equitable answers to their urgent problems remains very doubtful; but, to take a phrase from a different context, there is no alternative way forward.

Bibliography

Abel-Smith, B., 'Social Welfare', in B. Pimlott (ed.), *Fabian Essays in Socialist Thought* (Heinemann, 1984)

Adams, J., *Transport Planning: Vision and Practice* (Routledge & Kegan Paul, 1981)

Adley, M., Patch, A. and Tweedie, J., *Parental Choice and Educational Policy* (Edinburgh University Press, 1990)

Allardt, E., 'The Civic Conception of the Welfare State in Scandinavia', in R. Rose and R. Shiratori (eds), *The Welfare State East and West* (Oxford University Press, 1986)

Almond, G. A., *A Discipline Divided: Schools and Sects in Political Science* (Sage, 1990)

Arrow, K. J., *Social Choice and Individual Values* (John Wiley, rev. edn. 1963)

Arrow, K. J., 'Values and Collective Decision Making', in P. Laslett and W. G. Runciman (eds), *Philosophy, Politics and Society*, vol. 3 (Blackwell, 1967)

Arterton, F. E., *Teledemocracy: Can Technology Protect Democracy?* (Sage, 1987)

Ascher, K., *The Politics of Privatisation: Contracting out Public Services* (Macmillan, 1987)

Ashford, D. E., *The Emergence of the Welfare States* (Blackwell, 1986)

Axelrod, R., *The Evolution of Co-operation* (Basic Books, 1984)

Bacon, R. W. and Eltis, W. A., *Britain's Economic Problem: Too Few Producers* (Macmillan, 1976)

Baehr, P. R., 'The Netherlands Scientific Council for Public Policy', in B. Wittrock and P. R. Baehr (eds), *Policy Analysis and Policy Innovation* (Sage, 1981)

Baldwin, P., *The Politics of Social Solidarity: Class Bases of the European Welfare State 1875–1975* (Cambridge University Press, 1990)

Baldwin, R., 'Privatisation and Regulation: the case of British Airways', in J. Richardson, (ed.) *Privatisation and Deregulation in Canada and Britain* (Dartmouth, 1990)

Barr, N., *The Economics of the Welfare State* (Weidenfeld and Nicolson, 1987)

Barry, B., 'Political Ideas of Some Economists', in L. Lindberg and C. Maier (eds), *The Politics of Inflation and Economic Stagnation* (Brookings Institute, 1985)

Barry, N. P., *The New Right* (Croom Helm, 1987)

Batley, R., 'London Docklands: an analysis of power relations between UDC's and Local Government', *Public Administration*, 67:2, 167–89 (1989)

Bendick, M. Jr., 'Privatizing the Delivery of Social Welfare services: an idea to be taken seriously', in S. B. Kammerman and A. J. Kahn (eds), *Privatization and the Welfare State* (Princeton University Press, 1989)

Benjamin, R. W., 'Local Government in Post-industrial Britain: studies of the British Royal Commission on Local Government', in V. Ostrom and F. P. Bish (eds), *Comparing Urban Service Delivery Systems* (Sage, 1977)

Bentley, A. F., *The Process of Government* (reprinted, Indiana University Press, 1949)

Berle, A. and Means, G., *The Modern Corporation and Private Property* (Macmillan, 1932; revised edition, Harcourt, Brace & World, 1968)

Berlin, Sir I., 'Two Concepts of Liberty', in Berlin, Sir I., *Four Essays on Liberty* (Oxford University Press, 1969)

Black, D., *The Theory of Committees and Elections* (Cambridge University Press, 1958)

Blaug, M., 'Education Vouchers - it all depends what you mean', in J. Le Grand and R. Robinson (eds), *Privatisation and the Welfare State* (Allen & Unwin, 1984)

Blendon, R. J., and Taylor, H., 'Views on health care: public opinion in three nations', *Health Affairs*, 103–18, Spring (1989)

Borins, S. F., 'Public choice: "Yes, Minister" made it popular, but does winning the Nobel prize make it true?', *Canadian Public Administration*, 31: 1 12–26 (1988)

Boston, J.,'Chief Executives and the Senior Executive Service' in J. Boston *et al.* (ed.) *Reshaping the State: New Zealand's Bureaucratic Revolution* (Oxford University Press, 1991)

Boston, J., 'Reorganizing the Machinery of Government: Objectives and Outcomes' in Ibid. (1991)

Boston, J., Martin, J., Pallot, J. and Walsh, P., *Reshaping the State: New Zealand's Bureaucratic Revolution* (Oxford University Press, 1991)

Boudon, R., *The Analysis of Ideology* (Polity Press, 1989)

Braithwaite, V., Braithwaite, J. L., Gibson, D. and Makkai, T., *Regulatory Styles and Compliance in the Australian Nursing Home Industry* (Governability Program Working Paper No.5, Research School of Social Sciences, Australian National University, 1992)

Brandt Commission, *North-South: A Programme for Survival* (Pan, 1980)

Braybrooke, D., *Meeting Needs* (Princeton University Press, 1987)

Brennan, G. and Buchanan, J. M., *The Power to Tax: Analytical Foundations of a Fiscal Constitution* (Cambridge University Press, 1980)

Brennan, G. and Buchanan, J. M., *The Reason of Rules: Constitutional Political Economy* (Cambridge University Press, 1985)

Brennan, G. and Walsh, C., *Rationality, Individualism and Public Policy* (Centre for Research on Federal Financial Relations, Australian National University, 1990)

Breton, A., *The Economic Theory of Representative Government* (Aldine, 1974)

Breton, A. and Wintobe, R., 'The equilibrium size of a budget maximising bureau', *Journal of Political Economy*, 83, 197–207 (1975)

Bridge, G., 'Citizen Choice in Public Services: voucher systems', in E. S. Savas (ed.), *Alternatives for Delivering Public Services* (Westview Press, 1977)

Brindley, T., Rybin, Y. and Stoker, G., *Remaking Planning: The Politics of Urban Change in the Thatcher Years* (Unwin Hyman, 1989)

Brittan, S., 'The politics and economics of privatisation', *Political Quarterly*, 55: 2, 109–28 (1984)

Brown, M. C., *National Health Insurance in Canada and Australia* (Health Economics Research Unit, Australian National University, 1983)

Brown, M. K., (ed.) *Remaking the Welfare State* (Temple University Press, 1988)

Buchanan, J. M., *The Inconsistencies of the National Health Service* (Institute of Economic Affairs, 1965)

Buchanan, J. M., *Liberty, Market and State* (Wheatsheaf, 1986)

Buchanan, J. M., 'Post-Reagan Political Economy', in *Reaganomics and After* (Institue of Economic Affairs, 1989)

Buchanan, J. M. and Wagner, R. E., *Democracy in Deficit* (Academic Press, 1977)

Buchanan, J. and Tullock, G., *The Calculus of Consent* (Ann Arbor, University of Michigan Press, 1962)

Butler, S. M. (ed.), *Agenda for Empowerment* (The Heritage Foundation, 1990)

Cameron, D. R., 'Does Government Cause Inflation? Taxes, spending and deficits', in L. Lindberg and C. Maier (eds), *The Politics of Inflation and Economic Stagnation* (Brookings Institute, 1985)

Castles, F. G., *The Social Democratic Image of Society* (Routledge & Kegan Paul, 1978)

Castles, F. G., *The Working Class and Welfare* (Allen & Unwin, 1985)

Castles, F. G. and Dowrick, S., 'The impact of government spending levels on medium term economic growth in the OECD, 1960–1985', *Journal of Theoretical Politics*, 2:2, 173–204 (1990)

Castles, I., 'Living standards in Sydney and Japanese cities: a comparison', in K. Sheridan (ed.), *The Australian Economy in the Japanese Mirror* (Queensland University Press, 1992)

Chapman, B. J. and Chia, T. T., *Financing Higher Education* (Australian National University, Centre for Economic Policy Research, Discussion Paper 213, 1989)

Chubb, J. E. and Moe, T., 'Politics, markets and the organization of schools', *American Political Science Review*, 82 1065–87 (1988)

Clarke, Sir R., *New Trends in Government* (HMSO, 1971)

Connolly, W. E., *Appearance and Reality in Politics* (Cambridge University Press, 1981)

Cook, B. J. and Wood, B. D., 'Principal–agent models of political control of bureaucracy', *American Political Science Review* 83: 3, 965–78, (1989)

Crain, M. and Tollison, R., 'Campaign expenditure and political competition', *Journal of Law and Economics*, 19, 177–88 (1976)

Crain, W. H. and Tollison, R. D., *Predicting Politics: Essays in Empirical Public Choice* (Ann Arbor: University of Michigan Press, 1990)

Crouch, C., 'Conditions for Trade Union Wage Restraint', in L. Lindberg and C. Maier (eds), *The Politics of Inflation and Economic Stagnation* (Brookings Institute, 1985)

Crouch, C. and Dore, R. (eds), *Corporatism and Accountability: Organised Interests in British Public Life* (Oxford University Press, 1990)

Crozier, M., *The Bureaucratic Phenomenon* (University of Chicago Press, 1964)

Dahl, R. A., *A Preface to Economic Democracy* (University of California Press, 1985)

Dalfen, C. M., 'The Case of Teleglobe Canada', in J. Richardson (ed.), *Privatisation and Deregulation in Canada and Britain* (Dartmouth, 1990)

Davies, S., 'Beveridge Revisited: new foundations for tomorrow's welfare', in R. Haas and O. Knox (eds), *Policies of Thatcherism* (Centre for Policy Studies, 1991)

Day, P., 'Residential and nursing homes for the elderly', *Political Quarterly*, 59:1 44–55 (1988)

Day, P. and Klein, R., 'The politics of modernization: Britain's NHS in the 1980s', *The Milbank Quarterly*, 67:1 1–34 (1989)

Deakin, N., *The Politics of Welfare* (Methuen, 1987)

Department of the Environment, *Paying for Local Government* (HMSO, 1986)

Department of Education and Science, *The National Curriculum, Five to Sixteen, a Consultation Document* (HMSO, 1987)

Department of Health, *Working for Patients*, Cmnd 555 (HMSO, 1989)

Derthick, M. and Quirk, P. J., *The Politics of Deregulation* (Brookings Institute, 1985)

De Swaan, A. and Mokken, R. J., 'Testing Coalition Theories', in L. Lewis and E. Vedung (eds), *Politics as Rational Action* (D. Reichel, 1980)

Donahue, J. D., *The Privatization Decision* (Basic Books, 1989)

Donnison, D., 'The Progressive Potential of Privatisation', in J. Le Grand and R. Robinson (eds), *Privatisation and the Welfare State* (Allen & Unwin, 1984)

Dore, R., *Japan at Work* (OECD, 1989)

Dowding, K. H., *Rational Choice and Political Power* (Edward Elgar, 1991)

Downs, A., *An Economic Theory of Democracy* (Harper & Row, 1957)

Downs, A., *Inside Bureaucracy* (Little, Brown, 1967)

Dunleavy, P., *The Politics of Mass Housing in Britain 1945–75* (Oxford University Press, 1981)

Dunleavy, P., 'The growth of sectoral cleavages and the stabilisation of state expenditure', *Society and Space*, 42, 129–44 (1986)

Dunleavy, P., *Democracy, Bureaucracy and Public Choice* (Harvester Wheatsheaf, 1991)

Dunsire, A. and Hood, C., *Cutback Management in Public Bureaucracies* (Cambridge University Press, 1989)

Dye, T. R., *American Federalism: Competition among Governments* (Lexington Books, 1990)

Dye, T. R., *Understanding Public Policy* (Prentice Hall, 1972)

Easton, D., *The Political System* (Knopf, 1953)

Eckstein, H., *Division and Cohesion in Democracy: A Study of Norway* (Princeton University Press, 1973)

Efficiency Unit, U.K. Government, *Improving Management in Government: The Next Steps* (HMSO, 1988)

Elster, J., 'Further thoughts on Marxism, Functionalism and Game Theory, in J. Roemer (ed.), *Analytical Marxism* (Cambridge University Press, 1982)

Elster, J., *Making Sense of Marx* (Cambridge University Press, 1985)

Elster, J. (ed.), *The Multiple Self* (Cambridge University Press, 1986)

Enthoven, A. C., 'Internal market reform of the British health service', *Health Affairs*, 10. 3, 60–70 (1991)

Esping-Andersen, G., *The Three Worlds of Welfare Capitalism* (Polity Press, 1990)

Etzioni, A., *A Comparative Analysis of Complex Organisations* (Macmillan, 1961)

Etzioni, A., *The Moral Dimension: Toward a New Economics* (The Free Press, 1988)

Etzioni-Halevy, E., *Bureaucracy and Democracy* (Routledge & Kegan Paul, 1983)

Fainstein, S. S., 'The Changing World Economy and Urban Restructuring', in D. Judd and M. Parkinson, (eds), *Leadership and Urban Regeneration* (Sage, 1990)

Feigenbaum, H. B. and Henig, J. R., 'The political underpinnings of privatization: a typology' (Department of Political Science, George Washington University, 1992)

Fesler, J., 'The State and its study: the whole and the parts', in N. B. Lynn and A. Wildavsky, (eds), *Public Administration: The State of the Discipline* (Chatham House, 1990)

Fisk, D., Kiesling, H. and Muller, T., *Private Provision of Public Services: An Overview* (The Urban Institute, 1978)

Frey, B. S., *Democratic Economic Policy* (St. Martin's Press, 1983)

Friedman, M. and Friedman, R., *Free to Choose* (Macmillan, 1980)

Galbraith, J. K., *American Capitalism: the Concept of Countervailing Power* (Hamilton, 1957)

Galbraith, J. K., *The Affluent Society* (Penguin Books, 1978)

Galbraith, J. K., *The Culture of Contentment* (Houghton Mifflin, 1992)

Gamble, A., *The Free Economy and the Strong State* (Macmillan, 1988)

Gerth, H. H. and Mills, C. W., *From Max Weber: Essays in Sociology* (Kegan Paul, Trench, Trubner, 1948) pp. 77–128

Gilbert, N., *Capitalism and the Welfare State: Dilemmas of Social Benevolence* (Yale University Press, 1983)

Glazer, N., *The Limits of Social Policy* (Harvard University Press, 1988)

Goldthorpe, J. H., Lockwood, D., Bechhofer, F. and Platt, S. *The Affluent Worker: Industrial Attitudes and Behaviour* (Cambridge University Press, 1968)

Goodin, R. E. and Dryzek, J., 'Risk Sharing and Social Justice' in Goodwin, R. E. and Le Grand, J. (eds), *Not Only the Poor* (Allen & Unwin, 1987)

Goodin, R. E. and Le Grand, J. (eds), *Not Only the Poor* (Allen & Unwin, 1987)

Gottschalk, P., 'The Reagan Retrenchment in Historical Context', in M. K. Brown (ed.), *Remaking the Welfare State* (Temple University Press, 1988)

Grant, G. P., *Technology and Empire* (House of Anansi, 1969)

Gray, A., Jenkins, B., with Flynn, A. and Rutherford, B. 'The management of change in Whitehall: the experience of the FMI'', *Public Administration*, 69: 1, 41–59 (1991)

Green, D. G., *The New Right* (Brighton, Sussex: Wheatsheaf, 1987)

Green, T. H., 'Lectures on the Principles of Political Obligation', in R. Nettleship (ed.), *Collected Works of T. H. Green*, vol. 2 (Longmans Green, 1890)

Grodzins, M., 'The Federal System', in *Goals for Americans, Report of the President's Commission on National Goals* (Columbia University Press, 1960)

Gurin, A., 'Government Responsibility and Privatization', in S. B. Kammerman and A. J. Kahn (eds), *Privatization and the Welfare State* (Princeton University Press, 1989)

Haas, R. and Knox, C. (eds), *Policies of Thatcherism* (Centre for Policy Studies and University Press of America, 1991)

Hall, P., *Great Planning Disasters* (Weidenfeld & Nicholson, 1980)

Hall, P. G. (ed.), *The Political Power of Economic Ideas: Keynesianism across Nations* (Princeton Univerity Press, 1989)

Hanson, R. L., 'The Expansion and Contraction of the American Welfare State', in R. E. Goodin and J. Le Grand (eds), *Not Only the Poor* (Allen & Unwin, 1987)

Hardin, G., 'The tragedy of the commons', *Science*, 162: 3859 1243–8, (1968)

Harrington, M., *Socialism Past and Future* (Arcade Publishing, 1989)

Harrison, A. and Gretton, J. (eds), *Reshaping Central Government* (Policy Journals, 1987)

Hayek, F. A., *The Road to Serfdom* (Routledge & Kegan Paul, 1944)

Hayek, F. A., *The Constitution of Liberty* (Routledge & Kegan Paul, 1960)

Heath, A, Jowell, R. and Curtice, J., *How Britain Votes* (Pergamon, 1985)

Heclo, H. A., *A Government of Strangers: Executive Politics in Washington* (Brookings Institute, 1977)

Hede, A., 'The next step's initiative for civil service reform in Britain', *Canberra Bulletin of Public Administration*, 65, 32–40 (1991)

Heilbroner, R., *The Nature and Logic of Capitalism* (W. W. Norton, 1985)

Henig, J. H., Hamnett, C. and Feigenbaum, H. B., 'The politics of privatization: a comparative perspective', *Governance*, 1: 4, 442–68, (1988)

Hennessy, P., 'Prime Minister and Cabinet', in K. Minogue and M. Biddis (eds), *Thatcherism* (Macmillan, 1987)

Hennessy, P., *Whitehall* (Secker & Warburg, 1989)

Hirsch, F., *Social Limits to Growth* (Harvard University Press, 1976)

Hirschman, A., *Exit, Voice and Loyalty* (Harvard University Press, 1970)

Hirschman, A., *Shifting Involvements* (Princeton University Press, 1982)

Hollingsworth, J. R., Hage, J. and Hanneman, R. A., *State Intervention in Medical Care: Consequences for Britain, France, Sweden and the U.S., 1890–1970* (Cornell University Press, 1990)

Hollis, M. and Nell, E. J., *Rational Economic Man* (Cambridge University Press, 1975)

Hood, C., 'A Public Management for all Seasons?' *Public Administration*, 69:1, 21–39 (1991)

Hood, C., 'A Catastrophe for Government Growth Theory?', *Journal of Theoretical Politics* 3: 1, 37–63 (1991b)

Hoover, K and Plant, R., *Conservative Capitalism in Britain and the United States* (Routledge, 1989)

Jackson, P. M., *The Political Economy of Bureaucracy* (Philip Allan, 1982)

Joseph Rowntree Foundation, *Inquiry into British Housing*, 2nd report 1991

Joseph, Sir K. and Sumption, A., *Equality* (Murray, 1979)

Judd, D. and Parkinson, M., 'Urban Leadership and Regeneration', in D. Judd and M. Parkinson (eds), *Leadership and Urban Regeneration* (Sage, 1990)

Judge, K. and Knapp, M., 'Efficiency in the Production of Welfare: the public and the private sectors compared', in R. Klein and M. O'Higgins (eds), *The Future of Welfare* (Blackwell, 1985)

Kammerman, D. R., 'Does Government Cause Inflation? Taxes, spending and deficits', in L. Lindberg and C. Maier (eds), *The Politics of Inflation and Economic Stagnation* (Brookings Institute, 1985)

Kammerman, S. B. and Kahn, A. J. (eds), *Privatization and the Welfare State* (Princeton University Press, 1989a)

Kammerman, S. B. and Kahn, A. J., 'Childcare and privatization', in S. B. Kammerman and A. J. Kahn (eds), *Privatization and the Welfare State* (Princeton University Press, 1989b)

Kavanagh, D., *Thatcherism and British Politics: The End of Consensus* (Oxford University Press, 1987)

Kay, J. and Thompson, P.J., 'Privatisation, a policy in search of a rationale', *Economic Journal*, 96, 18–32 (1986)

Kent, T., *Getting Ready for 1990: Ideas for Canada's Politics and Government* (Institute for Research in Public Policy, 1989)

Kernell, S., *Going Public: New Strategies of Presidential Leadership* (Congressional Quarterly Inc., 1986)

Keynes, J.M., *The General Theory of Employment, Interest and Money* (Macmillan, 1936)

Kiewiet, D.R., *Macro-Economics and Micro-Politics* (University of Chicago Press, 1983)

King, D.S., *The New Right: Politics, Markets and Citizenship* (Macmillan, 1987)

Klein, R., 'Public expenditure in an inflationary world', in L. Lindberg and C. Maier (eds), *The Politics of Inflation and Economic Stagnation* (Brookings Institute, 1985)

Klein, R., *The Politics of the NHS*, 2nd edn. (Longmans, 1989)

Klein, R. and O'Higgins, M., (eds), *The Future of Welfare* (Blackwell, 1985)

Klein, R., 'The Political Price of Successful Cost Containment: the case of Britain's National Health Service', in *Health Care in the Nineties* (Blue Cross of California, 1991)

Lane, J.E. (ed.), *Bureaucracy and Public Choice* (Sage, 1987)

Lane, R., 'Market justice, political justice', *American Political Science Review*, 82, 383–402, (1986)

Lane, R., *The Market Experience* (Cambridge University Press, 1991)

Laver, M., *The Politics of Private Desires* (Penguin,1981)

Laver, M. and Schofield, N., *Multiparty Government* (Oxford University Press, 1990)

Leach, S., 'Strengthening Local Democracy? The Government's response to Widdicombe', in J. Stewart and G. Stoker (eds), *The Future of Local Government* (Macmillan, 1989)

Le Grand, J., *The Strategy of Equality* (Allen & Unwin, 1982)

Le Grand, J. and Robinson, R. (eds), *Privatisation and the Welfare State* (Allen & Unwin, 1984)

Le Grand J. and Winter, D., 'The Middle Classes and the Defence of the Welfare State', in R.E. Goodin and J. Le Grand (eds), *Not Only the Poor* (Allen & Unwin, 1987)

Letwin, O., *Privatising the World* (Cassell, 1988)

Levine, M., *The History and Politics of Community Mental Health* (Oxford University Press 1985)

Lewin, L., *Self-Interest and Public Interest in Western Politics* (Oxford University Press, 1991)

Lieberman, M., *Privatization and Educational Choice* (St. Martin's Press, 1989)

Lindberg, L. and Maier, C. (eds), *The Politics of Inflation and Economic Stagnation* (Brookings Institute, 1985)

Lindblom, C. E., *Politics and Markets* (Basic Books, 1977)

Lipsky, M. and Rathgeb-Smith, S., *Government Provision of Social Services through Non-profit Organisations* (Urban Research Program Working Paper no.21, Australian National University, 1990)

Locke, J., *The Second Treatise of Government*, ed. J.W. Gough (Blackwell,1946)

MacPherson, C. B., *The Political Theory of Possessive Individualism* (Oxford University Press, 1962)

MacRae, D. C., 'A political model of the business cycle', *Journal of Political Economy*, 85, 239–63, (1977)

March, J.G. and Olsen, J. P., 'The new institutionalism: organizational factors in political life', *American Political Science Review*, 78, 734–49, (1984)

Margolis, H., *Selfishness, Altruism and Rationality* (Cambridge University Press, 1982)

Marsh, I., *Globalisation and Australian Think Tanks* (Committee for Economic Development of Australia, 1991)

Marshall, T. H., 'Citizenship and Social Class', in T. H. Marshall, *Sociology at the Crossroads* (Heinemann, 1963)

Mayhew, D. R., *Congress: the Electoral Connection* (Yale University Press, 1974)

Maynard, A., *Whither the National Health Service?* (University of York, Centre for Health Economics, March 1989)

McAllister, J. and Studlar, D. T., 'Popular v. elite views of privatisation', *Journal of Public Policy*, 9: 2, 157–78 (1989)

McConnell, G., *Private Power and American Democracy* (A. A. Knopf, 1966)

McLean, I., *Public Choice: An Introduction* (Blackwell, 1987)

Miller, D., *Market, State and Community* (Clarendon, 1989)

Millet, J. D., *Organization for the Public Service* (1966)

Minogue, K. and Biddis, M. (eds), *Thatcherism* (Macmillan, 1987)

Mishan, E. J., *The Costs of Economic Growth* (Penguin, 1969)

Mishan, E. J., *The Economic Growth Debate* (Allen & Unwin, 1977)

Mishra, R., *The Welfare State in Capitalist Society* (Toronto: University of Toronto Press, 1990)

Moe, T.M., *The Organization of Interests* (University of Chicago Press, 1980)

Moe, T. M., 'The new economics of organization', *American Journal of Political Science*, 28 739–75, (1984)

Mokken, R. J., 'Political Aspects of Economic Power: a critique of the market concept', in L. Lewin and E. Vedung (eds), *Politics as Rational Action* (D. Preiddel, 1980)

Mueller, D. C., *Public Choice* (Cambridge University Press, 1979. Rev edn, 1989)

Musgrave, A., *The Theory of Public Finance* (McGraw-Hill, 1959)

Nathan, R.P. and Doolittle, F.C., *Reagan and the States* (Princeton University Press, 1987)

National Audit Office, *Competitive Tendering* (HMSO, 1987)

Navarro, V., 'Welfare states and their distributive effects', *Political Quarterly*, 59:2, 219–35 (1988)

New Yorker, 'Memoirs of the Reagan Era', 16 January 1989, 71–94

Niskanen, W.A. Jr., *Bureaucracy and Representative Government* (Aldine-Atherton, 1971)

Nordhaus, W.D., 'The political business cycle', *Review of Economic Studies*, 42, 169–90 (1975)

N.Z. Treasury, *Government Management* (Government Printer, 1987)

O'Connor, J., *The Fiscal Crisis of the State* (St. Martin's Press, 1973)

O'Higgins, M., 'Social Welfare and Privatisation: the British experience', in S.B. Kammerman and A.J. Kahn (eds), *Privatization and the Welfare State* (Princeton University Press, 1989a)

Olson, M., *The Logic of Collective Action* (Harvard University Press, 1965)

Olson, M., *The Rise and Decline of Nations* (Yale University Press, 1982)

Osborne, D. and Gaebler, T., *Reinventing Government* (Addison Wesley, 1992)

Ostrom, V., *The Intellectual Crisis in American Public Administration* (University of Alabama Press, 1973)

Ostrom, V. (ed.), *The Meaning of American Federalism* (San Francisco: Institute for Contemporary Studies, 1991)

Ostrom, V. and Ostrom, E., 'Structure and performance', in V. Ostrom and F.P. Bish (eds), *Comparing Urban Service Delivery Systems* (Sage, 1976)

Ostrom, V. and Ostrom, E., 'Public Goods – Public Choices', in E.S. Savas (ed.), *Alternatives for Delivering Public Services* (Westview Press, 1977)

Ostrom, V., Tiebout, C.M. and Warren, R., 'The Organization of Government in Metropolitan Areas: a theoretical enquiry', in V. Ostrom (ed.), *The Meaning of American Federalism* (Institute for Contemporary Studies, 1991)

Perrow, C., 'Economic theories of organization', *Theory and Society*, 15, 11–45 (1986a)

Perrow, C., *Complex Organizations: A Critical Essay* (Random House, 1986b)

Peters, B.G., 'Administrative Change and the Grace Commission', in C.H. Levine (ed.) *The Unfinished Agenda for Civil Service Reform* (Brookings Institute, 1985)

Peters, B.G., 'Politicians and Bureaucrats', in J.E. Lane (ed.), *Bureaucracy and Public Choice* (Sage, 1987)

Peterson, P., *City Limits* (University of Chicago Press, 1981)

Peterson, P.G., *On Borrowed Time* (Institute for Contemporary Studies, 1988)

Pfiffner, J.P., *The Strategic Presidency* (Dorsey Press, 1988)

Pint, E. M., 'Nationalisation and privatisation: a rational choice perspective on efficiency', *Journal of Public Policy*, 10: 3., 267–98, (1990)

Pirie, M., *Micropolitics* (Wildwood House, 1988)

Piven, F. F. and Cloward, R. A., 'Popular Power and the Welfare State', in M. K. Brown (ed.) *Remaking the Welfare State* (Temple University Press, 1988)

Pizzorno, A., 'On the rationality of democratic choice', *Telos*, 63, 41–69, (1985)

Pliatzky, Sir L., *The Treasury under Mrs Thatcher* (Blackwell, 1989)

Political Quarterly: special issue, *Is Britain becoming Authoritarian?*, 60: 1, January, 1989)

Pressman, J. L. and Wildavsky, A. B., *Implementation* (University of California Press, 1973)

Przeworski, A. and Sprague, J., *Paper Stones: A History of Electoral Socialism* (University of Chicago Press, 1986)

Pusey, M., *Economic Rationalism in Canberra* (Cambridge University Press, 1991)

Quest, C., *Equal Opportunity - a Feminist Fallacy* (Institute of Economic Affairs, 1992)

Raban, J., *God, Man and Mrs Thatcher* (Chatto & Windus, Chatto Counterblasts, 1989)

Ranson, S. and Thomas, H., 'Educational Reform: consumer democracy or social democracy?', in J. Stewart and G. Stoker (eds), *The Future of Local Government* (Macmillan, 1989)

Rawls, J., *A Theory of Justice* (Harvard University Press, 1971)

Reich, R. B. (ed.), *The Power of Public Ideas* (Bellinger, 1988)

Rein, M., 'The Social Structure of Institutions', in S.B. Kammerman and A. J. Kahn (eds), *Privatization and the Welfare State* (Princeton University Press, 1989)

Richard, S. S., 'The Financial Management Initiative', in A. Harrison and J. Gretton (eds), *Reshaping Central Government*, (Policy Journals, 1987)

Richardson, J. and Jordan, G., *Governing under Pressure: the Policy Process in a Post-parliamentary Democracy* (Blackwell, 1979)

Riker, W. H., *The Theory of Coalitions* (Yale University Press, 1962)

Riker, W., *Liberalism Against Populism* (W. H. Freeman, 1982)

Riker, W. H. and Ordeshook, P. C., *An Introduction to Positive Political Theory* (Prentice-Hall, 1973)

Rinehart, J. H. and Lee, J. E. Jr, *American Education and the Dynamics of Choice* (Praeger, 1991)

Ringen, S., *The Possibility of Politics* (Oxford University Press, 1987)

Robinson, J., *Economic Philosophy* (Penguin Books, 1962)

Robson, W. A., *Welfare State and Welfare Society* (Allen & Unwin, 1976)

Roemer, J., 'Rational Choice Marxism: some issues of method and substance', in J. Roemer (ed.), *Analytical Marxism* (Cambridge University Press, 1986)

Rose, R. and Shiratori, R. (eds), *The Welfare State East and West* (Oxford University Press, 1986)

Rose, R. (ed.), *Challenge to Governance: Studies in Overloaded Politics* (Sage, 1980)

Rose, R., 'Dynamics of the Welfare Mix in Britain', in R. Rose and R. Shiratori (eds), *The Welfare State East and West* (Oxford University Press, 1986)

Rose, R., *The Post-modern President* (Chatham House, 1988)

Rose, R. and Peters, G., *Can Government Go Bankrupt?* (Basic Books, 1978)

Royal Commission on Local Government in England Report, vols 1 & 2, Cmnd 4040 (HMSO, 1969)

Ryan, A., 'Liberty and Socialism', in B. Pimlott (ed.), *Fabian Essays in Socialist Thought* (Heinemann, 1984)

Salins, P. D. (ed.), *New York Unbound: The City and the Politics of the Future* (Blackwell, 1988)

Salamon, L., 'Partners in Public Service: toward a theory of government–nonprofit relations', in W. Powell (ed.), *The Nonprofit Sector: A Research Handbook* (Yale University Press, 1986)

Samuelson, P. A., 'The pure theory of public expenditure', *The Review of Economics and Statistics*, 36, 387–89 (1954)

Sartori, G., *The Theory of Democracy Revisited*, 2 vols, (Chatham House, 1987)

Savitch, H. V. and Thomas, J. C. (eds), *Big City Politics in Transition* (Sage, 1991)

Sawyer, M., 'Markets good, governments bad', *Current Affairs Bulletin*, 26–32, July 1987

Sayre, W. S. and Kaufman, H., *Governing New York City* (Russell Sage Foundation, 1960)

Schaffer, B. B. and Lamb, E. B., *Can Equity be Organised?* (Brighton: University of Sussex, Institute of Development Studies, 1979)

Schumpeter, J. A., *Capitalism, Socialism and Democracy* (Allen & Unwin, 1943)

Schumpeter, J. A., *The Great Economists* (Allen & Unwin, 1952)

Scott, G. and Gorringe, P., 'Reform of the core public sector: the New Zealand experience', *Australian Journal of Public Administration*, 48:1, 81–92, (1989)

Sears, D. O., Laes, R. R., Tyler, T. R. and Harris, M. A. Jr, 'Self-interest vs. symbolic politics in policy attitudes and presidential voting', *American Political Science Review* (1980) 670–84

Seldon, A., *Wither the Welfare State* (Institute of Economic Affairs, 1981)

Self, P., *Econocrats and the Policy Process* (Macmillan, 1975)

Self, P., *Administrative Theories and Politics*, 2nd ed. (Allen & Unwin, 1977)

Self, P., *Planning the Urban Region: A Comparative Study of Policies and Organisations* (University of Alabama Press, 1982)

Self, P., *Political Theories of Modern Government, Its Role and Reform* (Unwin Hyman, 1985)

Self, P. and Storing, H. J., *The State and the Farmer* (University of California Press, 1962)

Sen, A., *Choice, Welfare and Measurement* (Blackwell, 1982)

Shaw, G. B., *The Commonsense of Municipal Trading* (Fabian Society, 1908)

Shonfield, A., *The Use of Public Power* (Oxford University Press, 1982)

Simon, H., *Administrative Behaviour*, 2nd edn (Macmillan, 1957)

Spencer, H., *The Man Versus the State* (1884 reprinted London: Penguin, 1969)

Spencer, K. M., 'Local Government and the Housing Reforms', in J. Stewart and G. Stoker (eds), *The Future of Local Government* (Macmillan, 1989)

Starr, P., 'The meaning of privatization', in S. B. Kammerman and A. J. Kahn (eds), *Privatization and the Welfare State* (Princeton University Press, 1989)

Stewart, J. and Stoker, G. (eds), *The Future of Local Government* (Macmillan, 1989)

Stigler, G. L., 'Director's law of public income redistribution', *Journal of Law and Economics*, 13: 1, 1–10, (1970)

Stockman, D., *The Triumph of Politics: How the Reagan Revolution Failed* (Harper & Row, 1986)

Stoker, G., *The Politics of Local Government* (Macmillan, 1988)

Strange, S., *Casino Capitalism* (Blackwell, 1986)

Stretton, H., *Political Essays* (Georgian House, 1987)

Suleiman, E. N., *Politics, Power and Bureaucracy in France* (Princeton University Press, 1974)

Tawney, R. H., *Equality* (1935 reprinted London: Allen & Unwin, 1964)

Taylor-Gooby, P., 'The Politics of Welfare: public attitudes and behaviour', in R. Klein and M. O'Higgins (eds), *The Future of Welfare* (Blackwell, 1985)

Thurow, L., *Dangerous Currents: The State of Economics* (Random House 1983)

Tiebout, C. M., 'A pure theory of local expenditures', *Journal of Political Economy*, 64, 416–24 (1956)

Travers, T., 'Community Charge and Other Financial Changes', in J. Stewart and G. Stoker (eds), *The Future of Local Government* (Macmillan, 1989)

Truman, D., *The Governmental Process* (A. A. Knopf, 1951)

Tullock, G., *The Politics of Bureaucracy* (Public Affairs Press, 1965)

Tullock, G., *The Vote Motive* (Institute of Economic Affairs, 1976)

Tullock, G., *Wealth, Poverty and Politics* (Blackwell, 1988)

Veljanovski, C., *Selling the State: Privatisation in Britain* (Weidenfeld & Nicolson, 1987)

Vickers, Sir G., *Freedom in a Rocking Boat* (Penguin, 1970)

Volcker Commission, *Leadership for America: Rebuilding the Public Service* (Lexington Books, 1990)

Waldo, D., 'A theory of public administration means in our time a theory of politics also', in N. B. Lynn and A. Wildavsky (eds), *Public Administration: The State of the Discipline* (Chatham House, 1990)

Walsh, K., 'Competition and Service in Local Government', in J. Stewart and G. Stoker (eds), *The Future of Local Government* (Macmillan, 1989)

West, N., *Collected Works* (Penguin, 1975)

Whitbread, M., 'Department of the Environment', in A. Harrison and J. Gretton (eds), *Reshaping Central Government* (Policy Journals, 1987)

White, J. and Wildavsky, A., *The Deficit and the Public Interest* (University of California Press, 1989)

Wildavsky, A., *The Politics of the Budgetary Process* (Little, Brown, 1964)

Wildavsky, A., *The Art and Craft of Policy Analysis* (Macmillan, 1979)

Williams, A., *Creating A Health Care Market: Ideology, Efficiency, Ethics and Clinical Efficiency* (University of York, Centre for Health Economics, March 1989)

Williamson, O., *Markets and Hierarchies* (The Free Press, 1975)

Williamson, O., *The Economic Institutions of Capitalism: Firms, Markets, Relational Contracting* (The Free Press, 1985)

Wilson, J. A. (ed.), *The Politics of Regulation* (Basic Books, 1980)

Wilson, J. A., *Bureaucracy* (Basic Books, 1989)

Wiltshire, K., *Privatisation: The British Experience* (Longman Cheshire, 1987)

Yates, D., *The Ungovernable City* (MIT Press, 1977)

Zapf, W., 'Development, Structure and Prospects of the German Social State', in R. Rose and R. Shiratori (eds), *The Welfare State East and West* (Oxford University Press, 1986)

Index of Names

Index of Subjects